IMAGES
of America

HISTORIC HERITAGE SQUARE

ON THE COVER: The Rosson House, an 1895 Victorian brick mansion, is the crown jewel of Historic Heritage Square, the only preserved block of the original Phoenix townsite, platted in 1870. The affection for the Rosson House by a former Phoenix mayor ultimately led to its preservation and restoration, along with nine other historic buildings that now encompass the downtown park. (Rosson House–Heritage Square Foundation and Guild.)

IMAGES
of America

HISTORIC HERITAGE SQUARE

Donna J. Reiner, PhD, John Jacquemart,
and Douglas C. Towne

ARCADIA
PUBLISHING

ISBN 978-1-4671-3075-2

Published by Arcadia Publishing
Charleston, South Carolina

Printed in the United States of America

Library of Congress Control Number: 2013938127

For all general information, please contact Arcadia Publishing:
Telephone 843-853-2070
Fax 843-853-0044
E-mail sales@arcadiapublishing.com
For customer service and orders:
Toll-Free 1-888-313-2665

Visit us on the Internet at www.arcadiapublishing.com

To those who lived in the homes of Historic Heritage Square and their descendants, who graciously provided much of the block's history.

Donna Reiner thanks Edward Jensen for solving a problem with some photographs.

Douglas Towne would like to thank his wife, Maureen "Mo" Towne, who, for many years, has cheerfully supported his eclectic interests and provided invaluable critical commentary for his writing and art.

Contents

Acknowledgments 6

Introduction 7

1. Before the Phoenix Settlement 9

2. Early Phoenix Settlement 17

3. The Rosson House 37

4. The Rest of Block 14 55

5. It's Going to Be a Park 65

6. "Modern" Historic Heritage Square 103

ACKNOWLEDGMENTS

Even before the Rosson House–Heritage Square Foundation and Guild (RHHSFG) was founded in the early 1980s, dedicated Phoenicians volunteered hundreds of hours to ensure the preservation and restoration of one block of Phoenix's early history. The RHHSFG has continued to preserve this piece of history for present and future generations. Without these efforts, this book would not have been possible.

Unless otherwise noted, the images in this book appear courtesy of the Pueblo Grande Museum (PGM), the City of Phoenix Parks Department (PPD), and the Rosson House–Heritage Square Foundation and Guild (RHHSFG).

INTRODUCTION

The centerpiece of Phoenix history is Historic Heritage Square. The park serves to educate people about our city's past while also providing an oasis and recreation outlet downtown. Encompassing Block 14 and adjoining areas of the original Phoenix townsite, the park's creation included the preservation of the Victorian-era Rosson House and other period buildings. The project was a challenging task that involved the family of Mitt Romney, the 2012 Republican presidential candidate, and the Paris Peace Accord of 1973, which led to America's withdrawal from the Vietnam War.

My ties to the Rosson House go back many years. I was born in 1927 in the Mexican border town of Douglas, Arizona, where my grandfather established a bank that later became Western Savings and Loan. The following year, my family moved to Phoenix and lived at 2217 North Eighth Street in what is now the Coronado Historic District.

My family attended the Phoenix First Ward Church of Jesus Christ of Latter-day Saints (LDS), which was the first permanent Mormon building in Phoenix. The church was situated where the Lath House now stands in Historic Heritage Square and we went by the Rosson House every Sunday. I went on to graduate from Phoenix's North High School in 1945, enlisted in the Navy for a year, served a two-year LDS mission in New England, and then graduated from Stanford University before returning to Phoenix to work at Western Savings and Loan. During my subsequent years in the family banking business, I was active in civic groups and chaired the Phoenix Growth Committee that helped fund new municipal facilities.

I had lost track of the Rosson House until I was elected to the first of two terms as mayor of Phoenix in 1970, which coincided with the city's centennial. Few residents, however, were interested in Phoenix history and we were a historic preservation wasteland. To start the Phoenix Historical Society, I appointed a commission that included future US Supreme Court Justice Sandra Day O'Connor. As the country approached its bicentennial celebration, it seemed we should preserve the Rosson House. So I began to explore ways to save the beautiful, but dilapidated, Victorian residence.

The city was able to acquire the property using a Housing and Urban Development (HUD) grant in 1974. The agency director was the former Michigan governor George Romney, a distant cousin, family friend, and also the father of Mitt Romney. At Stanford, I escorted his eldest daughter to church every Sunday. Besides having this personal connection with Pres. Richard Nixon's administration, I was also approached by the White House to aid in their negotiations with the North Vietnamese delegation in Paris. Peace talks had bogged down during the early 1970s and one barrier to progress was considered the anti-war position that the US Conference of Mayors adopted in 1971. Because of this stance, the president's negotiators thought the North Vietnamese assumed the American public was also overwhelmingly anti-war because the mayors were considered the closest elected officials to the people.

President Nixon's chief deputy, John Erlichman, contacted me because I was one of the few Republican big city mayors, and asked if I would attempt to change the mayors' position on the Vietnam War. I agreed to try and, at our 1972 conference in New Orleans, I put forth the Driggs

Resolution that supported Nixon's proposal to withdraw US troops after a cease-fire throughout Indochina. When I asked for comments on the resolution, Mayor Richard Daley of Chicago rose to his feet. He was a very influential person but rarely spoke publicly.

"In the name of God, stand behind the President," a red-faced Daley said at the conference, according to an Associated Press wire account. "No one would work harder against a Republican president than me. But maybe I'm old-fashioned or behind the times. The question is whether we are going to stand behind the President in foreign affairs," Daley concluded. The Driggs Resolution was subsequently approved.

For the dedication of the nearby Phoenix Civic Plaza in 1974, Samuel Mardian Jr., the former Phoenix mayor who served two terms from 1960 to 1964, suggested we should invite President Nixon. The president, however, sent his daughter, Julie Nixon Eisenhower, to represent him. Mardian told me Nixon had said to him, "I'll do something else for Mayor Driggs by making sure he gets the $200,000 HUD grant." Of the HUD funds, we used $20,000 for condemnation of the Rosson House lot and $180,000 to relocate the 19 people who were living in the home. The other parcels on Block 14 were acquired using Community Development Block Grant funds until the city owned the entire block.

But we still needed to raise funds to restore the buildings located on what would become Historic Heritage Square. For the first donation, I persuaded my firm, Western Savings and Loan, on their 50th Anniversary, to donate $50,000 to restore the Silva House. My second target was A.J. "Jack" Pfister, who was the general manager of Salt River Project (SRP). I gave him a personal tour of the proposed park and Pfister subsequently appointed a committee of SRP board members to visit Block 14. They came out on a cold, rainy day and decided that they also wanted to sponsor the Silva House (I knew Western Savings would agree to switch its sponsorship to another house) and donated $50,000. SRP had a history museum in the Silva House for 20 years and paid the city one dollar per year and maintained the building.

Other businesses and institutions soon followed, with pledges including Arizona Public Service, First Interstate Bank, Mountain Bell Telephone, the Phoenix Rotary Club, and First Federal Savings, which each contributed $25,000. To help with the renovations, many firms provided in-kind services such as M.M. Sundt Construction, Cannon & Wendt Electrical, and J.R. Welch Plumbing. We promised a plaque would be placed on each building commemorating contributions but, unfortunately, that never happened.

Architect Bob Frankeburger was the chief advisor for the Historic Heritage Square architectural team. He also designed the Lath House Pavilion for outdoor events that was constructed to the east of the Rosson House. We had the opportunity to move to the square what was known as the Burgess Carriage House, which was owned by the mother-in-law of noted Phoenix attorney Richard Mallery. It was originally located kitty-corner to the Westward Ho on Central Avenue and Fillmore Street. An apartment building that had been a 1920s in-fill project on Sixth Street was demolished so that the Carriage House could be situated south of the Rosson House and serve as the park's headquarters. Valley National Bank, through my connections with Vice President Wilson Barnett Sr., donated $50,000 for this project and did get a bronze plaque on the building. The duplex that now houses both the city park and the foundation's offices was also considered for razing since it too was a later in-fill project. But we decided to keep the duplex so the square would reflect the evolution of downtown Phoenix and its increasing density.

My goal is to have Historic Heritage Square and the adjacent Arizona Science Center as key destinations in a history and tourism corridor that would stretch from the Arizona State Capitol to Papago Park. The corridor would be called the Arizona Second Century Initiative and synergistically combine venues from the past, voices of the present, and visions for the future. The El Zaribah Shrine Auditorium, Carnegie Library, Children's Museum, Tovrea Castle, National Guard Arsenal, and Arizona Historic Society Museum and the adjacent O'Connor House and Eisendrath House would be included. These buildings best reflect Phoenix's cultural heritage and will provide a lasting legacy for Arizona's second century.

—Former City of Phoenix mayor John Driggs

One

Before the Phoenix Settlement

Phoenix was the sixth-largest US city in 2010, with a population of 1.4 million. Yet, amazingly, the community had not existed only 150 years before. When former Confederate soldier Jack Swilling ventured into the area from Wickenburg while scouting for potential agricultural lands in 1867, he found the Salt River Valley unpopulated. Swilling recognized, however, the impressive ruins of an advanced agricultural society that came to be called the Hohokam, which is a Pima Indian word meaning "people who have gone."

Archeologists estimate the Hohokam lived in the valley for almost 2,000 years before eventually vanishing around 1450. Significantly, they were the only native North American culture to rely on irrigation to grow crops. To feed a population of up to 40,000, the Hohokam diverted the Salt River into a 135-mile canal system that irrigated up to 110,000 acres of farmland. The causes of the Hohokam's decline are not definitively known, though drought, floods, and soil salinity are considered contributing factors. Reusing Hohokam canals, Swilling and other settlers began farming in 1868 to supply the military post at Fort McDowell and mining camps in the Bradshaw Mountains. Their settlement was called various names, including Pumpkinville, until a well-educated world traveler and self-proclaimed "Lord," Darrell Duppa, suggested renaming the community Phoenix, because, like the bird of mythology, it rose from the ashes of an ancient civilization.

Hohokam ruins have been found throughout the Salt River Valley, prompting Phoenix in 1929 to become the first city with a staff archeologist and to establish the Pueblo Grande Museum. The city obtained Block 14 of the original Phoenix townsite in 1974 to create what would become Historic Heritage Square. Hohokam artifacts were encountered during limited archeological explorations in 1977. During park expansion in 1994, more extensive excavations were conducted. Archeologists working beneath an incongruous backdrop of skyscrapers found 63 prehistoric features, including pithouses, middens, thermal pits, postholes, hearths, and thousands of shards and projectile points. Most were from Pueblo Patricio, a major Hohokam settlement (100–500 AD), while fewer dated from 1350 AD, suggesting that the site was later only seasonally used by the Hohokam.

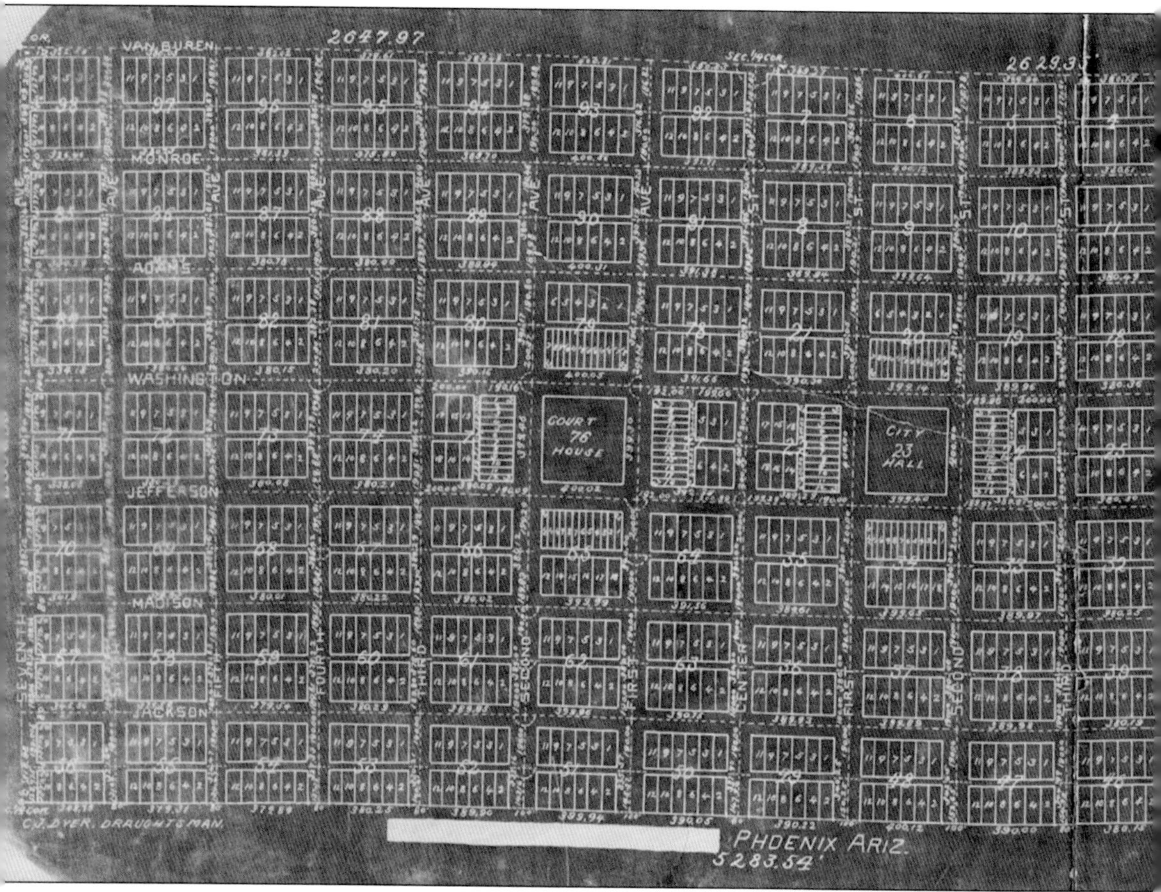

Blocks 13–16, which now encompass Heritage and Science Park, are located in the upper right corner of this map. This is the northeastern part of the original Phoenix townsite, platted in December 1870. The townsite was one-half square mile and contained 98 blocks. This plat was

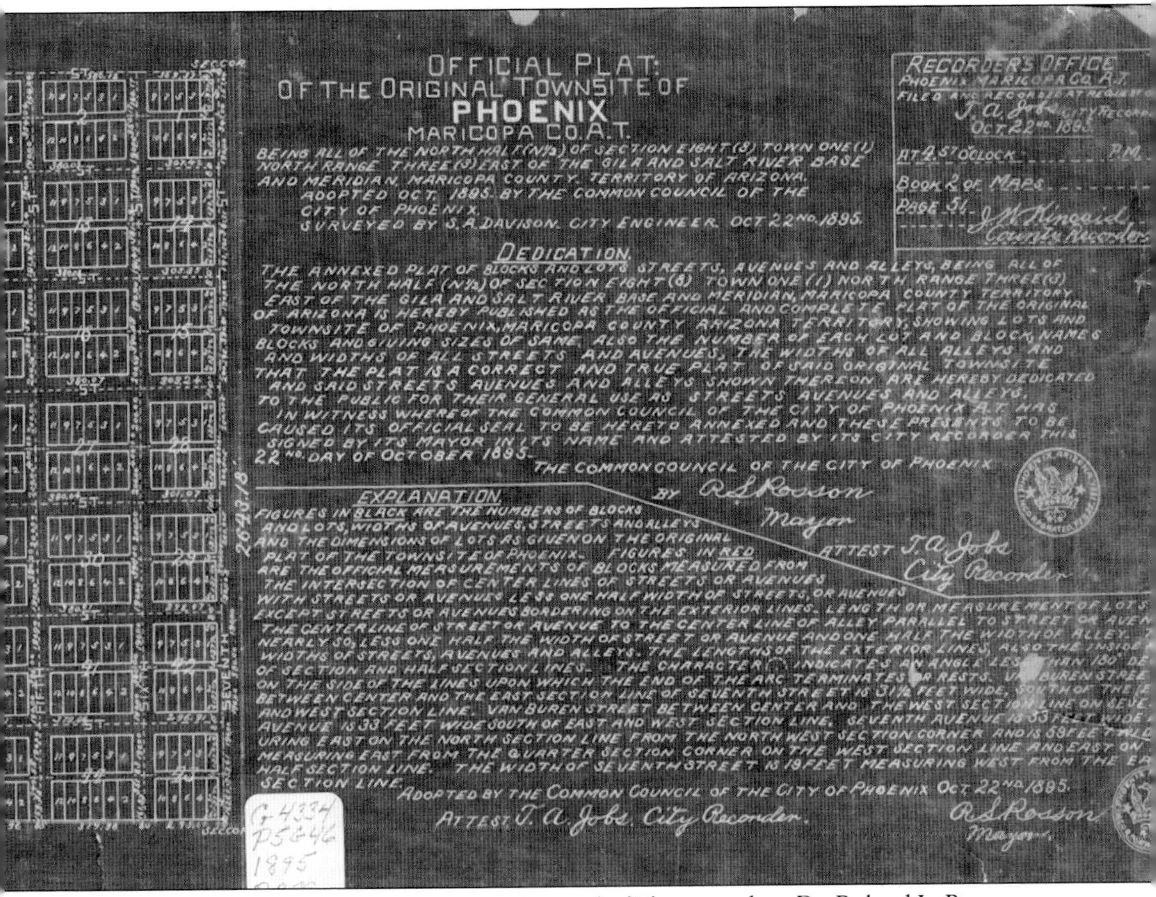

adopted in October 1895 by the Common Council of Phoenix when Dr. Roland L. Rosson was mayor. (Phoenix Public Library, Arizona Room.)

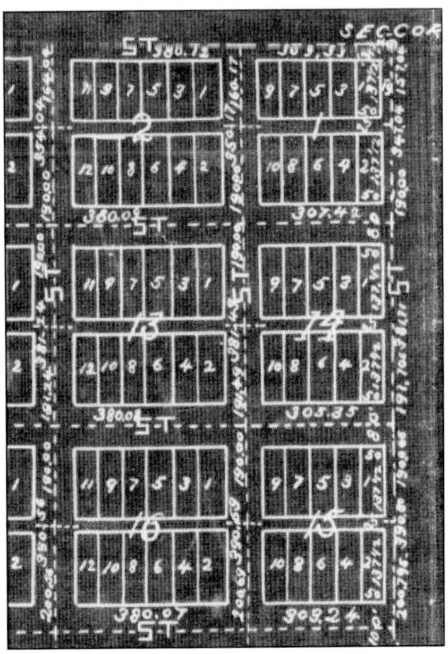

This section of the original Phoenix townsite map shows Blocks 13–16, the current location of Heritage and Science Park. The primary focus of this book is Block 14, now known as Historic Heritage Square. The majority of the archaeological findings shown in chapters one and two, however, come from digs conducted on Blocks 13 and 16. (Phoenix Public Library, Arizona Room.)

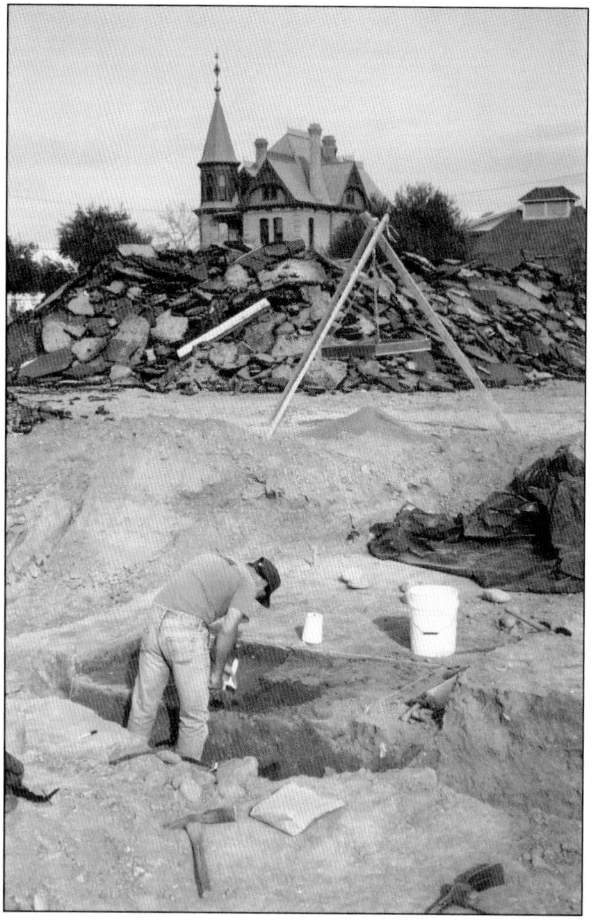

An archaeologist excavates a feature located in Block 13 during park expansion in 1994. The Rosson House is in the background, along with the roof of the Burgess Carriage House. This particular dig broadened understanding of the Hohokam settlement in this part of the Salt River Valley. (PGM.)

Half of a perforated plainware ceramic disc, this artifact is identified as a spindle whorl for cotton processing. Cotton pollen, however, was not found in flotation samples collected from Feature 805, an adobe-lined pithouse that dates to the Classic Hohokam Period of the 14th century. The results were based on archaeomagnetic and radiocarbon dating. (PGM.)

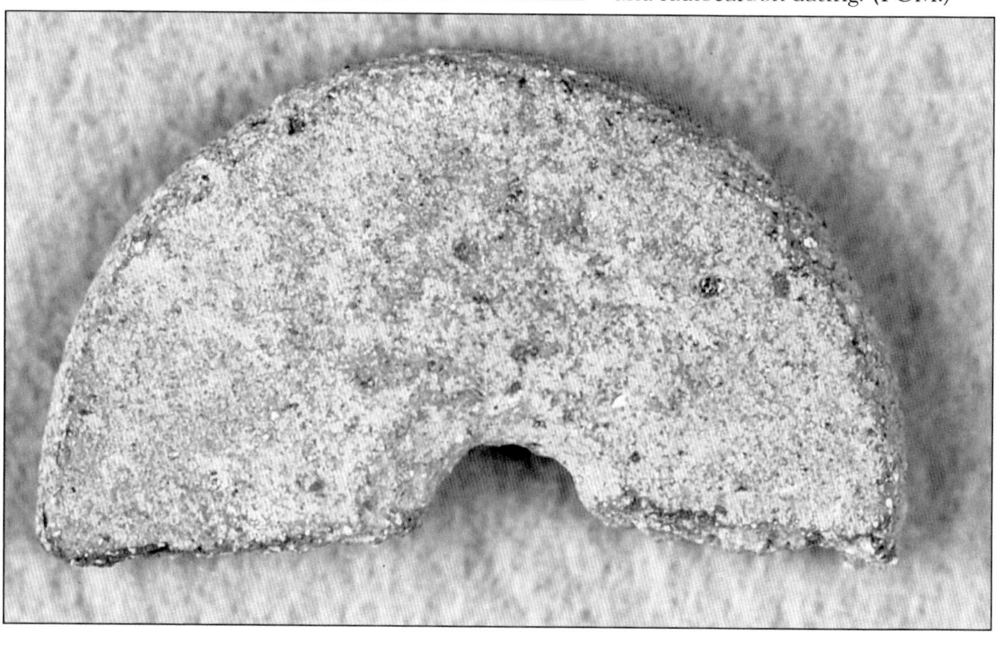

The right photograph, taken in 1994, shows students touring the excavations at Historic Heritage Square. In the upper portion of the photograph is the Mercado, where numerous prominent Phoenicians resided in large homes at the beginning of the 20th century. Once a small strip mall, it now serves as a classroom area for the downtown campus of Arizona State University. Below, students get a close-up view of the "discovery" of archeological history at Historic Heritage Square. (PGM.)

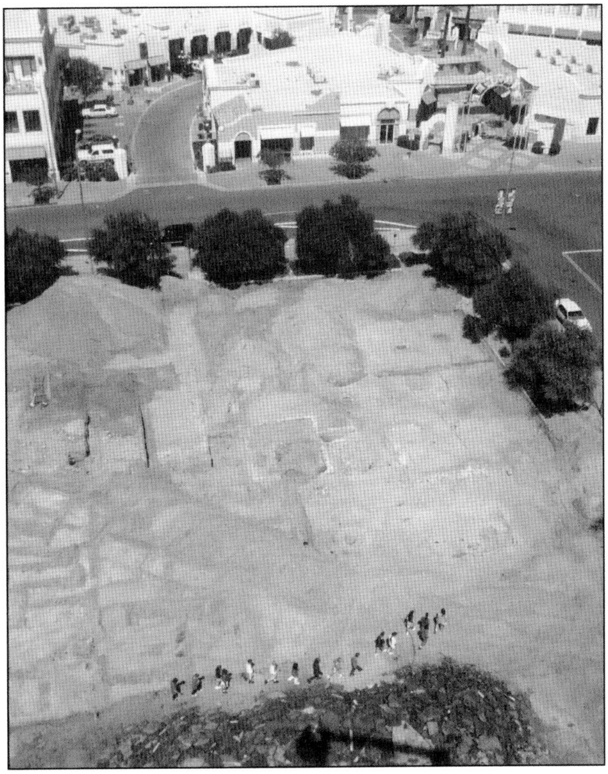

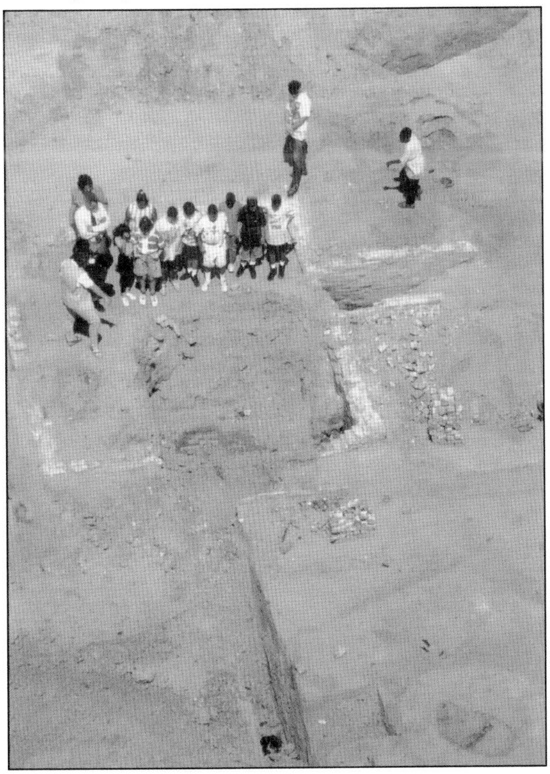

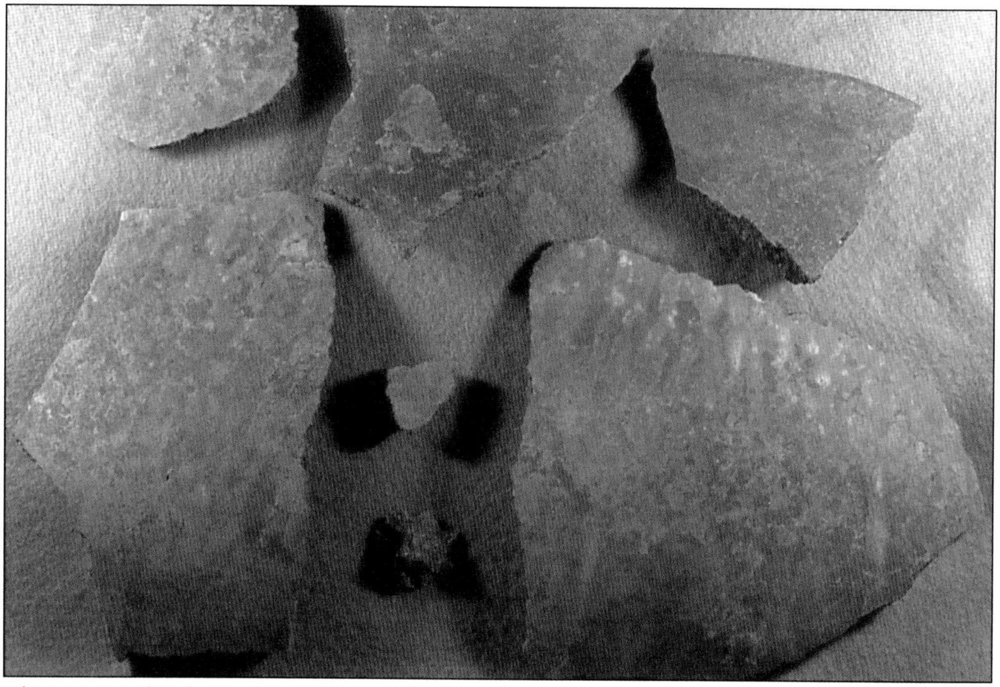

These seven shards are from a large redware wide-mouthed jar with a flaring rim. Found in an unused well on Block 13, such historic Native American ceramics in Heritage Square demonstrate interaction between the aboriginal inhabitants and the new settlers in Phoenix. This vessel was probably made by the Pima Indians, but classification remains problematic. The early settlers were fascinated with Indian relics they found in the nearby desert. (PGM.)

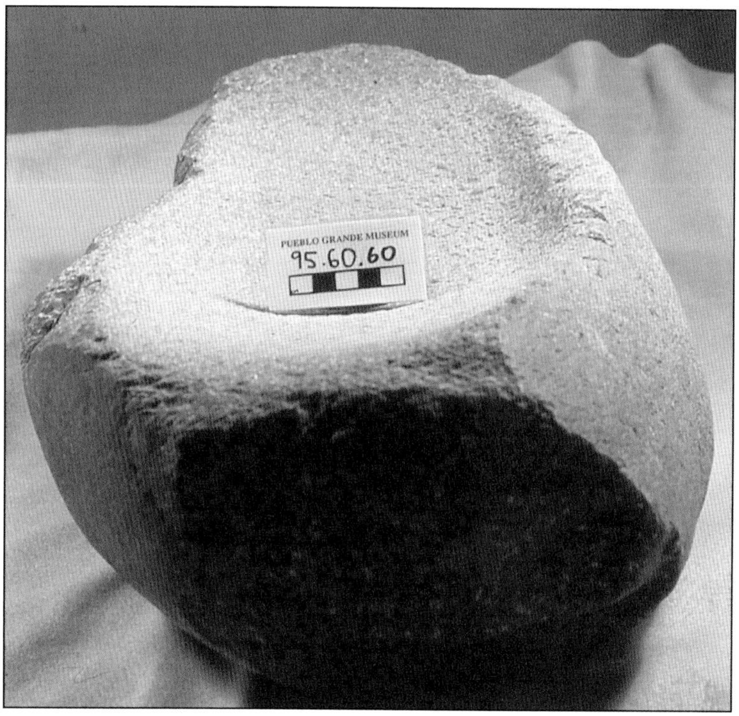

This is a large granite basin metate that is often associated with processing wild plant foods. Early settlers collected metates that they found in the region. This metate, which was found protruding from a large, bell-shaped pit in the floor of a pithouse, is dated to before 600 AD according to archaeomagnetic dating, with a radiocarbon date of 240–420 AD. (PGM.)

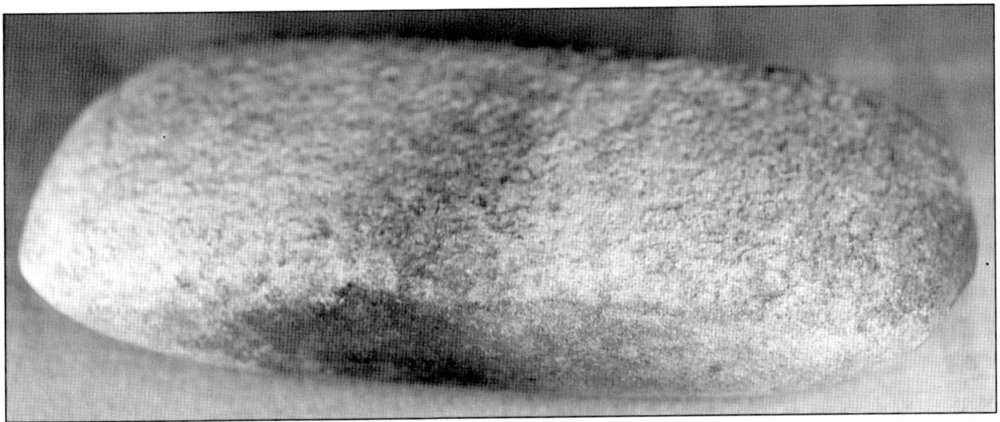

This quartzite mano has one grinding surface that has been pecked and, as a result, is a pale brown color, lighter than the rest of the mano. It was found in a thermal pit north of an undated pithouse on Block 13. The grinding surface on this mano is nearly 78 inches, which indicates the metate was also quite large. (PGM.)

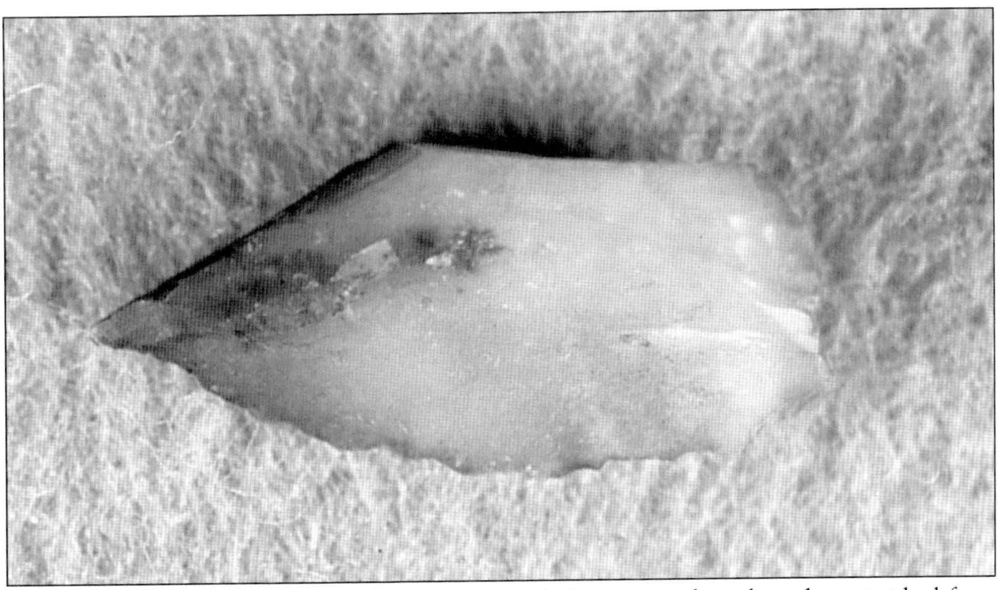

This point may have been burned or intentionally heat-treated, and its shape is ideal for a flake tool. The point was found in an insubstantial oval pithouse with a hearth and posthole. Morphology and low artifact quantity are consistent with early-period pithouses at Historic Heritage Square. (PGM.)

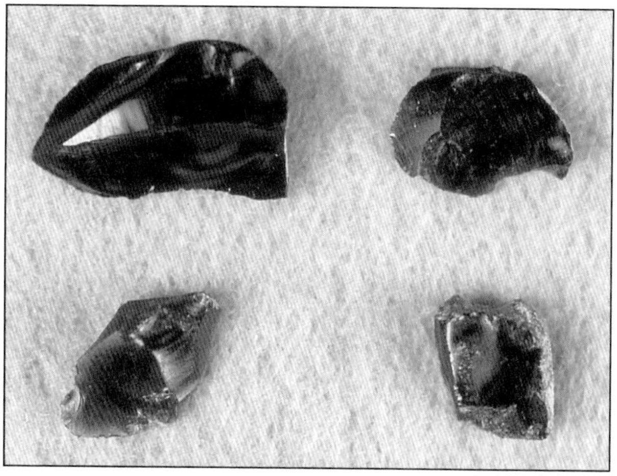

The largest of these four flakes of black obsidian appears to be a flake tool. There were several obsidian sources in northern Arizona. The flakes were found in a substantial rectangular, adobe-lined pithouse with postholes, two hearths, and a very large artifact assemblage. Archaeomagnetic dating places the pithouse in the 14th century, or the Classic Hohokam Period. (PGM.)

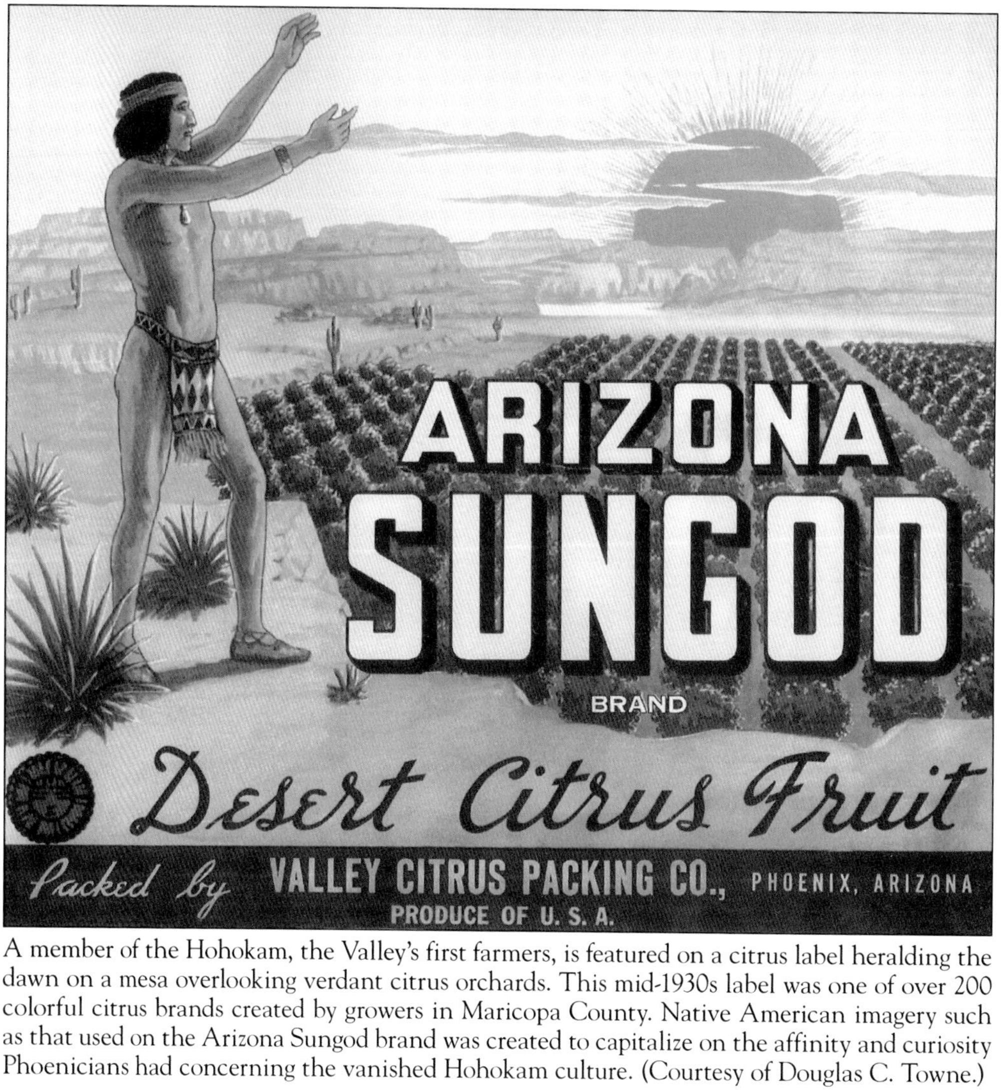

A member of the Hohokam, the Valley's first farmers, is featured on a citrus label heralding the dawn on a mesa overlooking verdant citrus orchards. This mid-1930s label was one of over 200 colorful citrus brands created by growers in Maricopa County. Native American imagery such as that used on the Arizona Sungod brand was created to capitalize on the affinity and curiosity Phoenicians had concerning the vanished Hohokam culture. (Courtesy of Douglas C. Towne.)

Two

Early Phoenix Settlement

The Phoenix township, established in 1870, encompassed 98 blocks in an area that would evolve into the city's downtown. Phoenix had a population of 2,453 by 1880 and was incorporated the following year. In 1887, the Southern Pacific Railroad reached the city via a branch line from the south originating at the town of Maricopa Wells. This transportation link boosted growth, helping Phoenix become the capital of the Territory of Arizona in 1889. The completion in 1911 of the Theodore Roosevelt Dam on the Salt River diminished the threat of flooding in Phoenix and provided water storage that allowed irrigated agriculture to dramatically expand in the valley. Arizona was granted statehood on February 14, 1912.

In the fledgling city, Block 14 was a mixed residential and commercial area located northeast of City Hall along Seventh Street, between Monroe and Adams Streets. Along with adjoining portions of Block 15, it would later become Historic Heritage Square. Initially, the area's undeveloped land was predominantly owned by three women: Annie S. Shaw, Laura E. Hawkins, and Margaret A. Richardson. In 1880, Richardson sold Block 14 to her sister, Flora Murray, who was married to Dr. Roland Lee Rosson. The couple had moved that year to Phoenix when the physician was 28 years old. The Rossons had an Eastlake Queen Anne–style Victorian mansion, called the Rosson House, built in 1894–1895.

The Rosson family gradually sold off portions of the block. Most of the additional homes were built around the early 1900s. The last residence, a duplex, was constructed in 1923. Block 14 was unusual in that 13 of its homes were originally owned by women. Another significant addition to the block was the first permanent Mormon building in Phoenix, the First Church of Latter-day Saints, built in 1918–1919.

To the south of Block 14, commercial enterprises developed along the north side of Washington Street, which had a major streetcar line. Prominent businesses there, in what were Blocks 15 and 16, included the Grand Hotel and the Shoup Lumber Yard. This area west was completely redeveloped for the construction of a new downtown convention center in 1972.

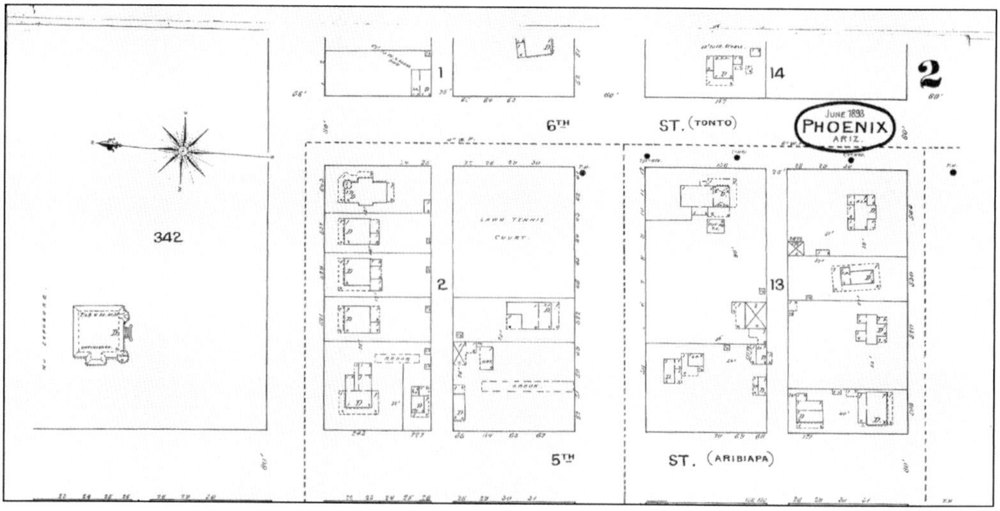

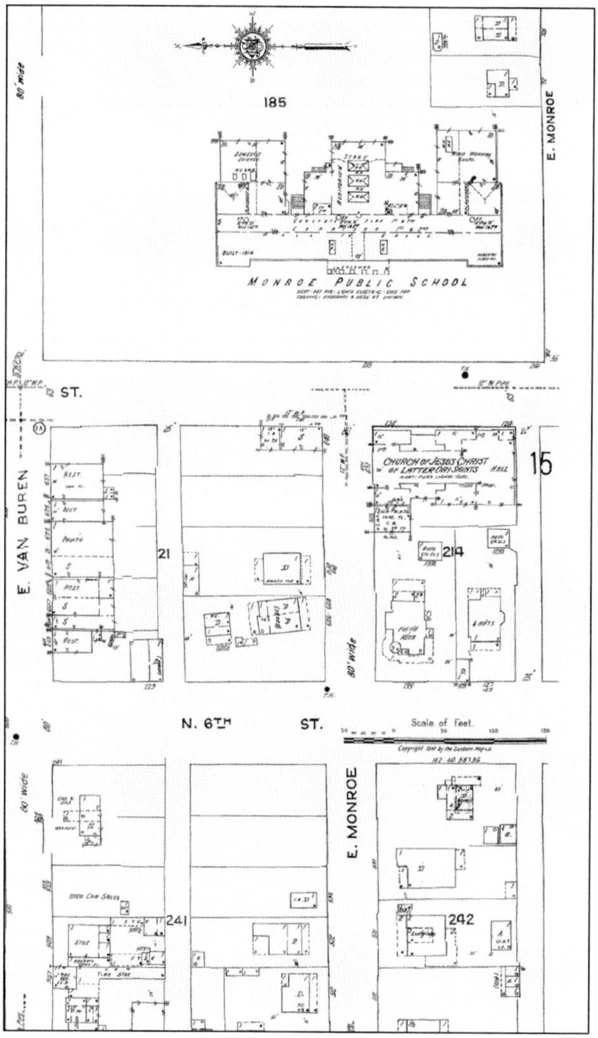

The Sanborn Fire Insurance map of 1893 (above) shows an adobe house on Block 14 (at the top of the section). According to city directories, the Rosson family lived on this block, so it is assumed that they originally lived in this dwelling. Block 13, between Fifth and Sixth Streets, is now part of Historic Heritage Square. A little over 50 years later, the 1946 Sanborn Fire Insurance map (left) shows major changes on Block 14. The Phoenix First Ward Church of Jesus Christ of Latter-day Saints occupies the east half of the north side of the block. There is a sign-painting shop between the church and the Rosson House, the latter of which was then offering furnished rooms. Across Seventh Street from the church is the Monroe Elementary School. A four-unit apartment house is located to the right of the Rosson House. (Courtesy of the City of Phoenix, Historic Preservation Office.)

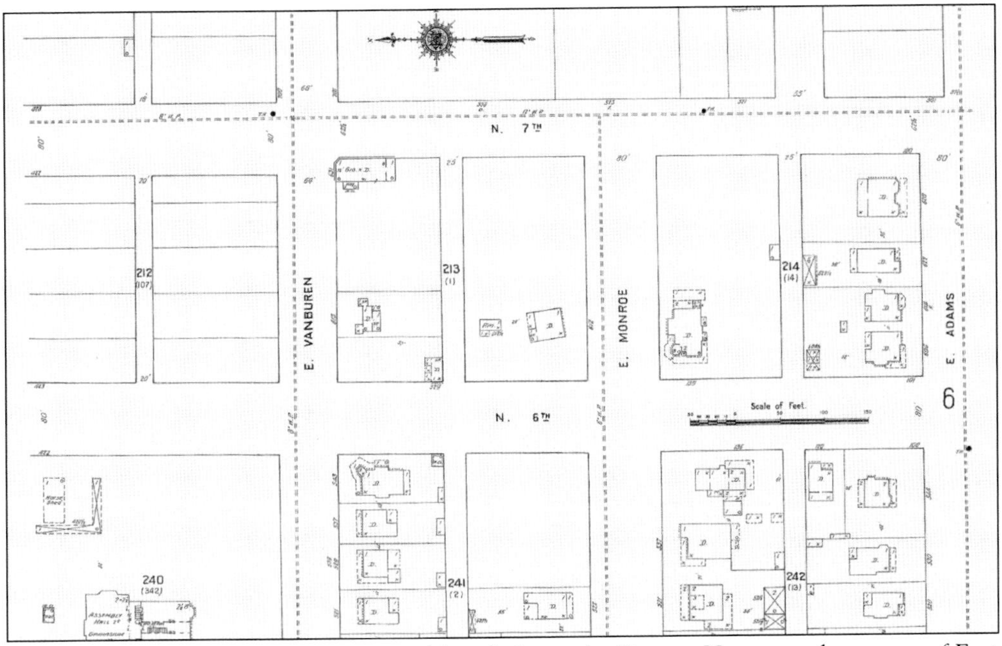

The 1911 Sanborn Fire Insurance map (above) shows the Rosson House on the corner of East Monroe and Sixth Streets. The houses on the south side of Block 14 along East Adams Street are still extant. At this time, an alley divided the block. The south half of Block 14 and all of Block 15 are seen 35 years later in the 1946 Sanborn Fire Insurance map section below. The Block 14 portion is unchanged and continues to be residential. Block 15 shows the commercial enterprises that have existed there from early in the city's history. Shoup's Lumber Yard is now part of the site of the Arizona Science Center. (Courtesy of the City of Phoenix, Historic Preservation Office.)

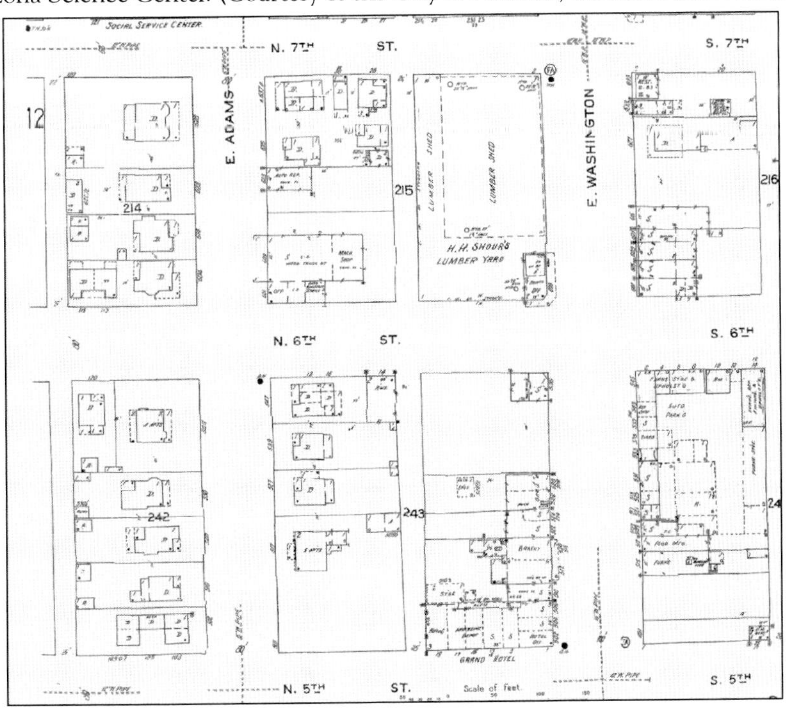

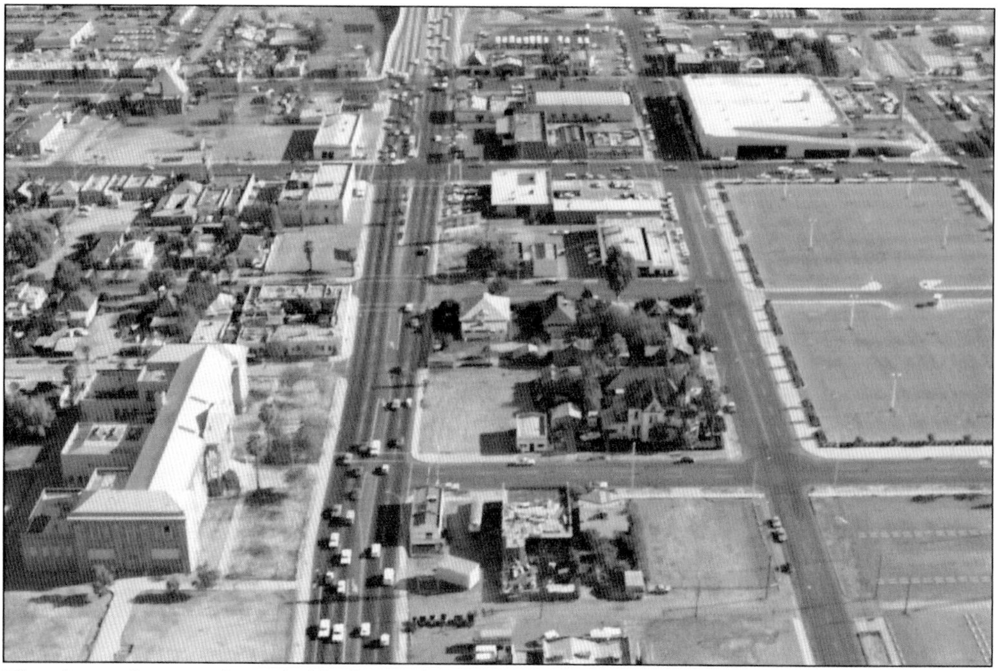

The above photograph, probably dating from the early 1970s, was taken prior to any restoration work on Historic Heritage Square. Looking south along Seventh Street, Monroe Elementary School is on the left. The center of the photograph is the future site of the park. Some of the buildings shown in the 1946 Sanborn Fire Insurance map are still standing in this photograph. The two surface parking lots on the right are Blocks 13 and 16 and became part of the park expansion in 1994. Below, a work crew takes on the difficult and sometimes tedious work of excavation. This photograph of Blocks 13 and 16 is looking south. The building on the right is the former convention center, which was recently razed. The parking lot in the background is now home to the Arizona Science Center. (Above, RHHSFG; below, PGM.)

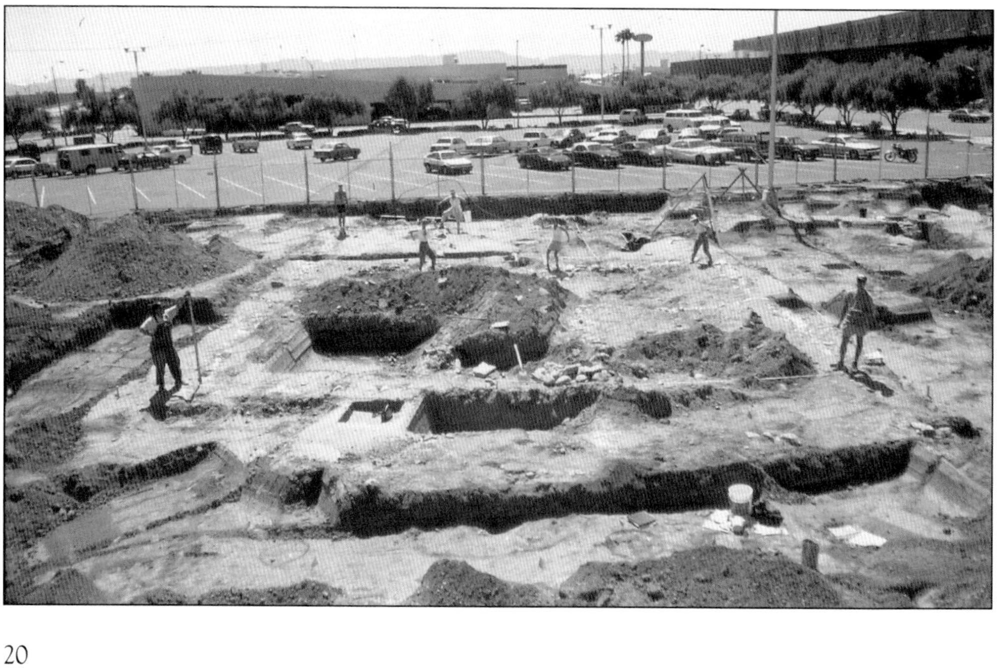

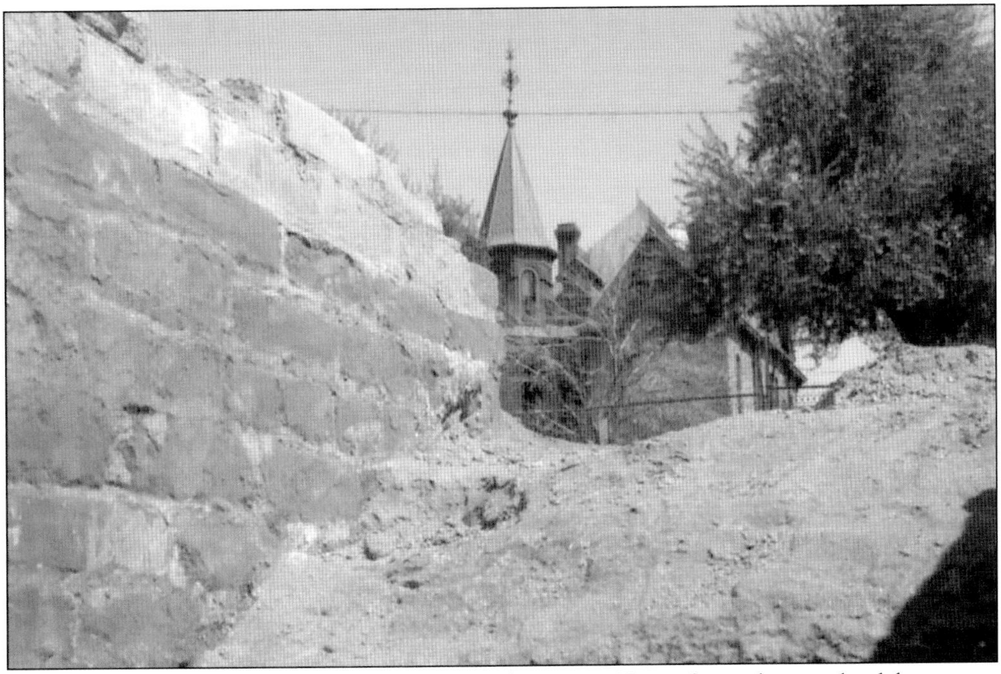

The above photograph offers an unusual view of the Rosson House from a historic brick basement. Brick was a popular building material in Phoenix in the latter part of the 19th century and the early part of the 20th century. It was not, however, the best building material to insulate against summer temperatures. Basements were not a common element in early Phoenix, due to the region's very hard caliche soil. The below photograph of the excavations on Block 13 show the Rosson House on the left and Monroe Elementary School, just visible at far left. The Lath Pavilion roofline is also visible. Cars are parked on Sixth Street, which was closed to traffic when the expansion of the park was completed. (PGM.)

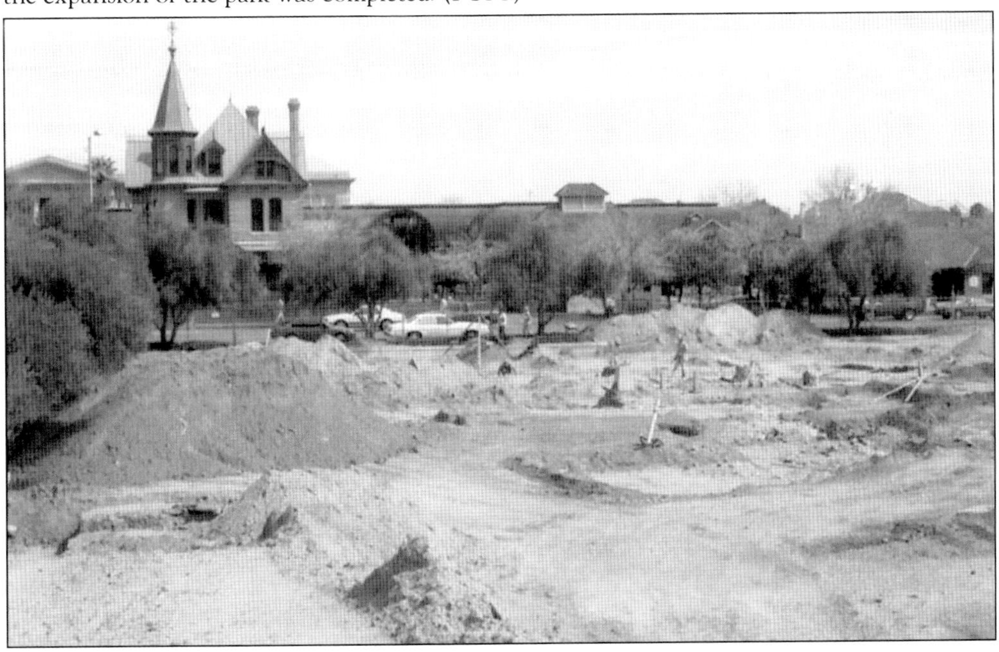

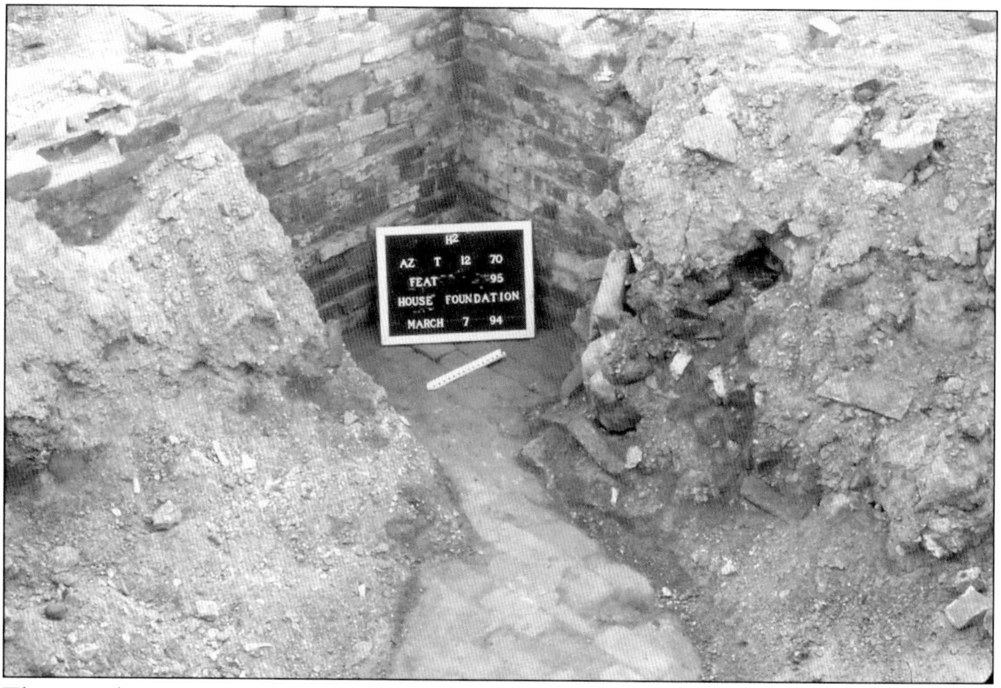

This is a close-up view of a historic brick basement. The excavations provided information, especially regarding personal items that the Sanborn Insurance Maps did not reveal, thus enriching the history and stories of the buildings. (PGM.)

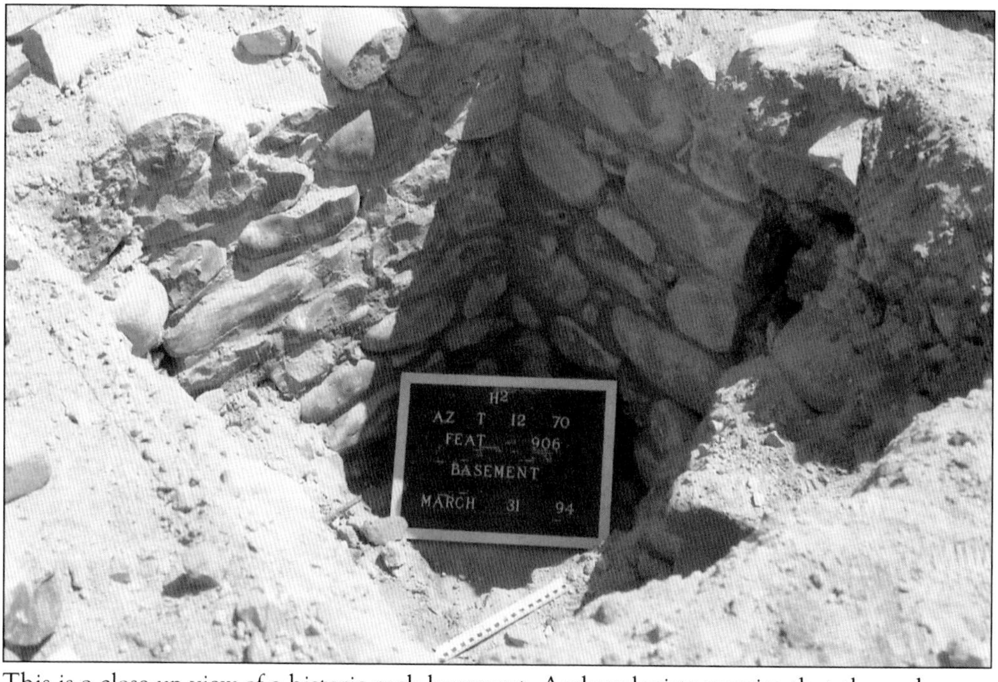

This is a close-up view of a historic rock basement. Archaeologists surmise that the rock came from the nearby Salt River. In contrast to the rock basement, the house was brick, as determined from the information on the Sanborn Insurance Maps. (PGM.)

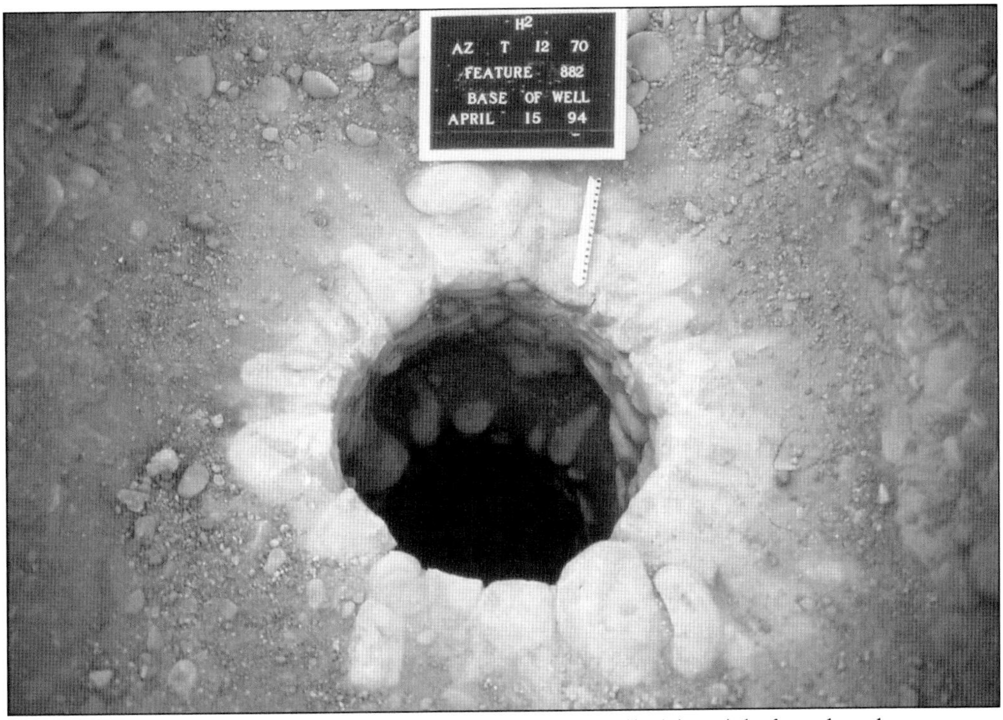

Some of the early residents of Block 13 had hand-dug wells (above) before their homes were connected to the city water system. The water level was very shallow in the area because of the proximity of the Salt River to the south. Consequently, if a house did not have running water, it had a privy or outhouse (below). For the archaeologists on this excavation, the privies became a fabulous source of artifacts, as people sometimes used them to discard unwanted items. (PGM.)

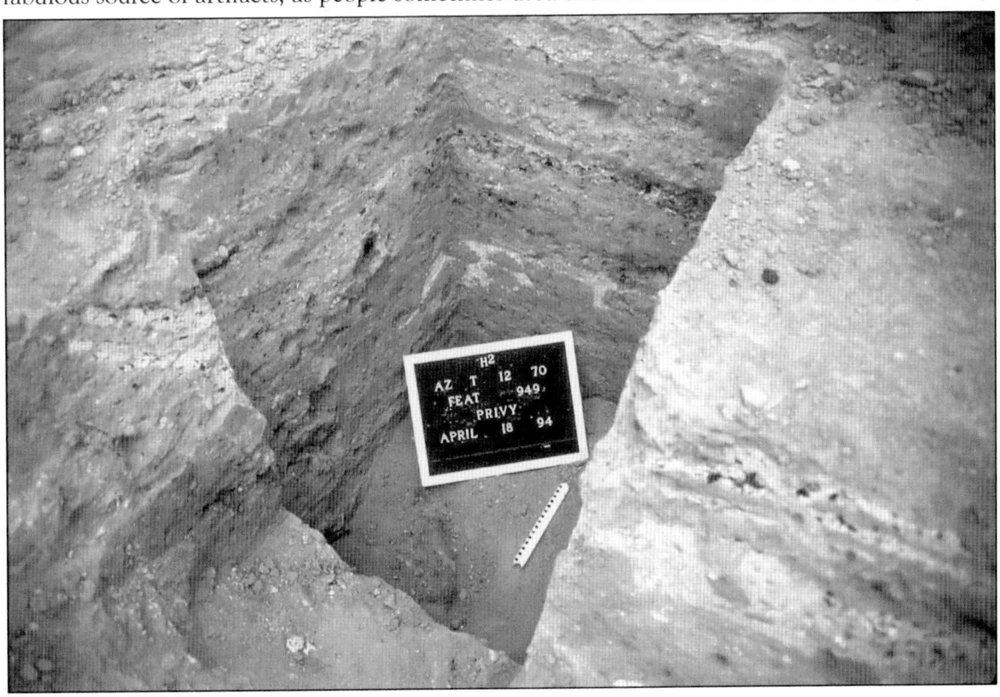

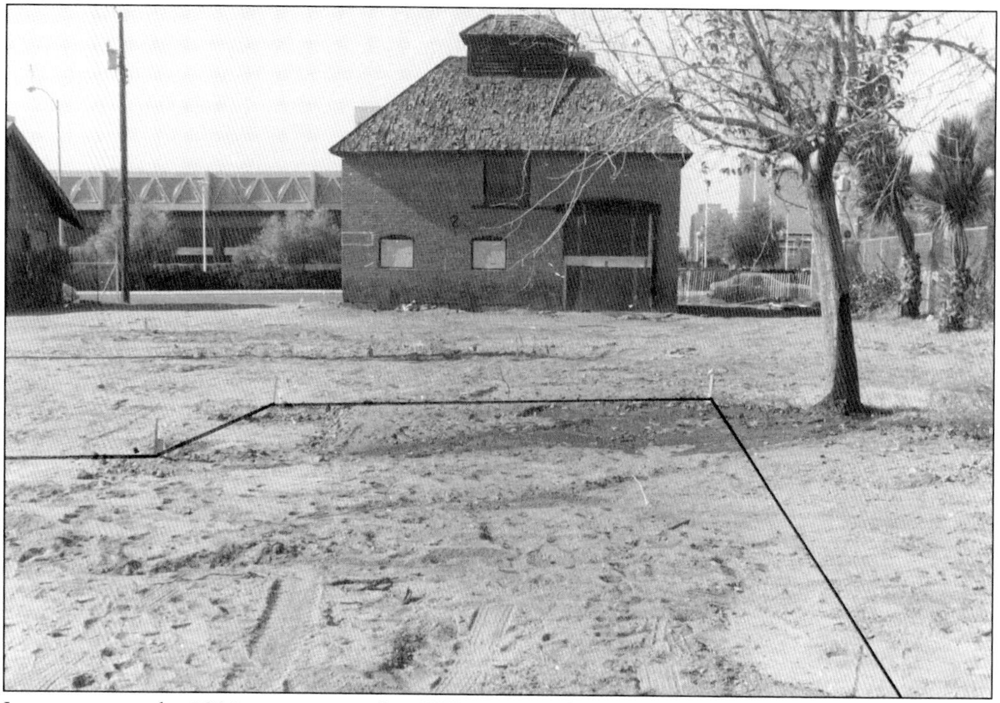

In contrast to the 1994 excavation, the 1977–1978 work looked only at a small area of Block 14. The above photograph is a view of the east side of the Burgess Carriage House. The black outline on the ground is the footprint of an outbuilding where some of the excavations took place. The Phoenix Convention Center is visible in the background. The below photograph, taken from the southeast corner of the Burgess Carriage House, shows the back porch of the Rosson House and a view of the Monroe School building across Seventh Street. The three black outlines are the footprints of several outbuildings. (PGM.)

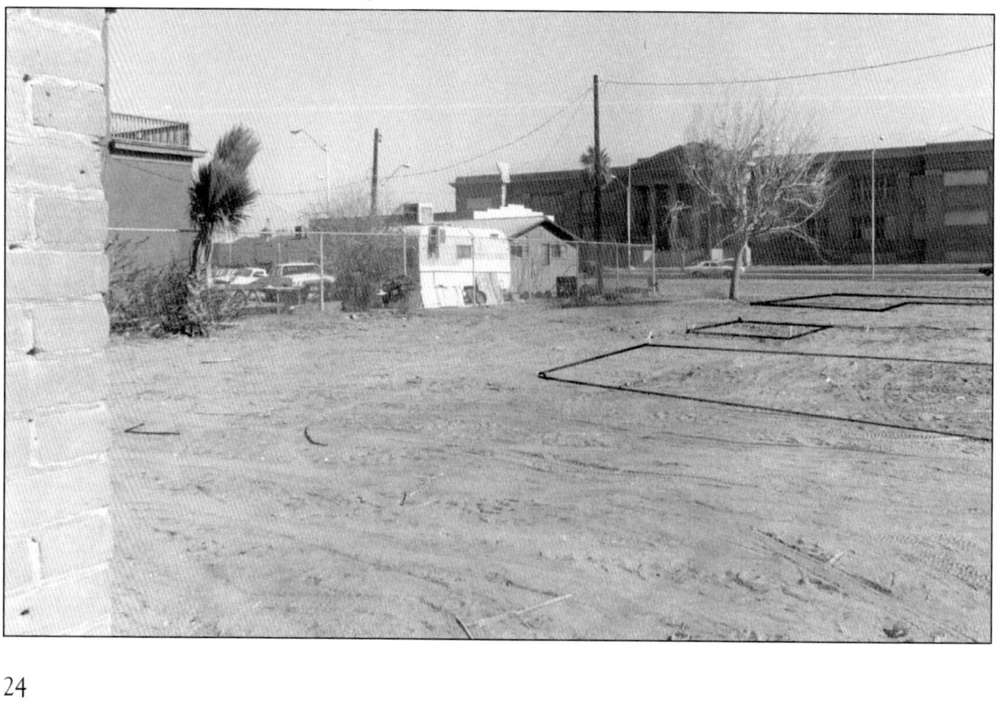

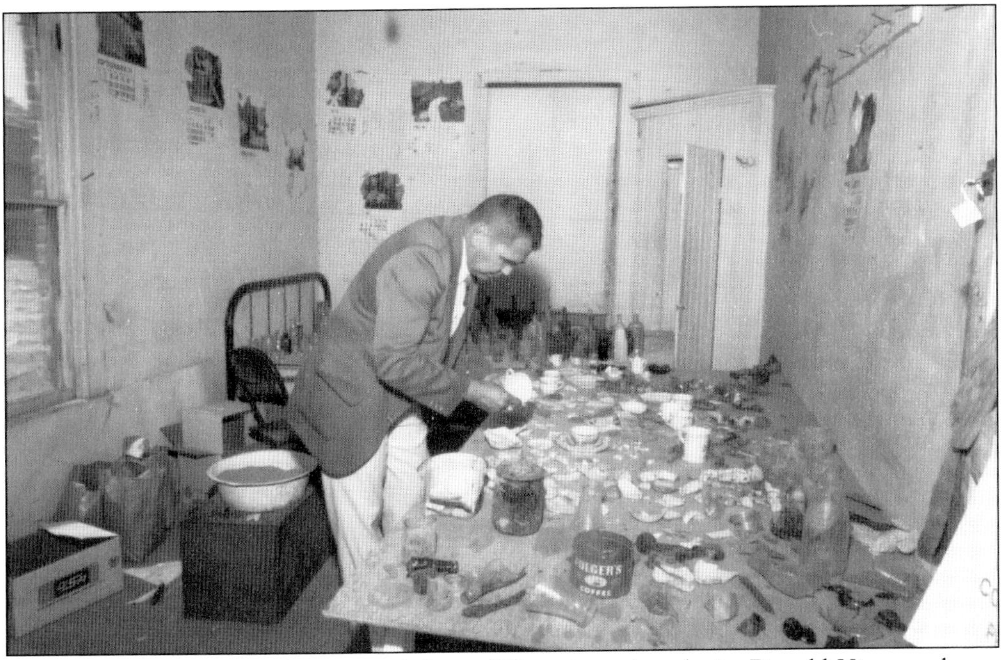

Pueblo Grande Museum director and City of Phoenix archaeologist Donald Hiser works on objects collected during the 1977–1978 excavations at Historic Heritage Square (above). The objects may have been found in an unused well. The Burgess Carriage House can be seen through the window at left. The photograph was taken inside one of the park's buildings, possibly the Teeter Carriage House or another small building near the temporary trailer behind the Rosson House. The below photograph shows a collection of glass bottles obtained during the 1977–1978 excavations, possibly from an unused well. (PGM.)

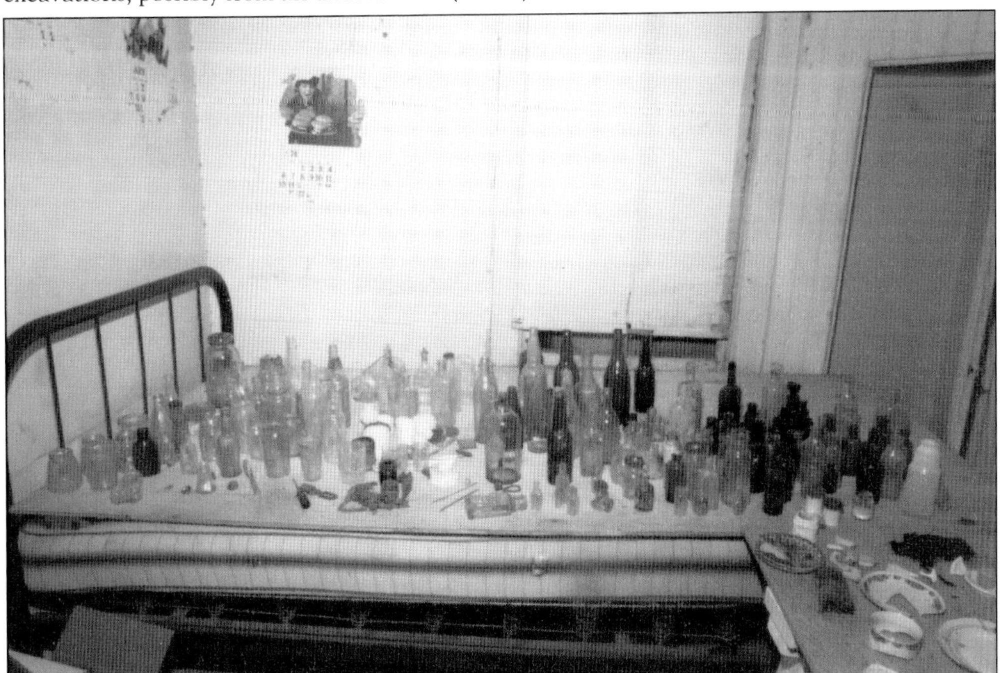

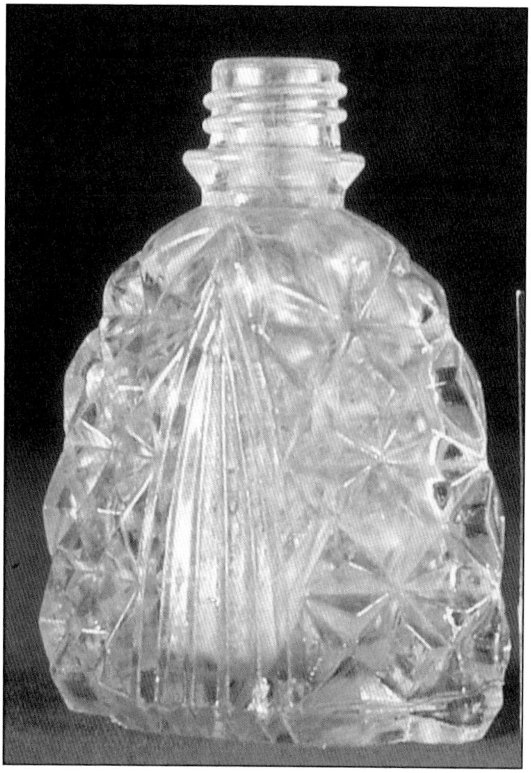

This clear, pressed-glass perfume bottle has a post-1903 date of fabrication, because it was manufactured by an automatic bottle machine. It was found in the brick-lined basement in the house of Leon Bouvier on Block 13, Lot 11, which was constructed in 1911. Bouvier is also associated with the Teeter House on Block 14. (PGM.)

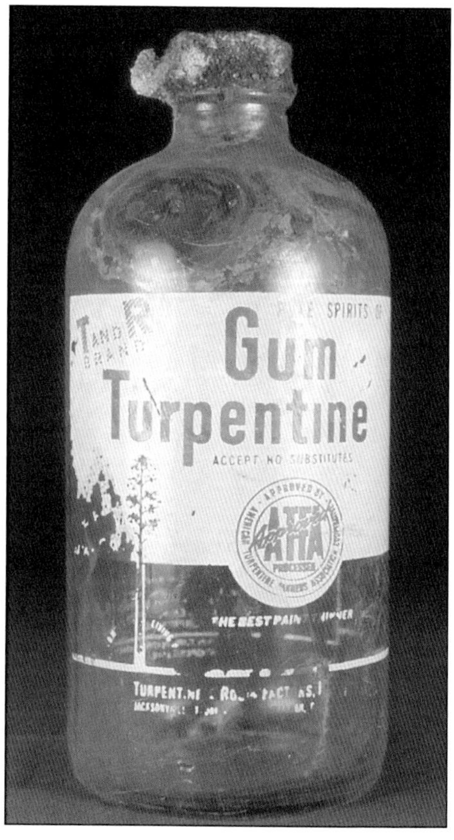

This is a cylindrical, machine-made, clear-glass bottle with rounded shoulders and a pyroglaze label used for gum turpentine. The bottle probably dates between 1940 and 1954 and was found in the former basement of Leon Bouvier's house on Block 13. (PGM.)

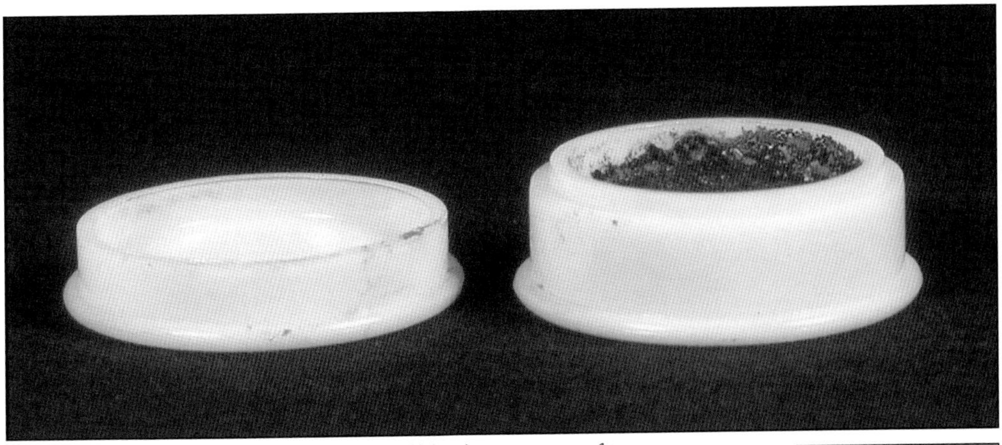

This white glass cosmetic container still had remnants of its contents, probably rouge. The container was recovered from Feature 923, a privy from Block 13, Lot 4, that was associated with a rental property. Although its age was not determined, it likely falls into the 1907–1918 period. (PGM.)

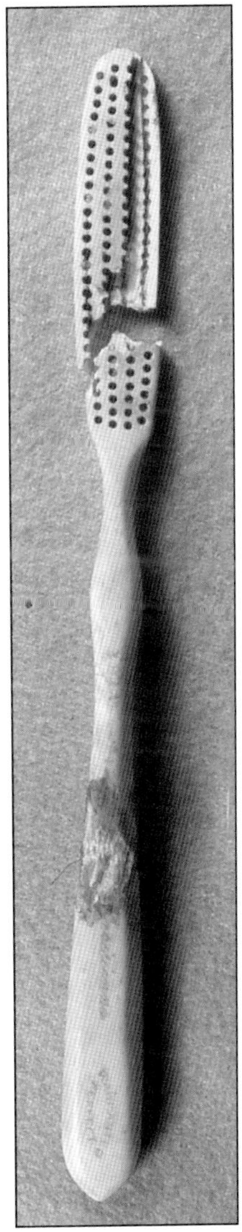

This toothbrush handle, manufactured from bone, was found in a privy from Block 13, Lots 4 and 6, with other items dated between 1900 and 1907. The inscription on the handle indicates it is of French origin. Margaret Jones owned both lots after 1902, using Lot 6 as a rental property. (PGM.)

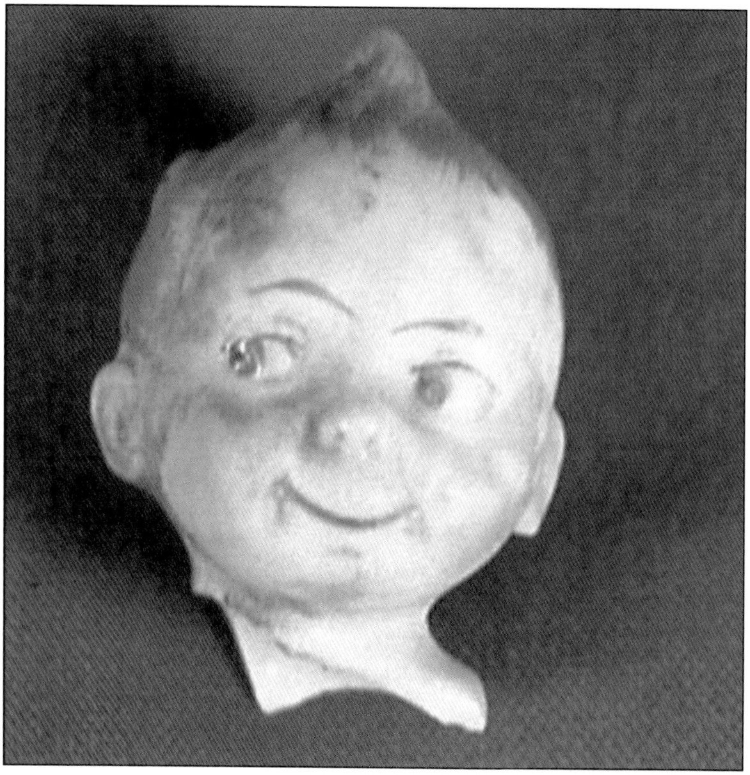

This hollow, thin-walled, molded porcelain doll head is that of an impish baby, similar to a Kewpie doll. The artifact was recovered from a trash-filled pit in Block 13, Lot 5, and dates from between 1900 and 1909. Material cultural items provide vital insight into the lives and status of the home owners. (PGM.)

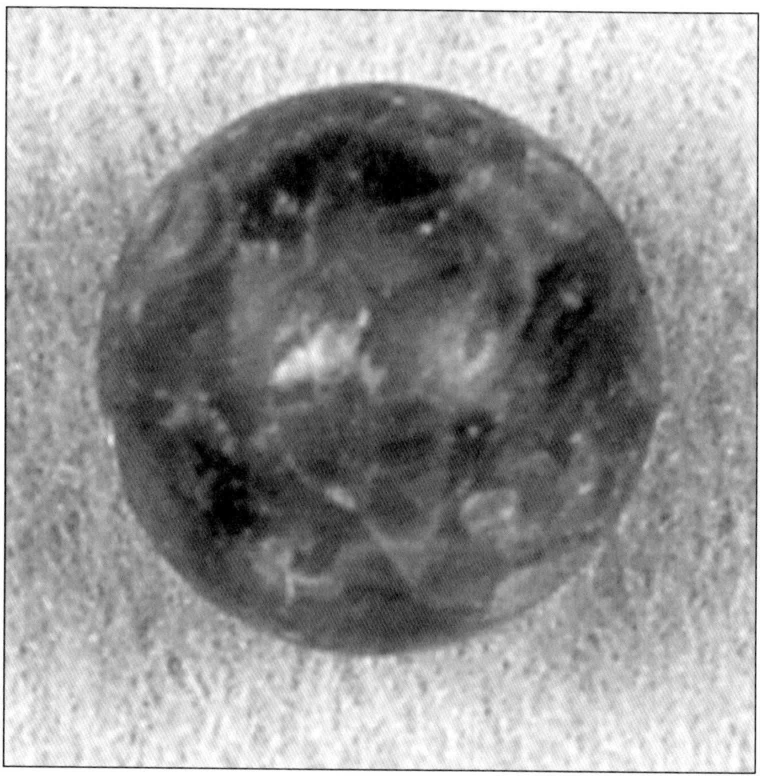

This marble, mostly blue with white swirls, has some cracking near the surface. The toy was found in a basement below a home's detached summer kitchen, located on Block 13, Lots 1 and 3. That house was constructed in 1887 or 1888. (PGM.)

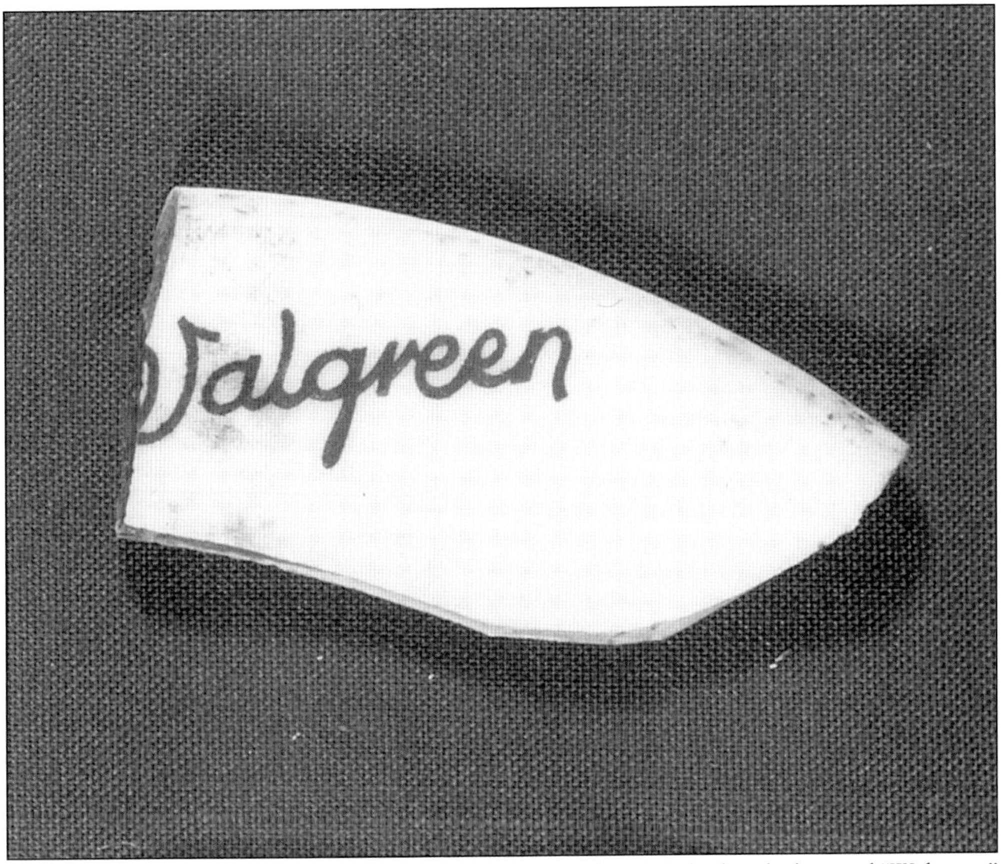

This white glazed porcelain fragment of a tableware vessel is inscribed with the word "Walgreen" in green cursive under the glaze. The original vessel was probably a plate or bowl from a Walgreen lunch counter. The porcelain fragment, found in a trash pit from Block 13, Lot 11, is dated between 1932 and 1943. (PGM.)

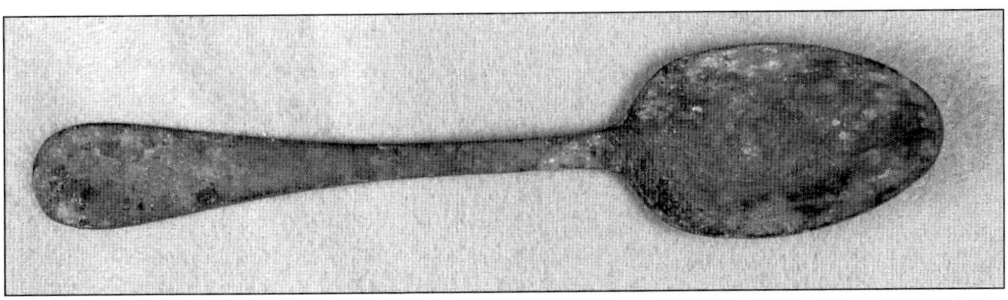

This nickel silver teaspoon is discolored due to corrosion. The utensil was found in a trash pit from Block 13, Lot 11, and is dated between 1932 and 1943. As with many found items, researchers will never know if it was disposed of accidentally or deliberately. It does raise the question as to whether someone in the house got in trouble when it went missing. (PGM.)

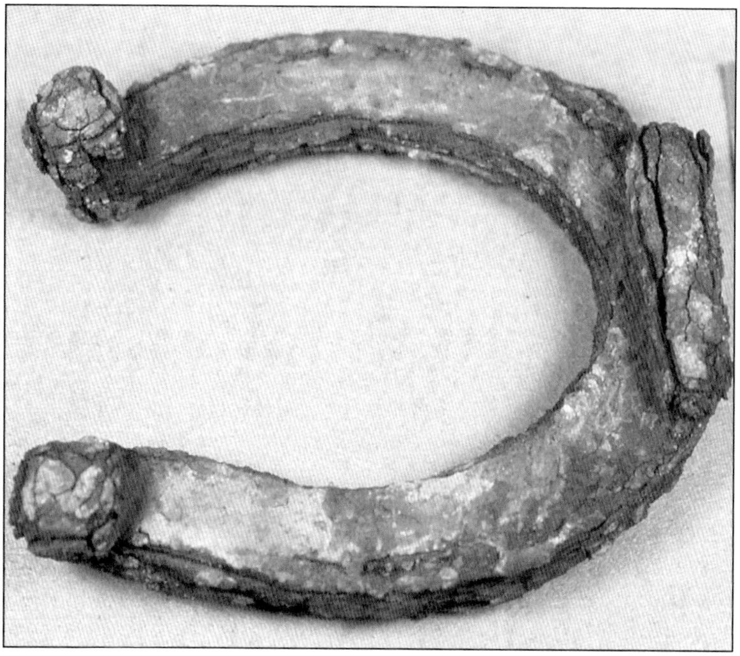

This large, extremely corroded horseshoe was probably made for a front hoof, due to the rounded toe. The horseshoe is at the upper end of sizes for premade shoes, which could, at the time, be custom fitted to the hoof. Based on the physical characteristics, it appears to be a shoe for a horse as opposed to a mule. The artifact was found in a trash pit from Block 16, Lot 11. (PGM.)

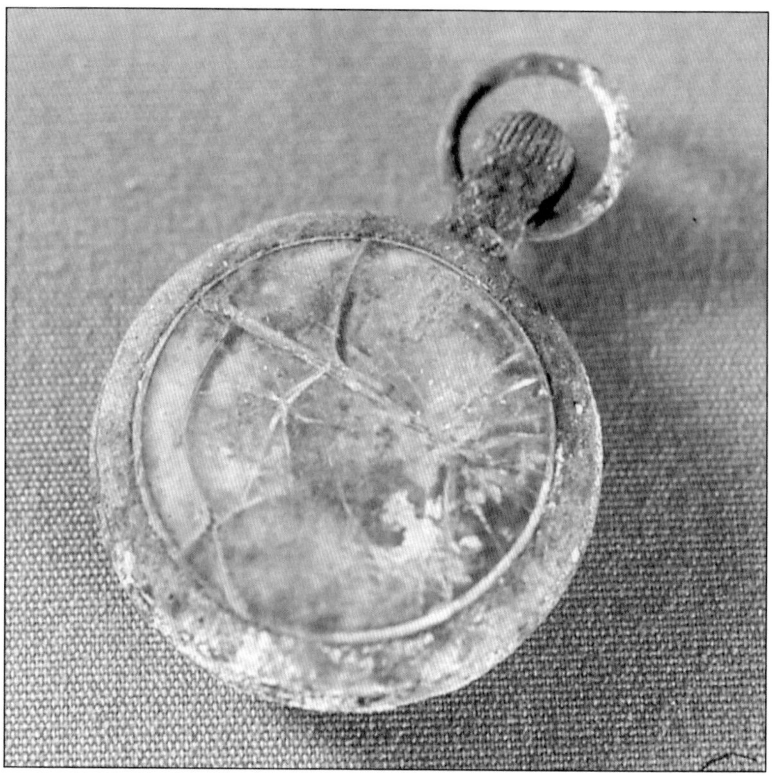

This small pocket watch, found in a privy from Block 13, Lots 4 and 6, might have been a boy's watch. The 1897 *Sears Roebuck Catalogue* illustrates a similar boy's watch. In consideration of the price range of watches presented in the catalog, it appears that this would have been a less expensive model. (PGM.)

This circular, one-hole bone button was found in a trash pit from Block 13, Lot 9, that contained glass and metal items dating from 1915 to 1970. With such a wide hole, it is not known how this button functioned. Perhaps it was a compound button, with an insert or shank that went into the center hole. (PGM.)

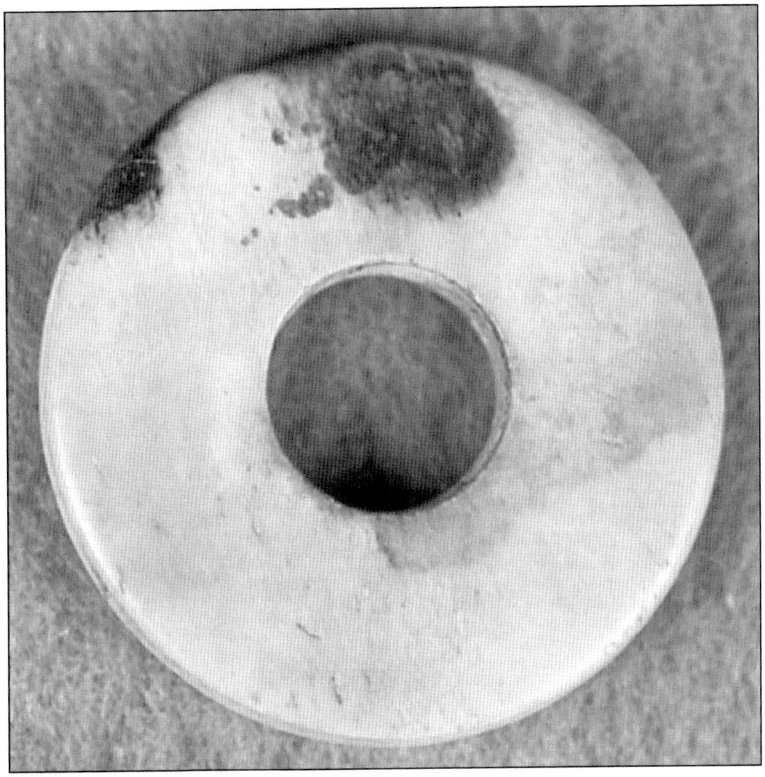

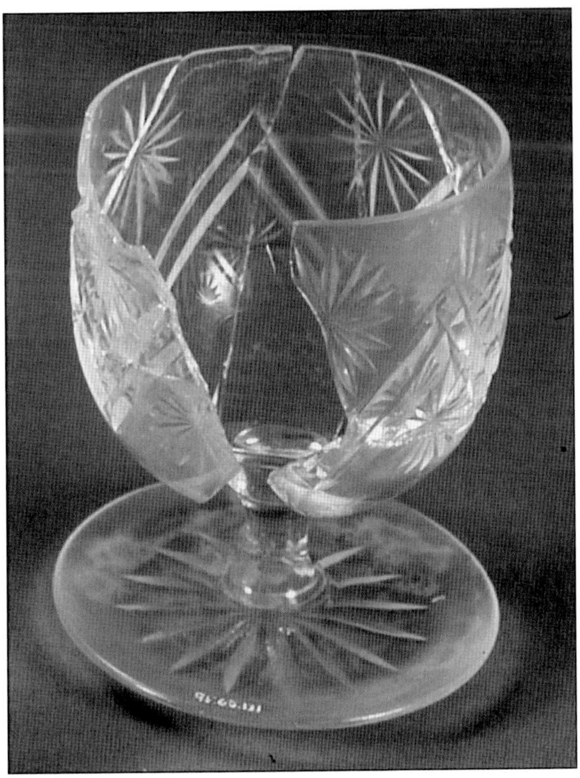

This is a reconstructed cut/imitation cut-glass stemmed tableware. Distinctions in glass tableware are one measure of socioeconomic status. This artifact was found in a privy located on Block 16, Lot 9, which had an address of 509 and 517 East Adams Street. The privy was associated with the most prominent resident of the project area, John Y.T. Smith. His house was constructed in 1892. (PGM.)

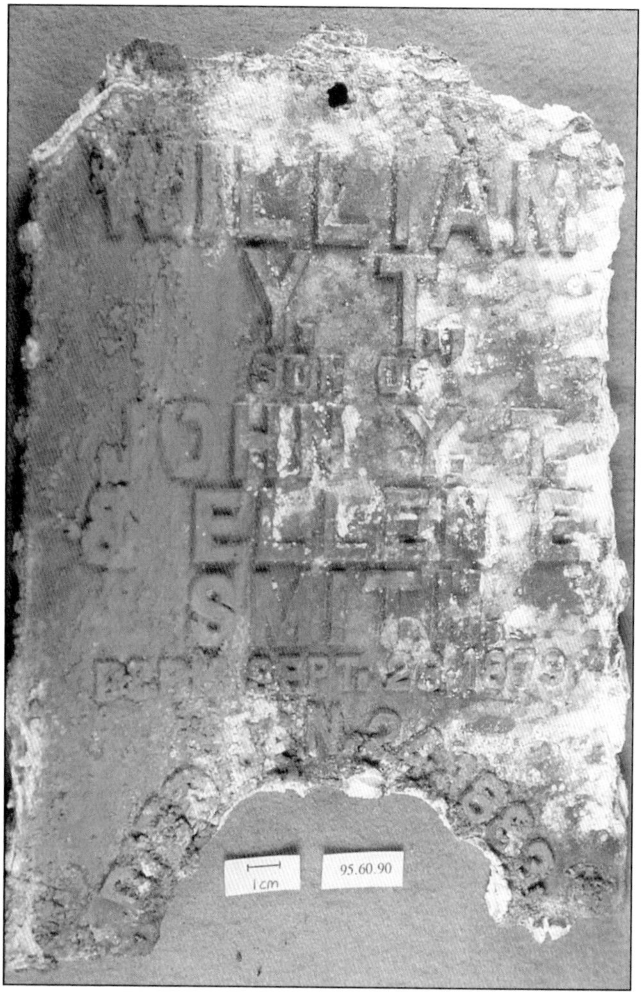

This flat, rectangular-cast, lead alloy commemorative plaque (or possibly a gravestone plaque) was found in a privy on Block 16, Lot 9. The exact nature of the plaque has not been determined, such as where it would have been hung following the death of William Y.T. Smith, son of John Y.T. Smith, who owned the property from 1886 to 1909. The privy was capped around 1907. (PGM.)

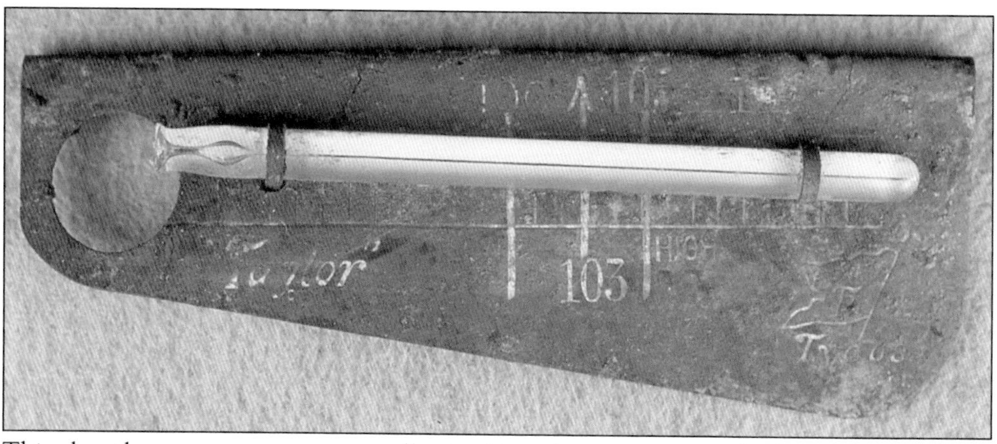

This glass thermometer on a copper alloy backing plate is not a standard item. Based on the markings, it was probably used to monitor the ambient temperature for a special purpose requiring temperatures between 100 and 105 degrees Fahrenheit. The thermometer was found in an undated trash pit from Block 13, Lot 7. (PGM.)

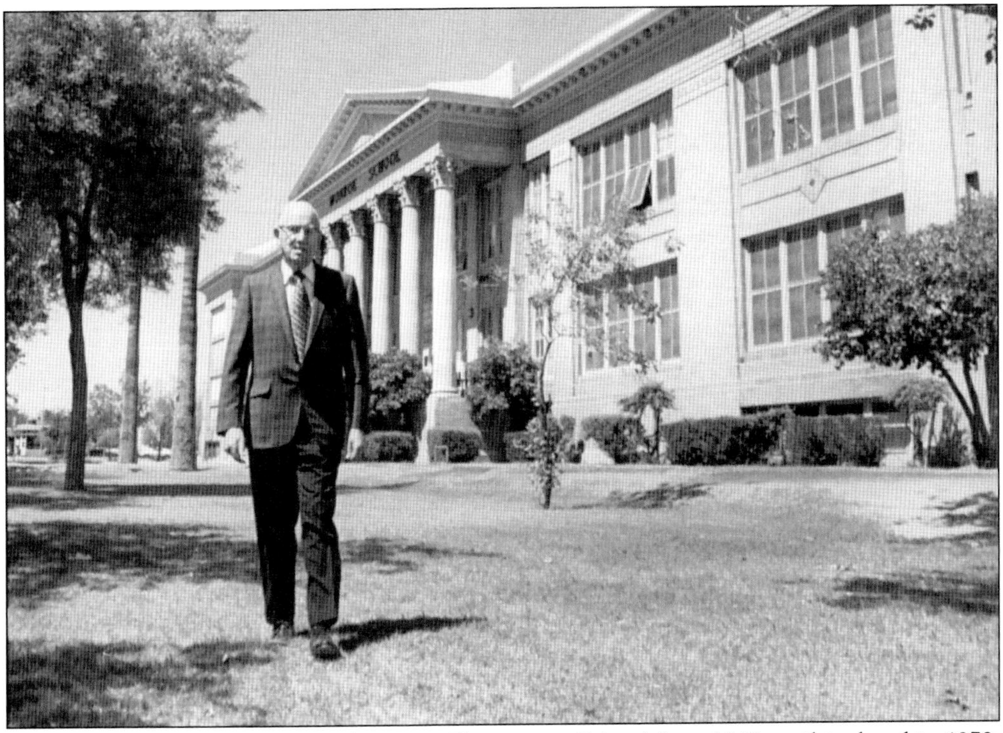

Clifford Armack was principal of Monroe Elementary School from 1949 until it closed in 1972. The school was built in 1914 and was attended by neighborhood children. Following its closure, Monroe School served as offices for a number of years until the building was rehabilitated to serve as the Phoenix Children's Museum. (Courtesy of Phoenix Elementary School District.)

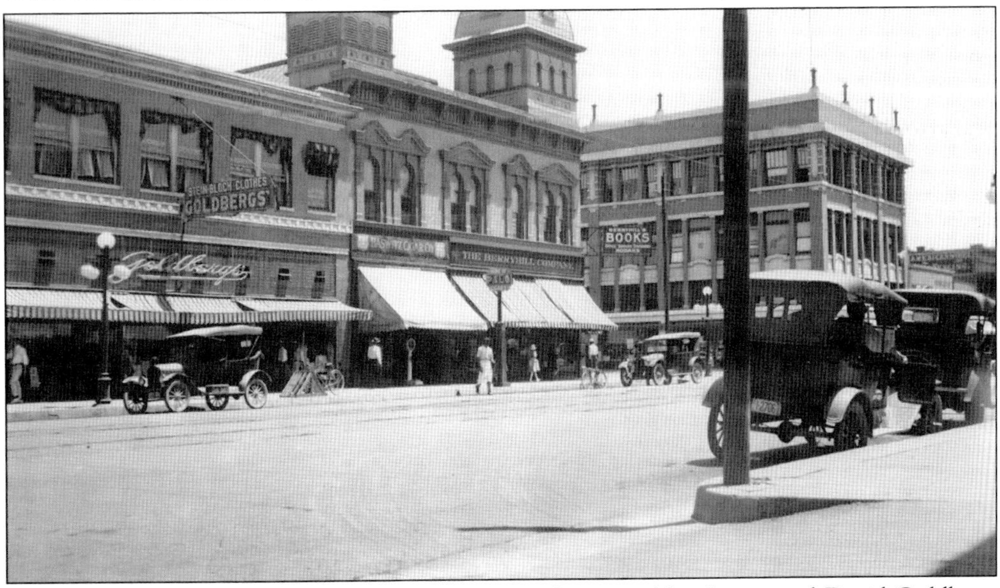

Goldberg's was the men's clothing store owned and operated by Aaron and David Goldberg. Located on Washington Street, the apparel shop was considered one of the finest in Phoenix. In 1897, Aaron Goldberg purchased the Rosson House from the Rosson family. (Courtesy of the Collection of Jeremy Rowe Vintage Photography, vintagephoto.com.)

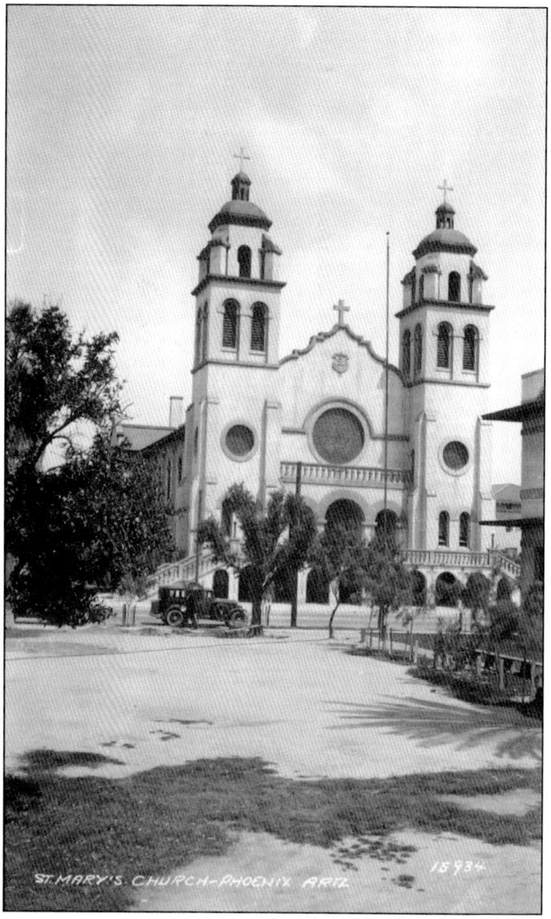

St. Mary's Church is located at 231 North Third Street, two blocks west of the Rosson House on the northeast corner of Third and Monroe Streets. Now classified as a minor basilica, St. Mary's was completed in 1914. In this area of Monroe Street, there were many large homes like the Rosson House. (Courtesy of the Collection of Jeremy Rowe Vintage Photography, vintagephoto.com.)

This 1914 photograph of Phoenix Union High School shows Van Buren Street still as a dirt road. Van Buren Street was the northern boundary of the original Phoenix townsite, just one block north of Monroe Street. The children of two families that lived in the Rosson House, the Higley boys and the Gammel girls, likely attended this high school. (Courtesy of the Collection of Jeremy Rowe Vintage Photography, vintagephoto.com.)

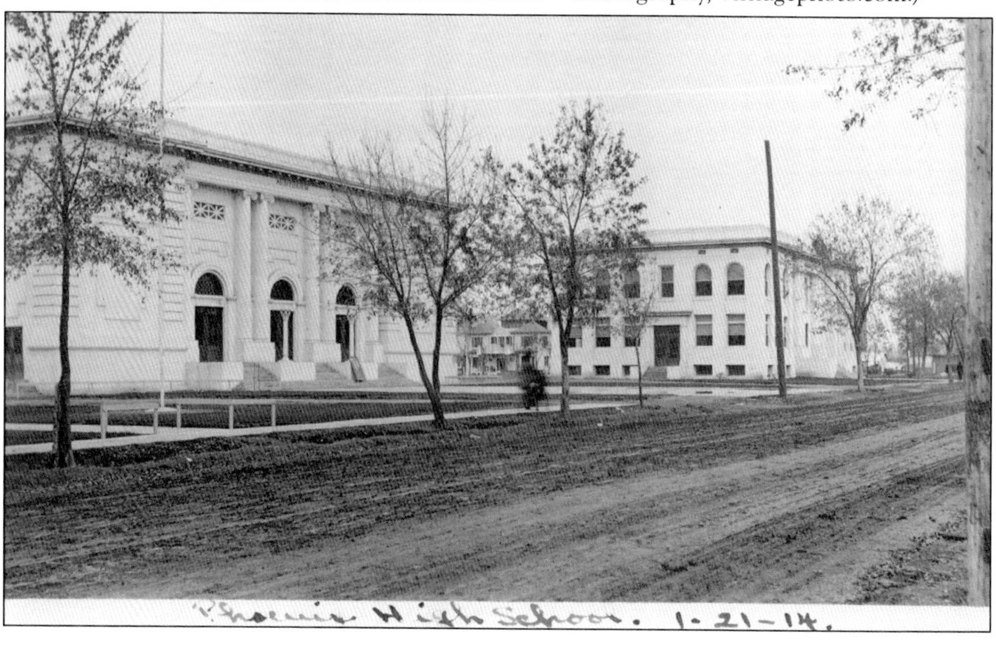

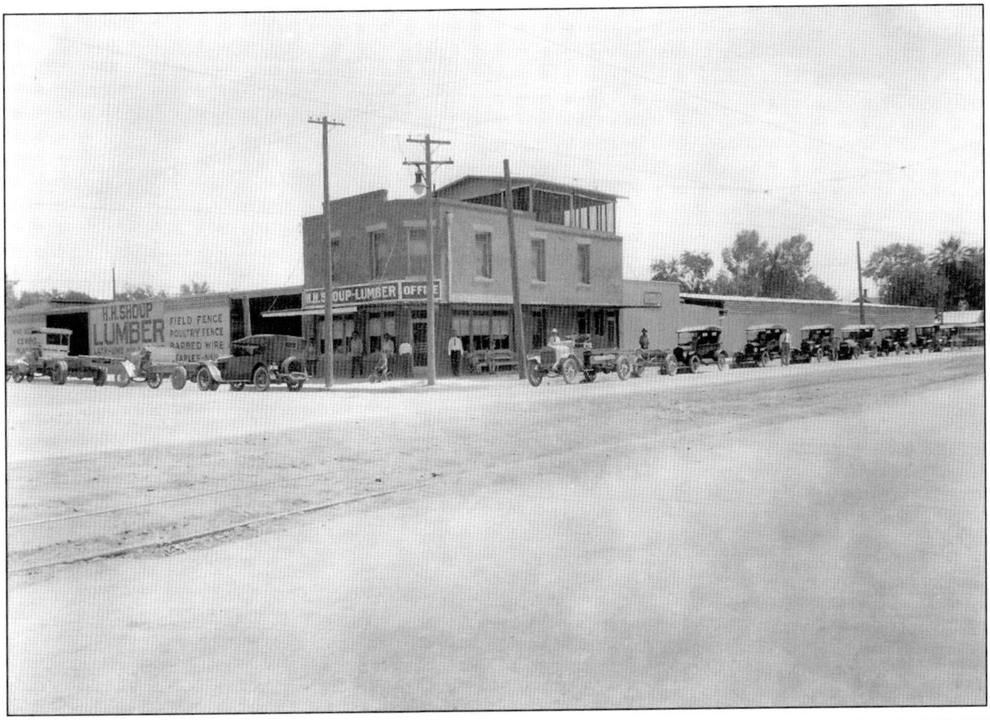

The Shoup Lumber Yard was an extremely busy place, judging by the number of vehicles surrounding it. A 1930 *Arizona Republican* advertisement touted, "Now Was the Time to Build," even though it was the start of the Great Depression. Constructed on what is the south half of Block 15, the business remained in operation until the early 1950s. (RHHSFG.)

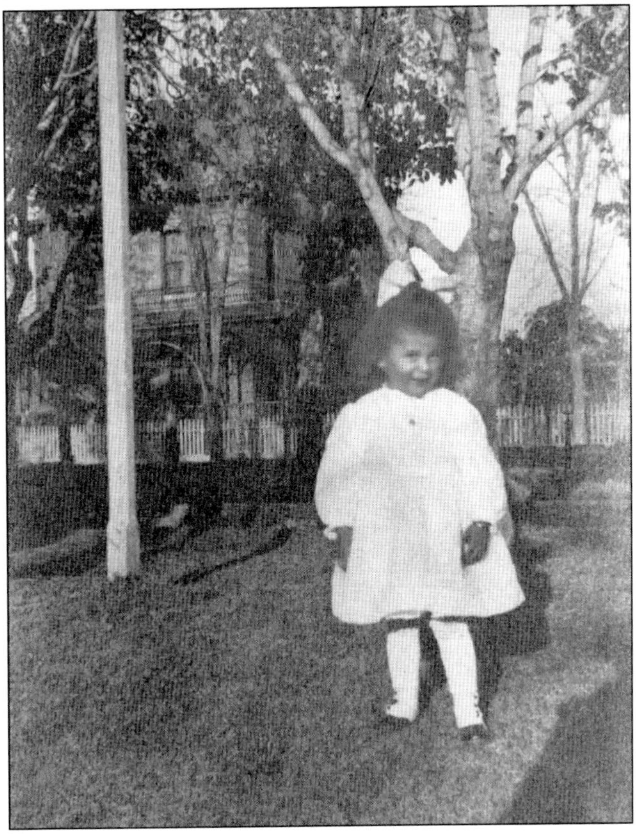

This photograph, taken in 1909, shows three-year old Benita Yaeger, with the Rosson House in the background. Her grandparents lived across the street, at 136 North Sixth Street. Benita became a volunteer when the Rosson House opened as a museum in 1980. (RHHSFG.)

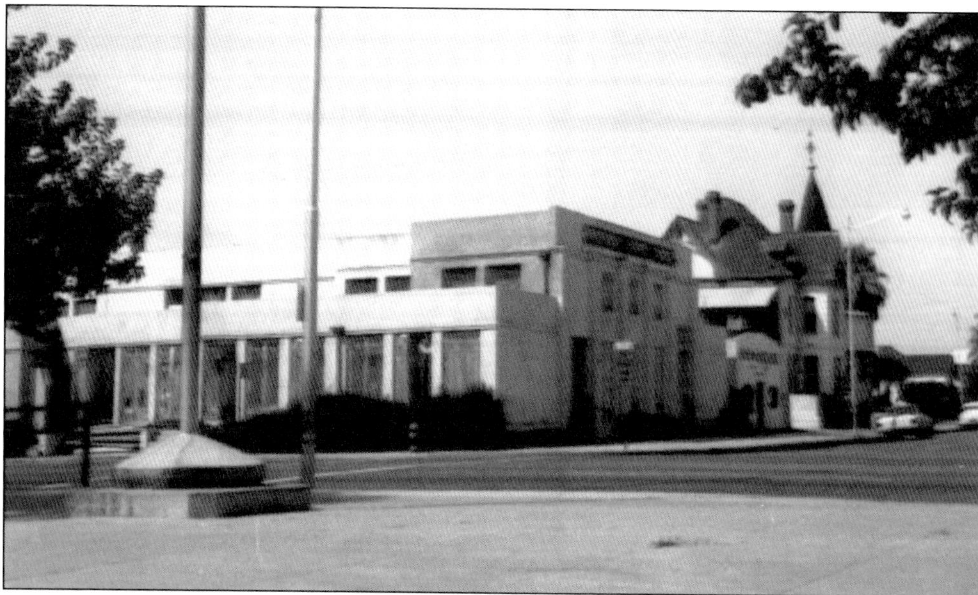

The 1969 photograph above, taken from the steps of Monroe Elementary School on the east side of Seventh Street, looks westward. The large structure in the foreground is the former Phoenix First Ward Church of Jesus Christ of Latter-day Saints (LDS). The initial building was constructed in 1918–1919. As the congregation increased, so did the building. The LDS First Ward occupied the building until 1948, when it moved to a larger site a couple of miles away. The building was sold to another church, the Phoenix Gospel Temple (below), which used the building until 1968. It was razed in 1969. The Lath Pavilion in Historic Heritage Square is located on the site of the former church. (Courtesy of the Church of Jesus Christ of Latter-day Saints.)

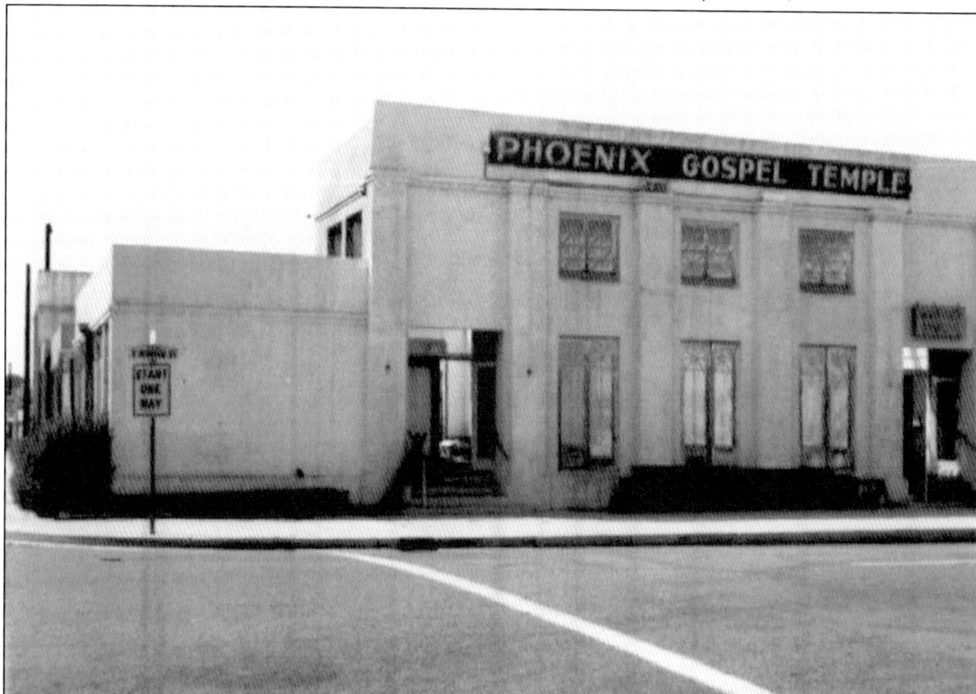

Three

The Rosson House

The centerpiece of Block 14 was the Rosson House. The Victorian mansion continues as the centerpiece of today's Historic Heritage Square. The house was designed by A.P. Petit, a noted architect from San Francisco who died before its completion. The architecture, which displays multicultural attributes such as an Asian moon gate, Italianate hooded windows, and a French octagonal tower, may not have been a unique design. Exact plans for the house had been previously published in 1891 in George Franklin Barber's *The Cottage Souvenir No. 2: Containing 120 Original Designs in Cottage and Detail Architecture*.

In the frontier city of Phoenix, the impressive Victorian mansion undoubtedly aided the political career of Dr. Rosson, who became the ninth mayor of Phoenix, serving from 1895 to 1896. The house featured many conveniences that were rare for the time, including electrical lights, cold and hot water, an upstairs bathroom, and a telephone. The mansion may have caused the Rosson family financial difficulties, however, as they owned the house for only two years. During this period, they rented the Rosson House for two winters to Whitelaw Reid, the longtime editor of the *New York Tribune*, the 1892 Republican vice presidential nominee, and the US ambassador to France and the United Kingdom. Reid temporarily moved to Phoenix to relieve his respiratory problems. Reid's correspondence while he lived in the Rosson House provides invaluable information regarding its original design.

Three other families, the Goldbergs, Higleys, and Gammels, owned and lived in the home before its transition to a boardinghouse by the late 1940s. Each family made changes to the house through remodeling and the construction of outbuildings. Downtown Phoenix, however, gradually became less desirable as a location for upscale residences, so the single-family dwelling was subdivided into multiple rooms to rent. The Rosson House evolved from a respectable boardinghouse to a flophouse frequented by skid row itinerants by the 1960s. The house was purchased by the City of Phoenix in 1974.

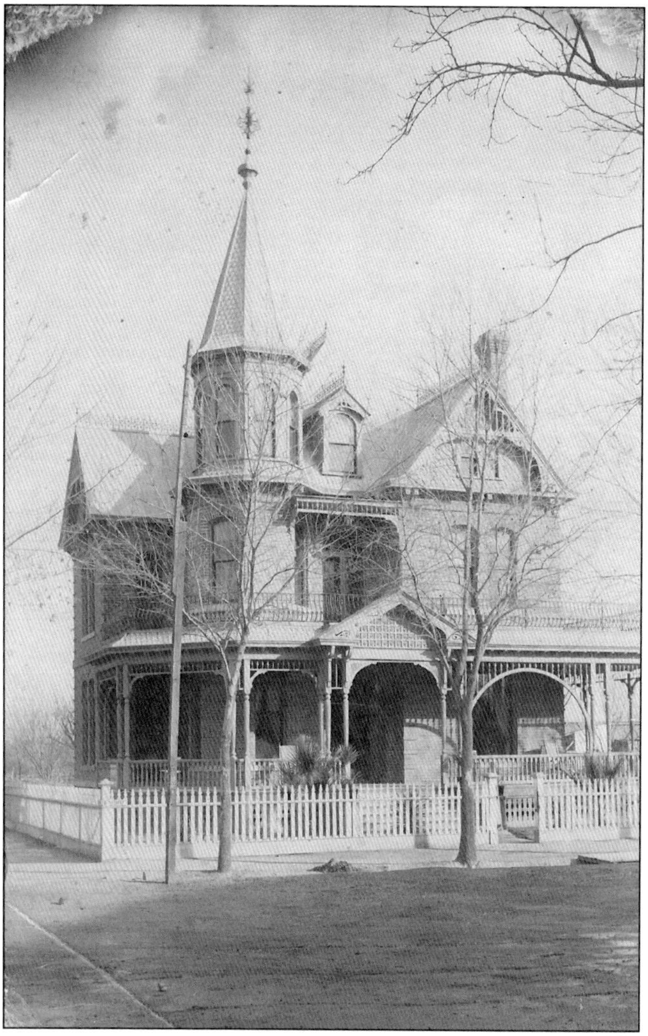

This c. 1900 postcard of the Rosson House indicates the stately presence of the Victorian mansion on the southeast corner of Monroe and Sixth Streets. A.P. Petit was the architect of this Eastlake/Stick brick home, which was completed in early 1895 at a cost of $7,525. (RHHSFG.)

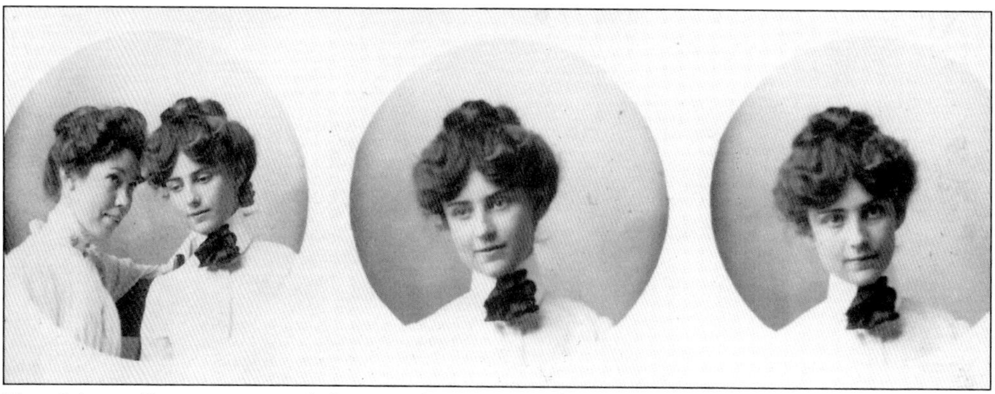

Flora Murray Rosson, pictured alone in the center and right photographs, poses with one of her sisters on the left. Her family moved to Phoenix in 1870 when she was a young girl. Flora purchased Block 14 from one of her older sisters in 1882 for $1,000. Her husband, Dr. Roland Lee Rosson, was the ninth Phoenix mayor; her brother-in-law, John Alsap, was the first. (RHHSFG.)

Depicted here in his military uniform, Dr. Roland Lee Rosson came to the Arizona Territory in late 1875 from Virginia to serve with the US Army as an assistant surgeon. He was stationed at several posts, including Camp McDowell near Phoenix. He left the Army in March 1879, married Flora B. Murray in August 1880, continued to practice medicine, and had a successful political career. He was Phoenix's ninth mayor. (RHHSFG.)

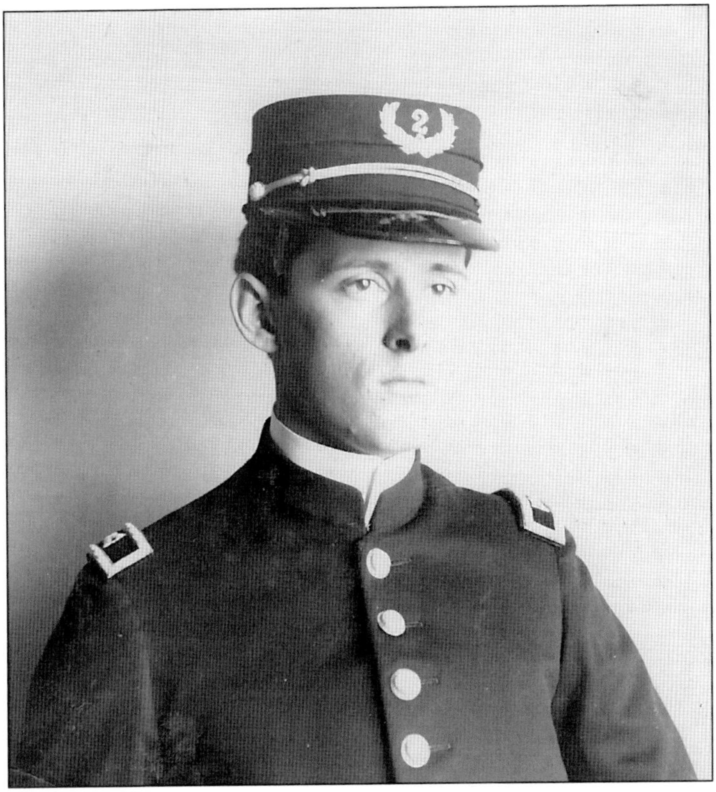

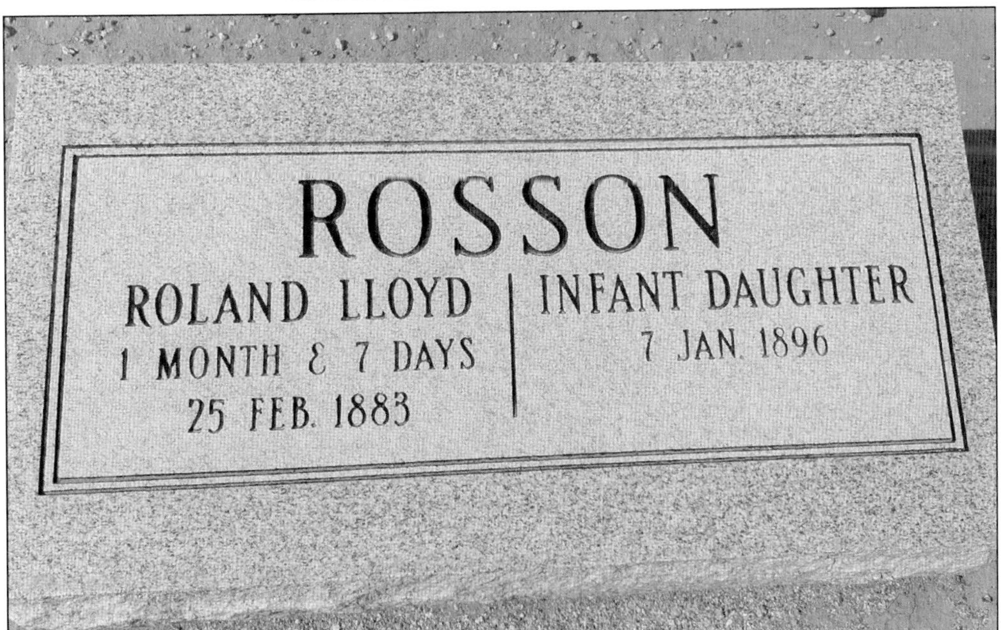

The Rossons had five children who lived to maturity: Clyde, Irene, Vivien, Floy, and Norma. This headstone, for their two children who died in infancy, rests in the Pioneer and Military Cemetery, located at Fifteenth Avenue and West Jefferson Street. The headstone is a replacement for the original marker. (RHHSFG.)

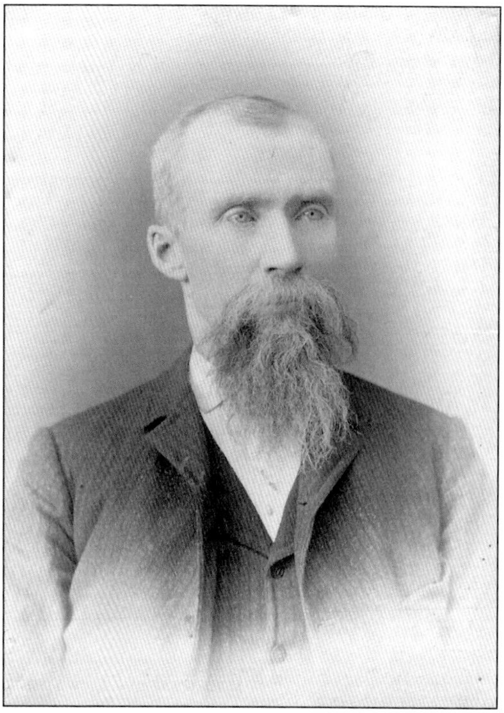

George Cisney was the contractor who built the Rosson House. He established his construction firm in 1893 after moving to Phoenix from Indiana. Cisney's son, Claud, who carried on the business following his father's death, built the Thomas House, which was later moved onto Historic Heritage Square. (RHHSFG.)

This undated photograph of the Rosson House was probably taken before 1910, as evidenced by the dirt streets. The octagonal tower with its decorative finial atop the gable is a prominent feature. The California architect A.P. Petit was familiar with brick technology and helped transform Phoenix from its reliance on wood-frame and adobe construction to this much sturdier material. (RHHSFG.)

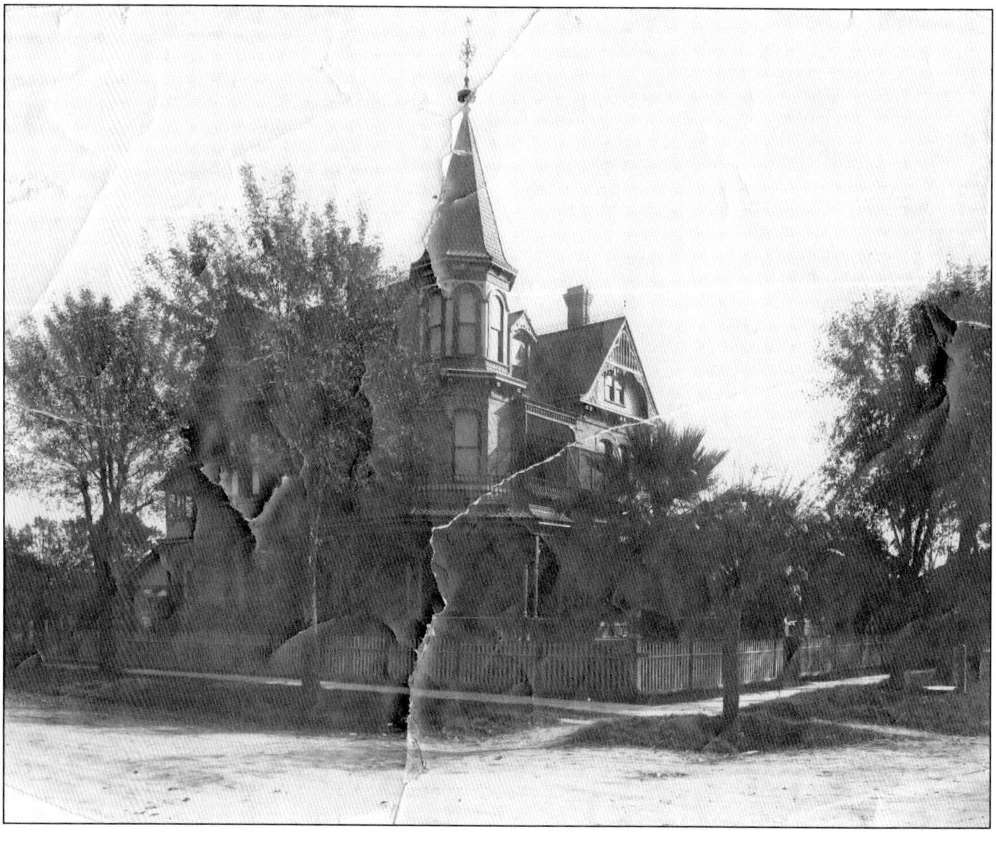

Whitelaw Reid, the prominent *New York Tribune* editor, rented the Rosson House in the fall of 1895 when his doctor told him that he needed a warm, dry climate to aid his health. Reid stayed for a number of months and rented the Rosson House the following winter. His letters and editorials provide invaluable information on life in Phoenix at the time. (RHHSFG.)

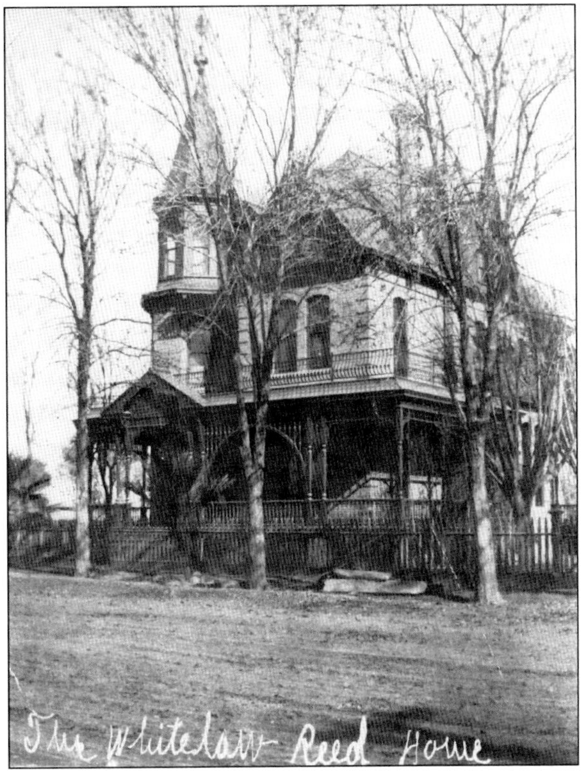

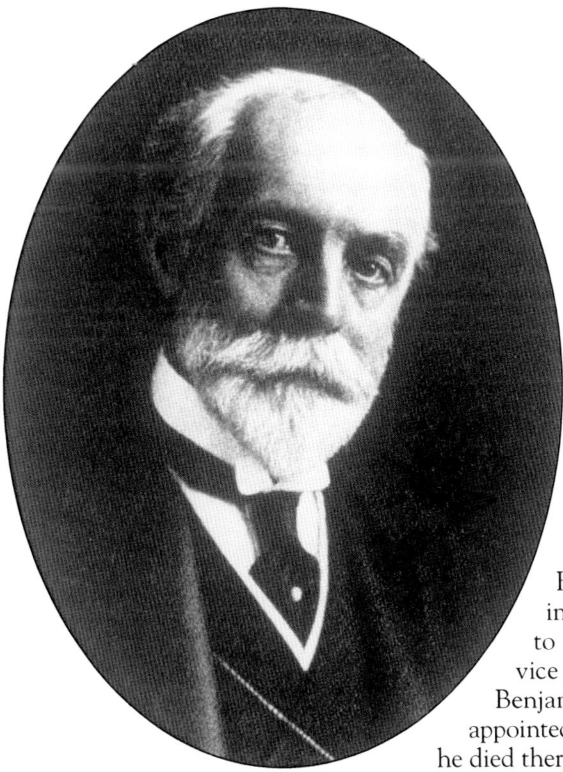

Before arriving in Phoenix for the first time in 1895, Whitelaw Reid had been ambassador to France and had run unsuccessfully for vice president on the Republican ticket with Benjamin Harrison. Pres. Theodore Roosevelt appointed Reid ambassador to England in 1905, and he died there in 1912 at the age of 75. (RHHSFG.)

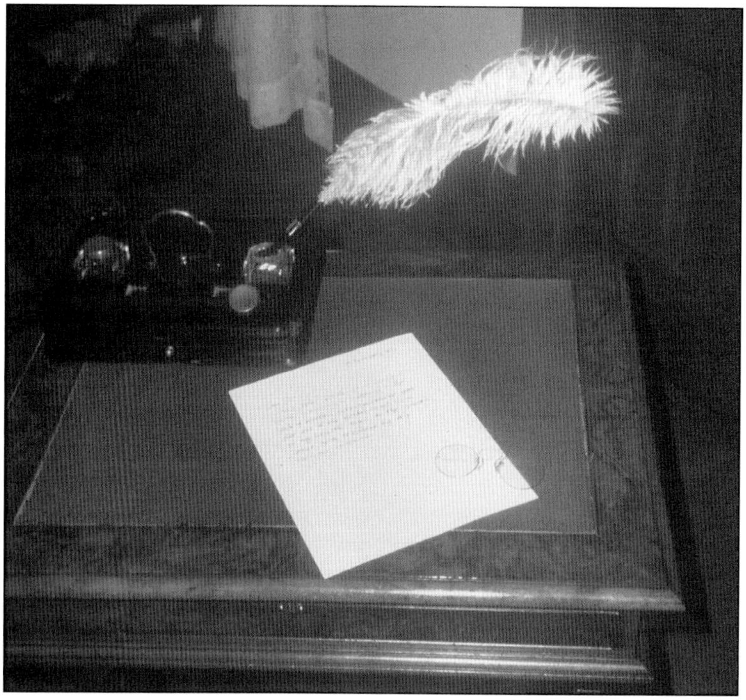

Featured in the library of the Rosson House Museum is Whitelaw Reid's pen set. The prolific Reid wrote battlefront reports during the Civil War, published the two-volume *Ohio in the Civil War* in 1867, and worked with Horace Greeley for several years at the *New York Tribune* before purchasing it in 1872. (RHHSFG.)

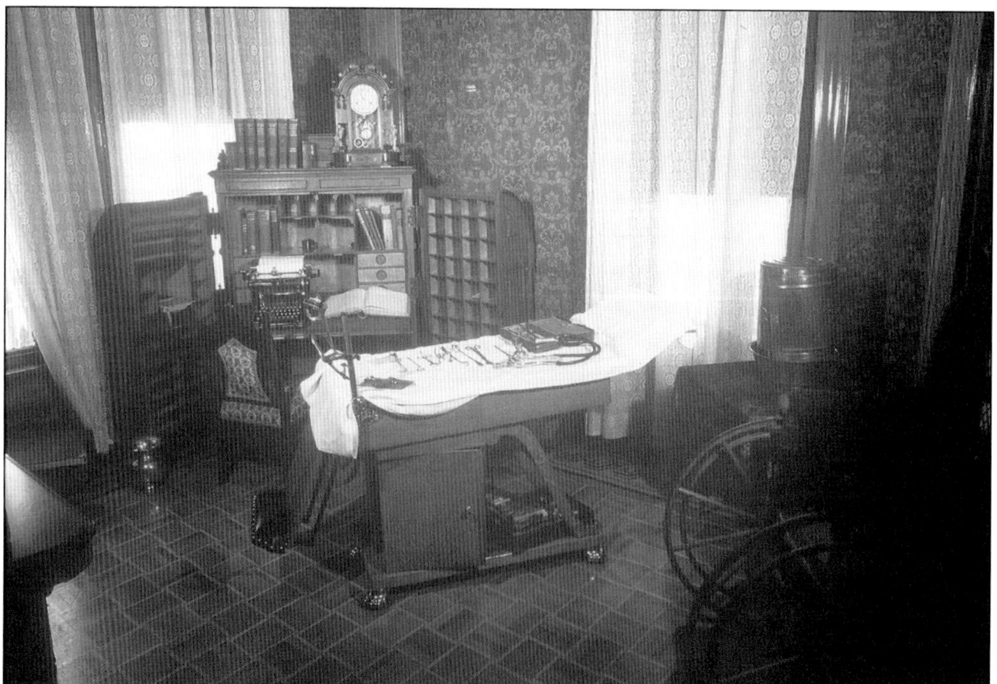

Dr. Roland Rosson had an office nearby at 325 East Monroe Street. It is not known whether he also used one of the rooms at the Rosson House as an office. If Rosson did, he may have had some of this equipment. Rosson is credited for performing, with another physician, the first successful hairlip repair in the Arizona Territory. (RHHSFG.)

Aaron Goldberg, who moved to Phoenix with his parents when he was 16, may have been the Barry Goldwater of his day. He served in the Arizona Territorial Legislature, was instrumental in moving the territorial capital to Phoenix, and was the legislative liaison for the construction of the capitol building. He and his brother, David, co-owned Goldberg's clothing store. The Goldbergs purchased the Victorian mansion from the Rossons in June 1897. (Courtesy of Arizona State Library, Archives and Public Records, History and Archives Division, #98-1543.)

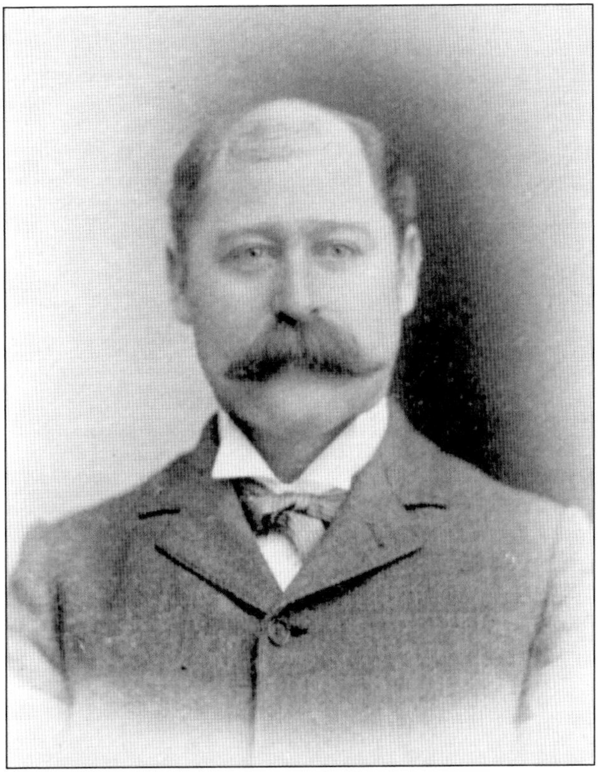

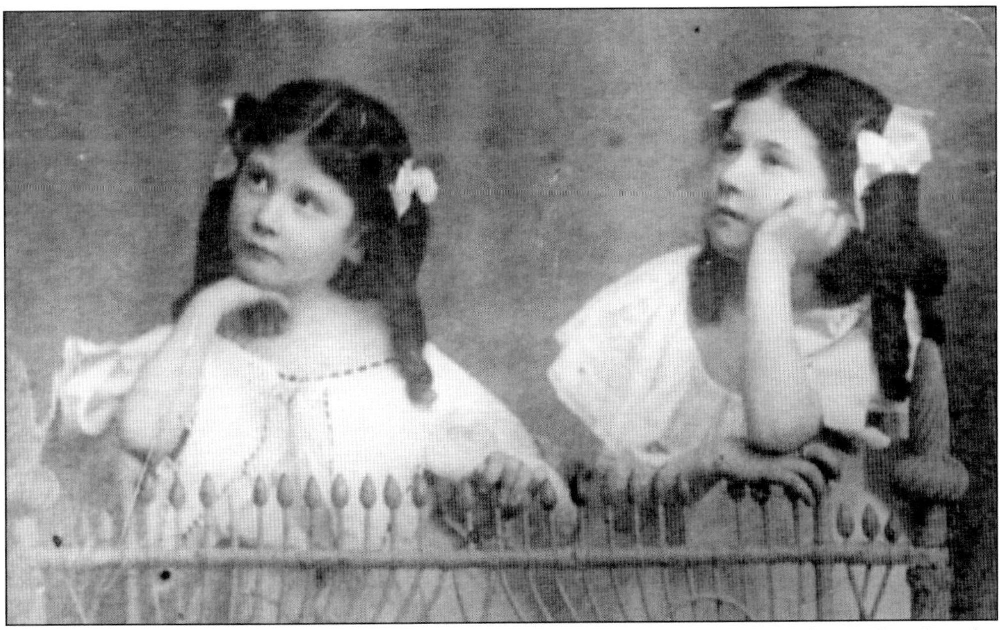

Selma and Hazel Goldberg, daughters of Aaron and Carrie Goldberg, pose in this undated studio photograph. The daughters occupied the upstairs, north bedroom of the Rosson House. Hazel married Joseph T. Melczer on Arizona Statehood Day, February 14, 1912, with Barry Goldwater as the ring bearer. Selma later married Albert Rosenberg. (Courtesy of Arizona State Library, Archives and Public Records, History and Archives Division, #02-0104.)

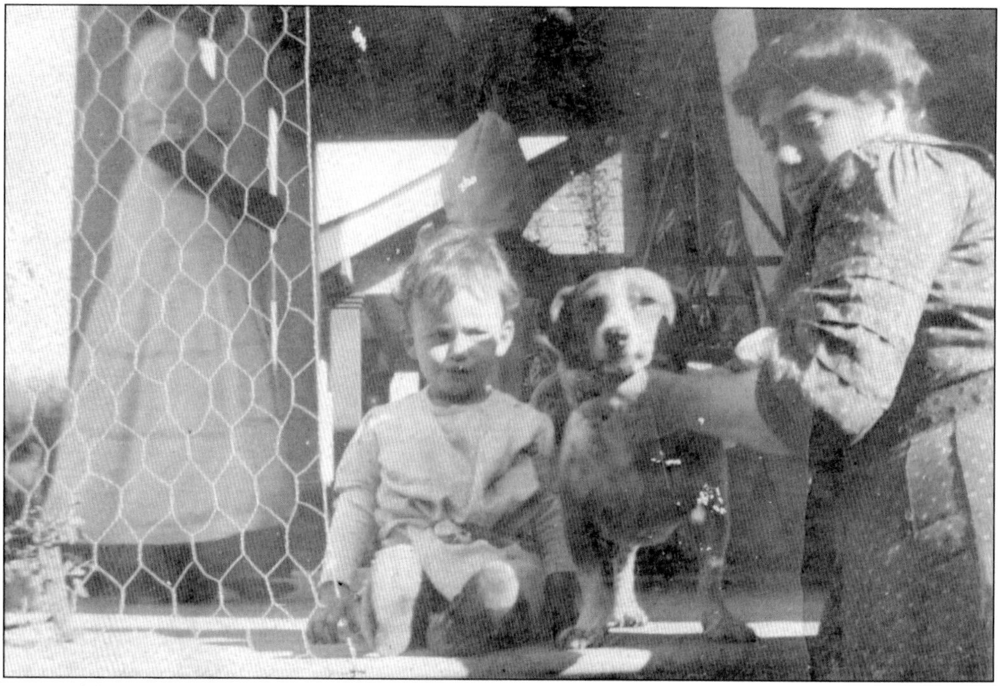

Pictured here on what may be one of the porches of the Rosson House are Chester "Chet" Goldberg and his mother, Carrie. Aaron and Carrie Goldberg were a social couple; detailed information on the parties they attended could be found in the *Arizona Republican*. Chet Goldberg eventually took over his father and uncle's clothing business, Goldberg Brothers. (Courtesy of Arizona Historical Society, Goldberg Family Collection, PPM55244.)

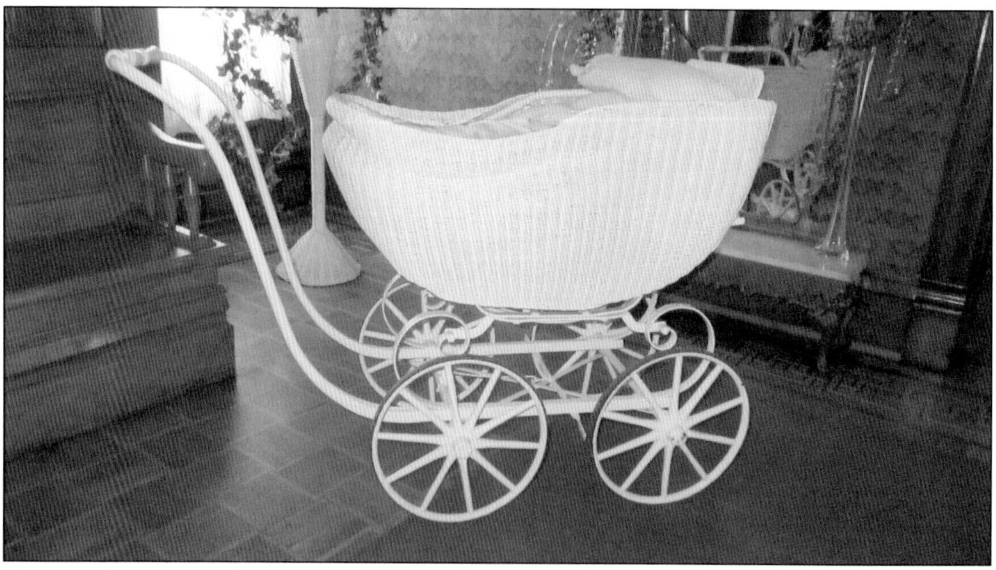

The Goldbergs were the owners of the Rosson House at the time of their only son, Chester's, birth in April 1899. This photograph shows Chester's white, painted wicker baby carriage, which is on display in the foyer of the Rosson House Museum. (RHHSFG.)

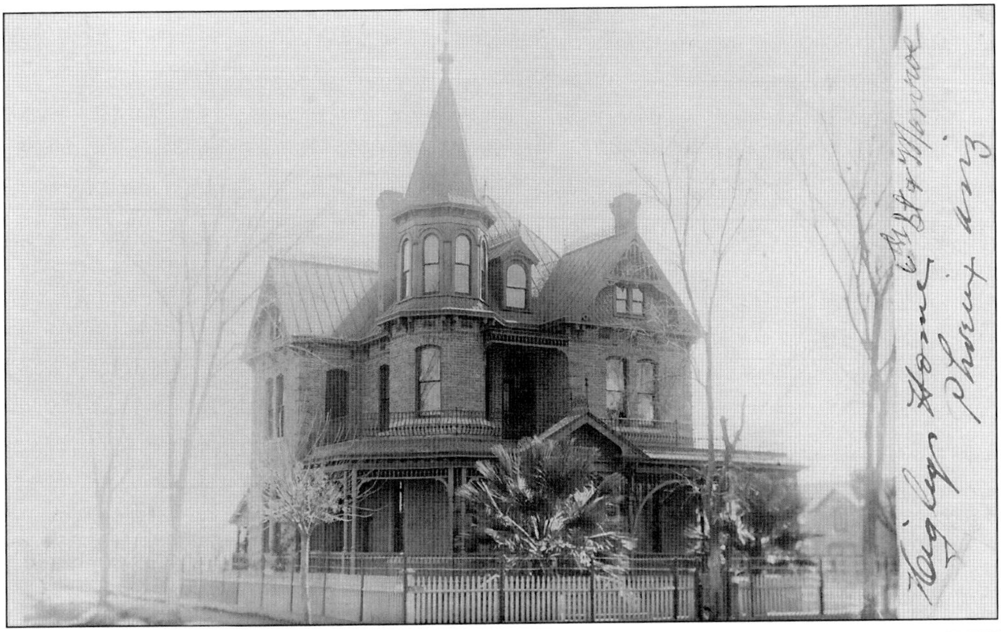

This undated postcard identifies the Rosson House as the Higley House on the corner of Sixth and Monroe Streets. The Higleys were the third owners of the house, having purchased it from the Goldbergs in 1904. The Higley family had moved to Phoenix from Prescott, Arizona, just before the turn of the 20th century. (RHHSFG.)

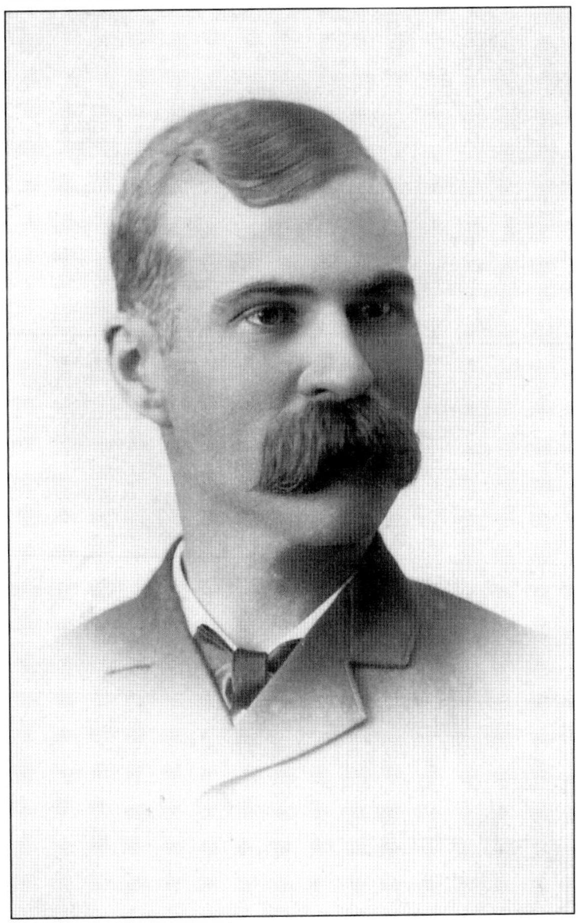

Young Stephen Higley's photograph was taken in 1889 in Prescott, Arizona, when he worked for the Santa Fe, Prescott & Phoenix Railway. After moving to Phoenix, he eventually purchased the *Arizona Republican* newspaper, now the *Arizona Republic*, and became its editor. The unincorporated community of Higley in southeastern Maricopa County is named for Stephen Higley, who owned over 8,000 acres in that area. (Courtesy of Sharlot Hall Museum Photos.)

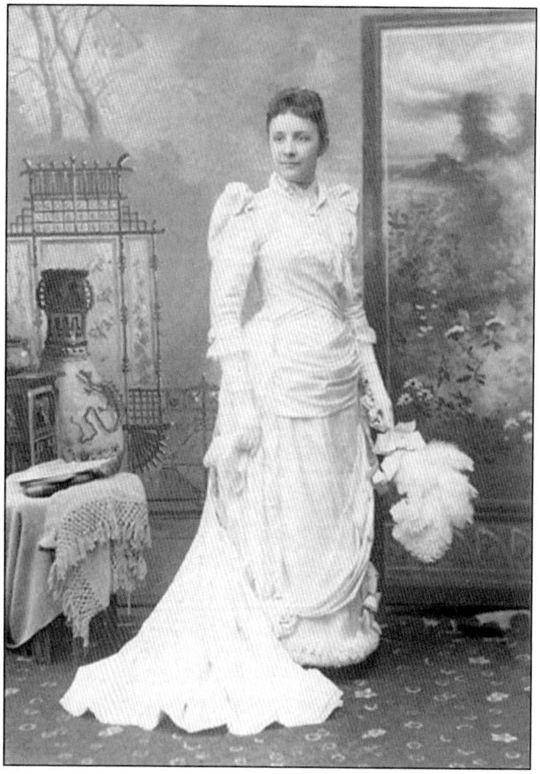

Jessie Howe, daughter of Civil War Union general John H. Howe, poses in her wedding dress in a photograph taken in November 1890. A large, gold-framed version of this photograph hung on the north wall of the parlor when the Higleys lived in the Rosson House. To help maintain their new home, the Higleys employed a live-in cook, Mary Johns, a Maricopa Indian whose services may have come from Phoenix Indian School. (Courtesy of the Higley family.)

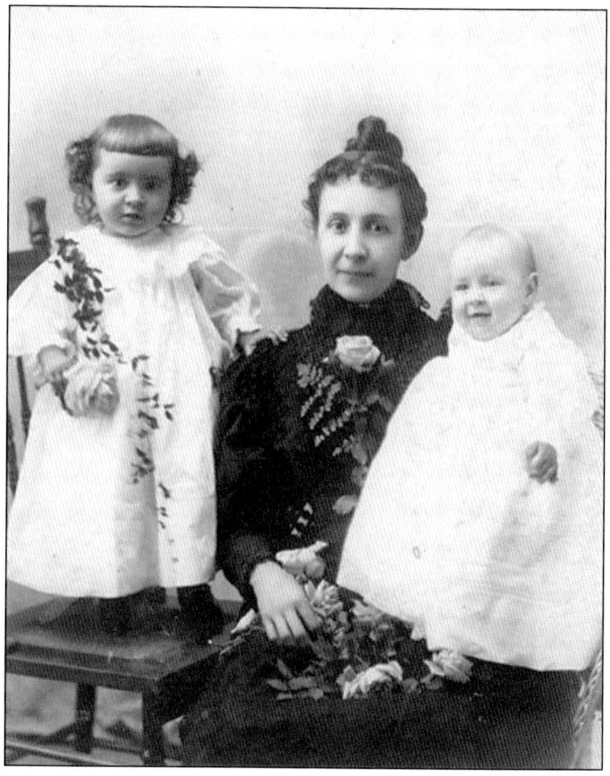

Jessie Howe Higley, the second wife of Stephen Higley, is seated between the couple's two children, 18-month-old Jessie Jean "JJ" (left) and five-month-old James. Both children were born in Prescott, Arizona, prior to the family's move to Phoenix. (Courtesy of the Higley family.)

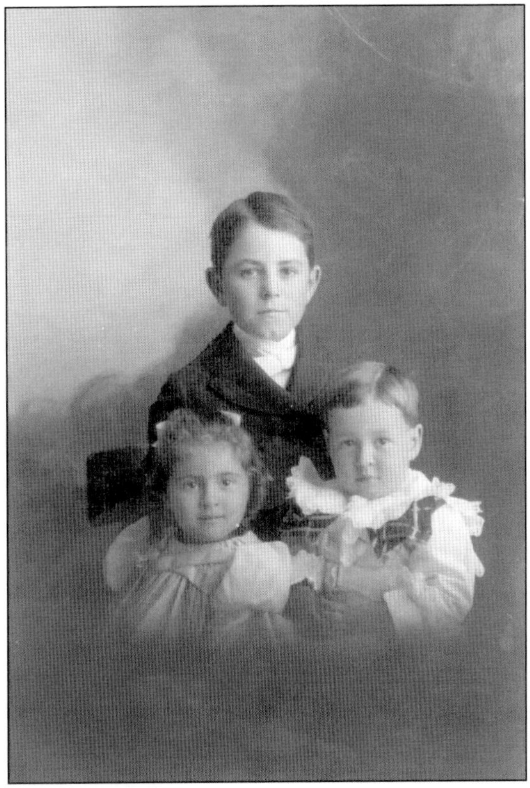

In an undated photograph of the three Higley children (right), Thomas, approximately five years older than JJ, sits in the back. JJ is on the left and her younger brother, James, is on the right. Thomas was the oldest son of Stephen Higley from his first marriage. Below, Thomas Higley (left), Pauline Johns (center), and Bert Johns pose by their bikes near Prescott in 1894. Thomas Higley served with the Marines in World War I. In 1929, he founded Tom's Tavern, now a historic Phoenix bar and restaurant that has long been a gathering spot for politicians, lawyers, judges, and other professionals. (Right, courtesy of the Higley family; below, courtesy of Sharlot Hall Museum Photos.)

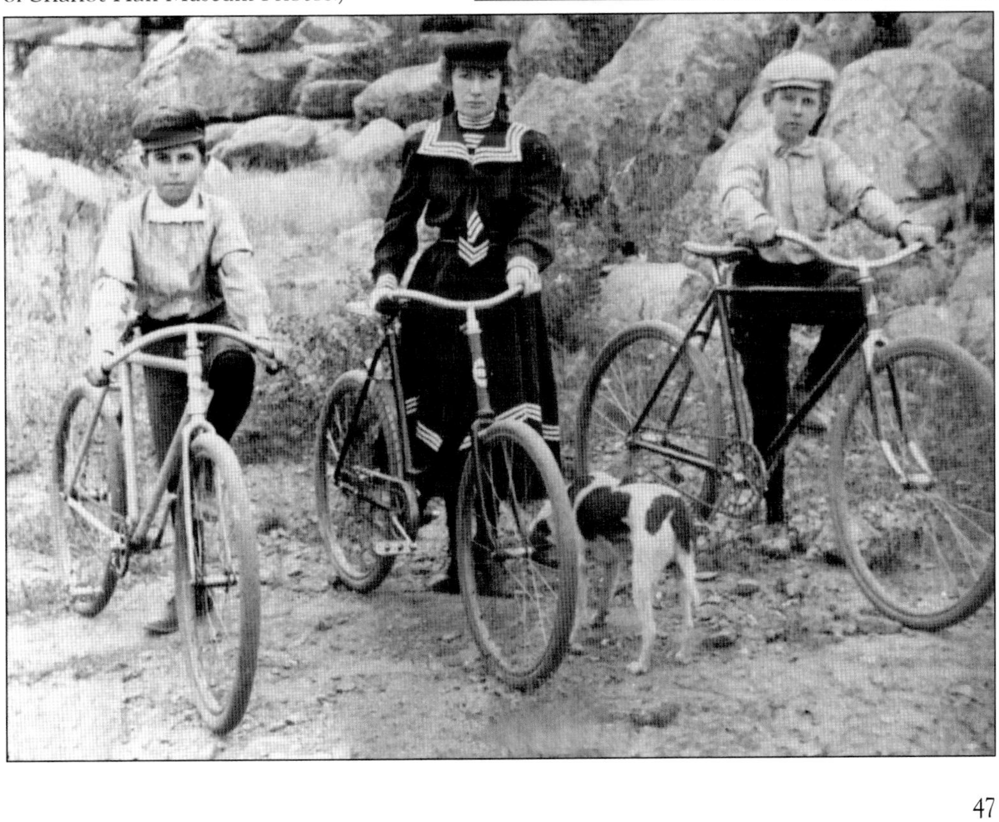

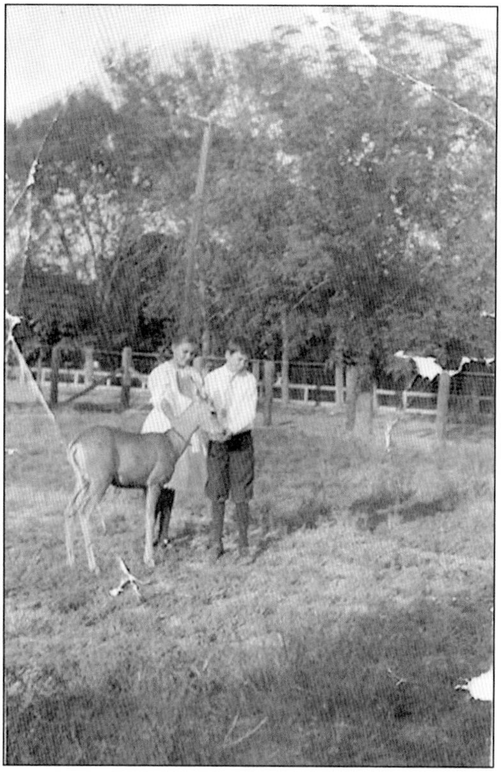

JJ Higley and her brother, James, pose with their pet deer in the backyard of the Rosson House (left). In an interview, JJ recalled sneaking the deer into the house and up the back stairs to her room on the second floor. She said, however, that it was quite difficult to get the deer back downstairs and outside. Below, JJ and two of the family dogs play in front of the house during the winter. (Courtesy of the Higley family.)

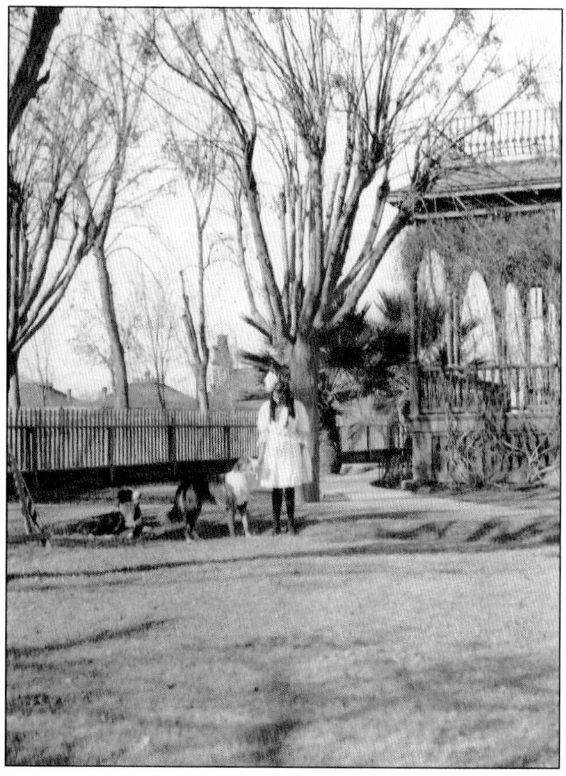

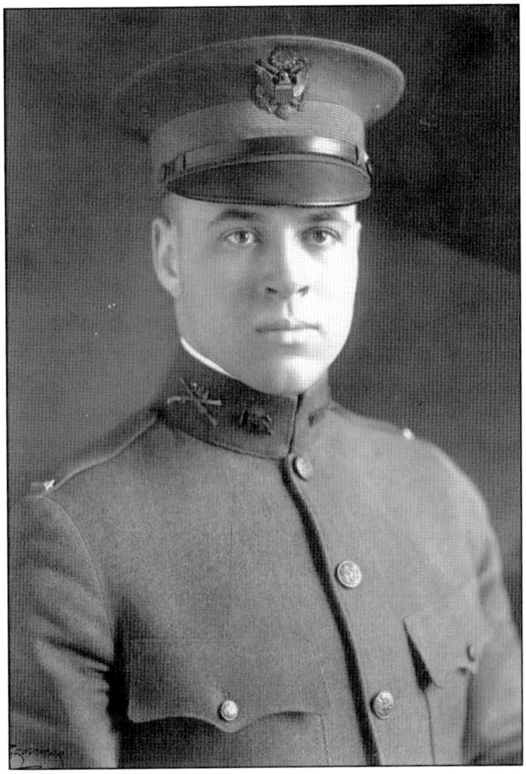

Following graduation from high school, James Stephen Higley (right, in uniform) attended Stanford University in California. When World War I broke out, he joined an Army officer's training camp and was commissioned a second lieutenant. He reached the rank of first lieutenant. James, the youngest son of Jessie and Stephen Higley, died in France and was buried there (below). (Courtesy of the Higley family.)

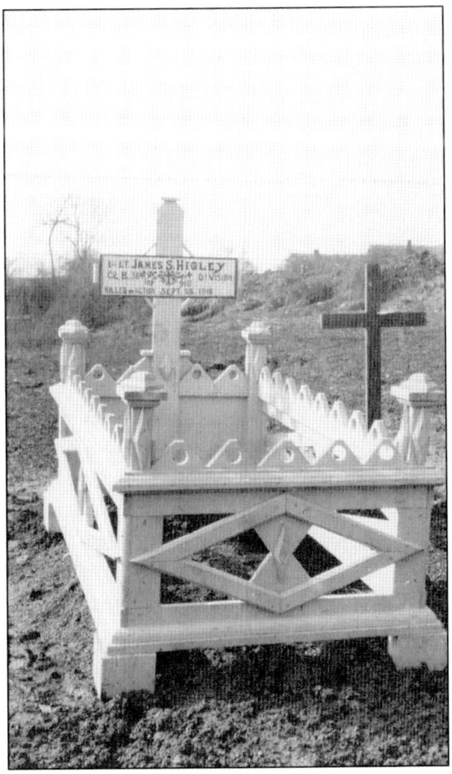

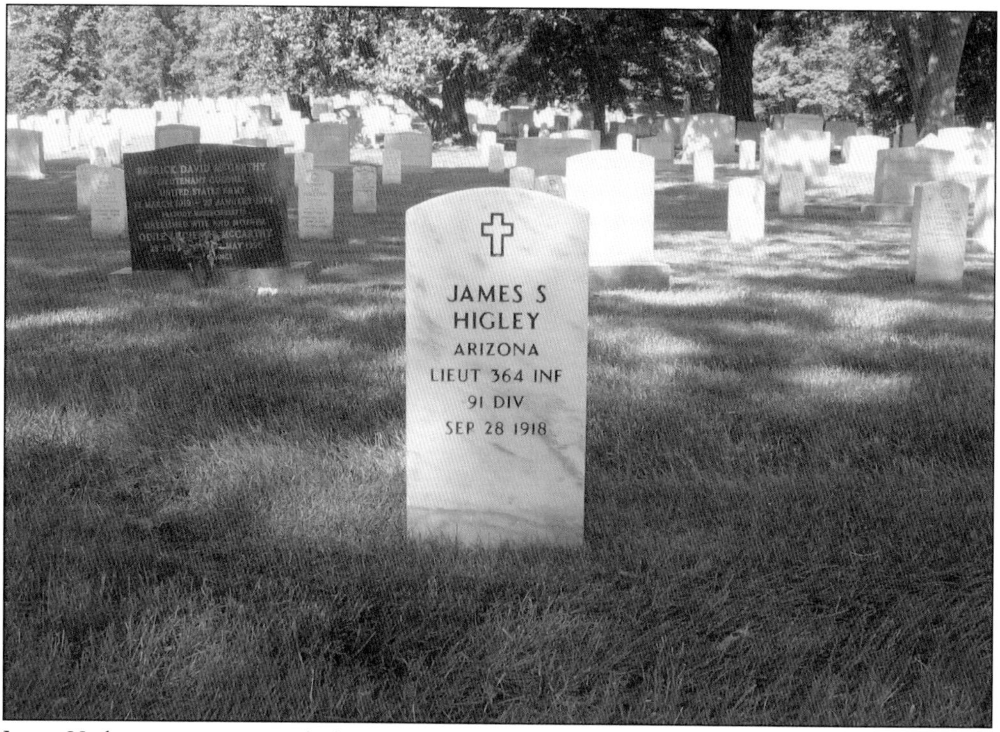

James Higley was in command of Company B of the 364th Infantry during the Battle of Argonne Forest when he was mortally wounded. Letters from fellow officers and men who served with him praised James for his bravery. Higley was posthumously awarded the Medal of Valor and was later re-interred in Arlington National Cemetery. (Photograph by Donna Reiner.)

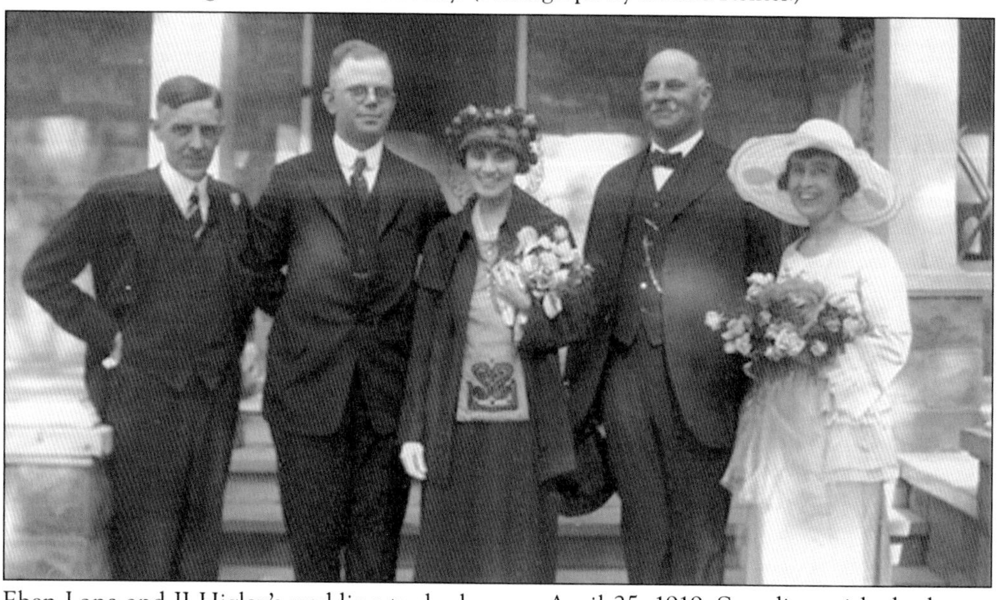

Eben Lane and JJ Higley's wedding took place on April 25, 1919. Standing with the happy couple (center) are JJ's father, Stephen Higley (second from right); a good friend, Naomi Stephenson (far right); and Naomi's husband (far left). The Lanes resided in Phoenix. (Courtesy of the Higley family.)

This is a formal portrait of Frances (Frankie) Gammel, wife of William Gammel. Frankie, of Mexican descent, was born in Tucson, Arizona. She ran a rooming house in her home at 136 North Sixth Street starting in the late 1920s, but, according to her daughter Georgia, the tenants did not eat in the house. (RHHSFG.)

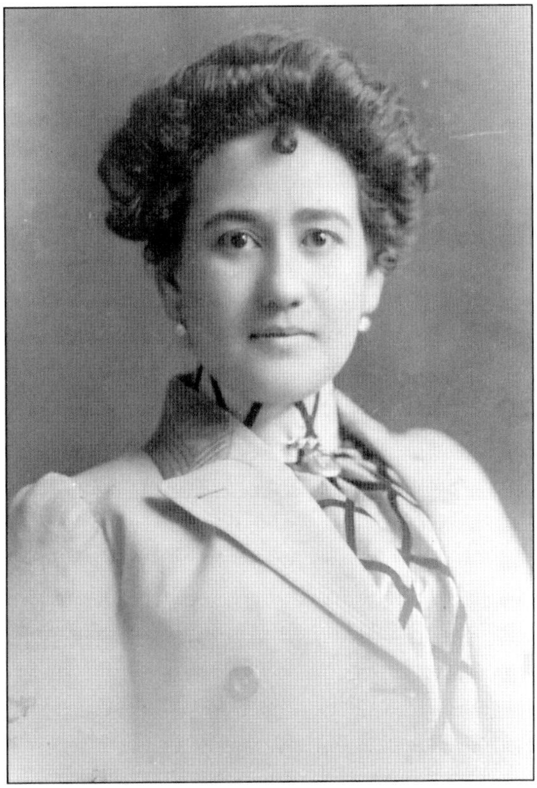

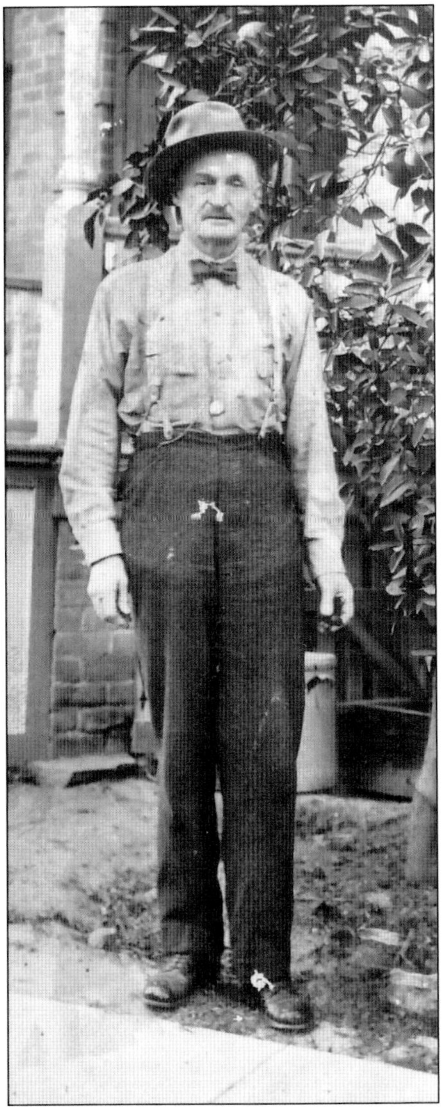

This is an undated photograph of William (Billy) Gammel, who was co-owner of the Capitol Saloon in downtown Phoenix. He purchased the Rosson House in August 1914. Arizona became a dry state on January 1, 1915, which caused Gammel to rename his business the Capitol Buffet and sell soft drinks. Gammel had trouble, however, making the new business format profitable. (RHHSFG.)

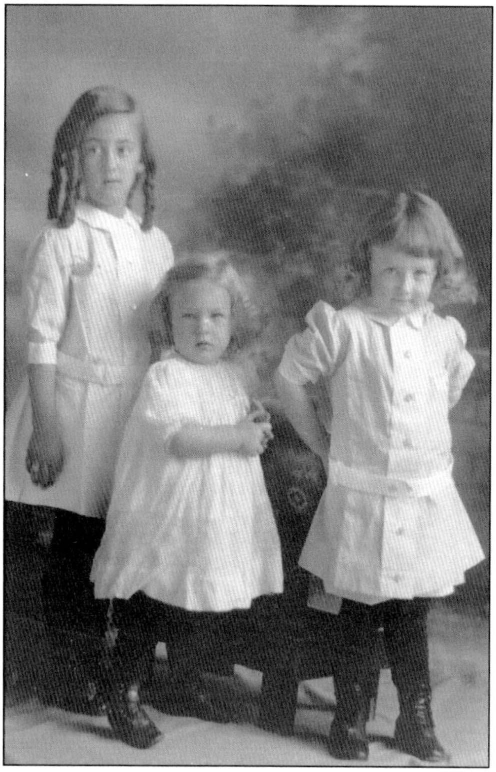

The Gammel sisters pose for a photograph in 1906. They are, from left to right, Annie (six), Georgia, (three), and Wilma (four). Much of what is known about the Gammel residence stems from a 1986 interview with Georgia. This photograph was taken prior to the Gammels' purchase of the home from the Higleys. (RHHSFG.)

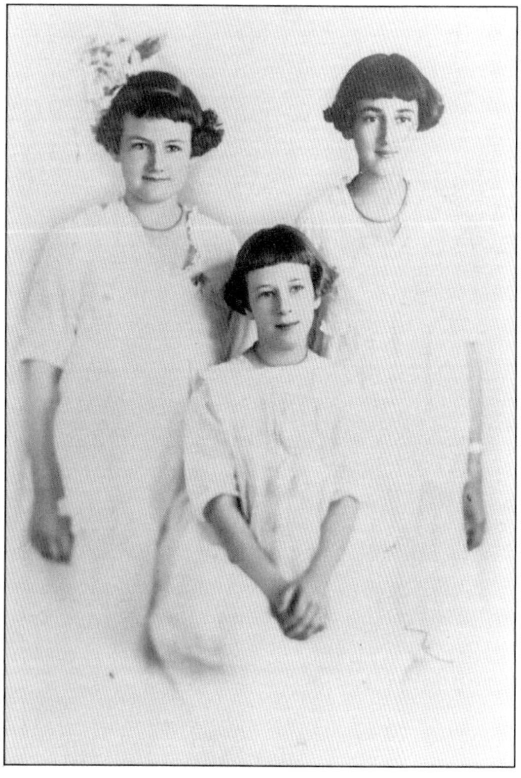

This photograph of, from left to right, Anna, Georgia, and Wilma Gammel was taken around 1916. The three sisters shared a downstairs room, which is now considered the library room of the Rosson House Museum. Like the Higley children, the Gammel girls had unusual pets, such as peacocks, an opossum, and two parrots. The students from Monroe Elementary School across Seventh Street loved to come to see the menagerie. (RHHSFG.)

This is an undated photograph of Anna Gammel, who married Milton Ponder in the Rosson House in 1925. Ponder's brother, Newell, had been a boarder in the Gammel household, which is likely how Anna and Milton became acquainted. Ponder later purchased the land and built a sign shop just behind the Rosson House, at 615 East Monroe Street. (RHHSFG.)

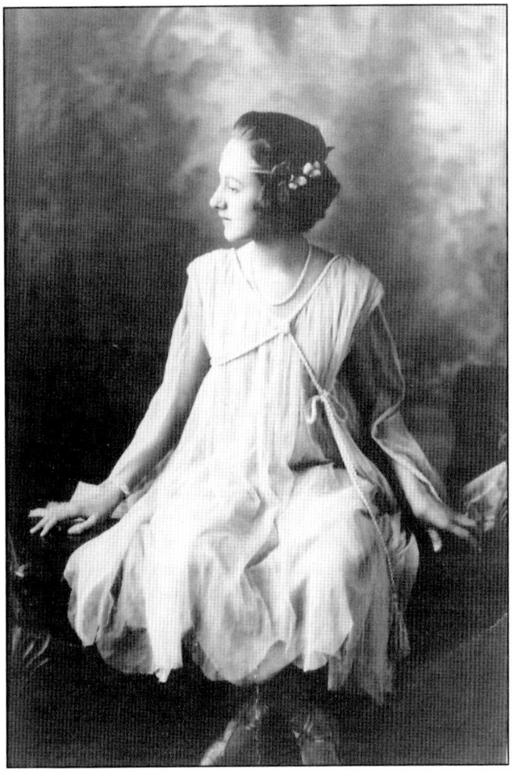

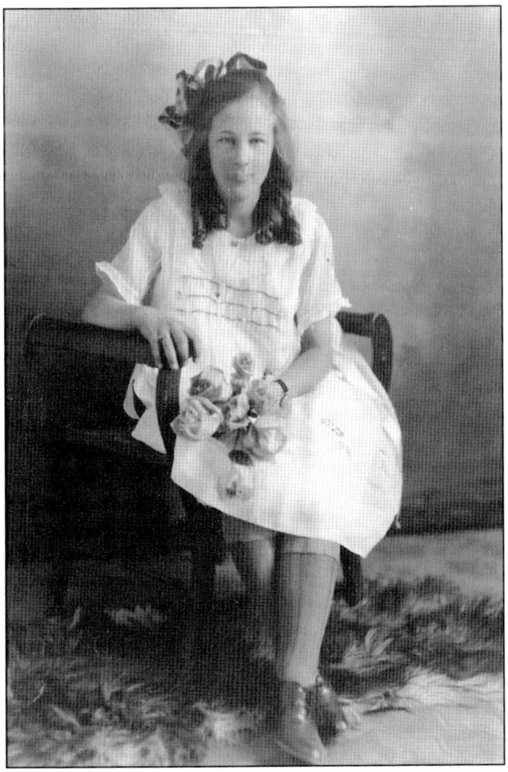

Georgia Gammel is shown in a formal portrait. She married Edward Sewell in 1929, and they continued to live with her parents even after their son, Edward Jr., was born in 1931. They divorced in 1939, and Georgia married George Valliere in 1941. George's carpentry skills aided Frankie Gammel when she upgraded the interior and improved living areas for her roomers in the Rosson House. (RHHSFG.)

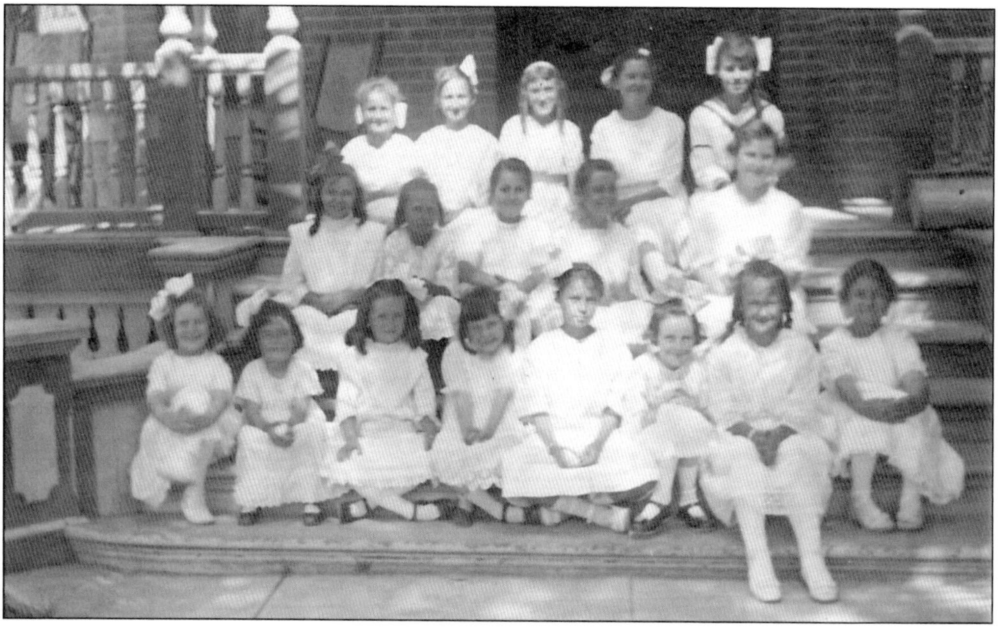

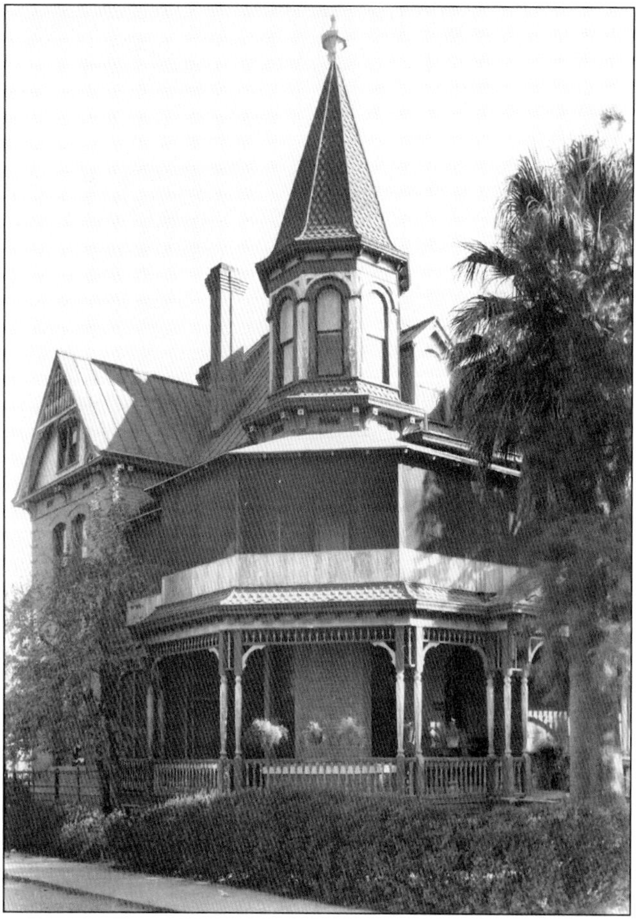

Apparently, the home on Sixth and Monroe Streets was a popular place for children's parties. Here, the unidentified attendees pose on the front steps. All of these young ladies are delightfully dressed in white, and many have large white bows in their hair. Arizona governor George W.P. Hunt often visited the Gammel family on his way to his home near Sixteenth Street and East McDowell Road during his last term. (RHHSFG.)

This c. 1918 photograph of the house shows the front upstairs porch screened in, which was done at the direction of Frankie Gammel. She merely expanded a small screened area that had previously been enclosed by the Higley family. The metal cresting on the roof seen in earlier pictures no longer exists. Apparently, it often fell off and was not replaced when roof repairs were done. (RHHSFG.)

Four

The Rest of Block 14

Historic Heritage Square is comprised of ten buildings, eight of which are original to Block 14. Among these is the Rosson House, finished in 1895. Other surviving buildings include four bungalows located along the north side of Adams Street, and the Teeter Carriage House, all constructed from 1899 to 1901. Later additions to Block 14 include the duplex located on Sixth Street, built in 1923, and the Baird Machine Shop on the south side of Adams Street on Block 15, constructed in 1929. Buildings relocated to the park are the Burgess Carriage House in 1976 and the Thomas House in 1985.

The four Adams Street bungalows include the Silva House, built by Phoenix liquor dealer A.F.C. Kirchoff. Alejandro Silva, a Glendale rancher, purchased the house in 1906, and his family lived in the home until 1977. Next door, the Teeter House was built by Leon Bouvier, a cattleman and flour miller, who used it as a rental property. Bouvier sold the home to Eliza Teeter in 1911, and she, in turn, rented the property until moving into the house in 1919. Further west, the Stevens-Haustgen House was built as a rental property by Constance Stevens in 1901. In 1911, Edward Haustgen purchased the house for his sisters, Marguerite and Anna. Marguerite Haustgen, a dressmaker, lived there from 1937 to 1952. Next door, the Stevens House was also built as a rental property by Stevens, who worked in Korrick's New York Department Store. The one-story brick house is interesting in that it has an irregular, raised roof that creates a gap above the attic for air circulation.

Block 14's other original buildings include the Carriage House, which sheltered the horses and vehicles of the Teeter House residents. The duplex on Sixth Street, an in-fill project built by Anna and Marguerite Haustgen, had sleeping porches constructed with canvas and wood panels that were opened at night to let in the cool desert air. The Baird Machine Shop, a brick building on the south side of Adams Street, illustrates the commercial aspect of the neighborhood.

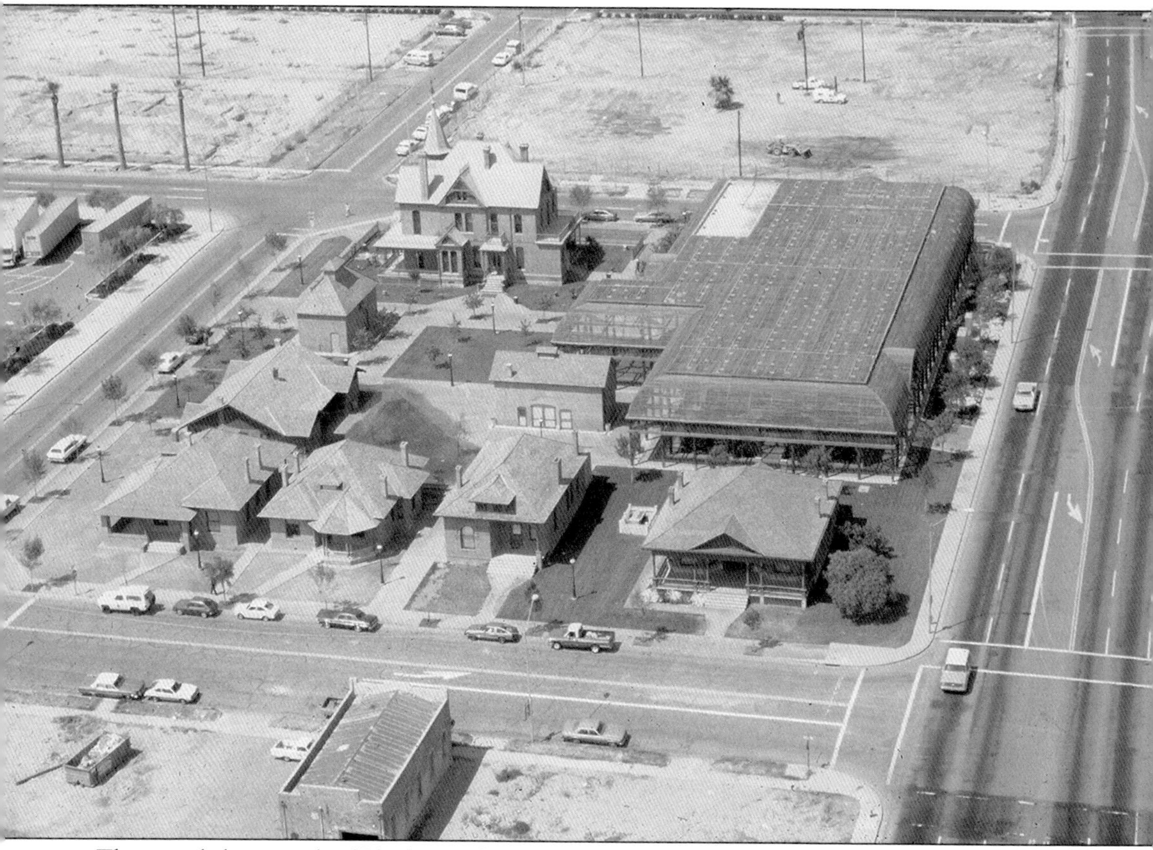

This aerial photograph of Block 14, taken in 1981, looks north. The block is bounded by Seventh Street on the right, Adams Street in the foreground, Sixth Street on the left, and Monroe Street above. From left to right on the north side of Adams Street are the Stevens House, the Stevens-Haustgen House, the Teeter House (with its carriage house to the rear), and the Silva House. The single building on the south side of Adams Street is the Baird Machine Shop. The duplex is on Sixth Street just north of the Stevens House, and the Rosson House is in the upper left corner of Block 14. The large structure north of the Silva House is the Lath Pavilion, the site of the former Phoenix First Ward LDS Church. (RHHSFG.)

This 1928 photograph was taken in front of the duplex at 113 and 115 North Sixth Street. The Rosson House is in the background. From left to right are Mae Gemmel and her brother, Jimmy Gemmel, who lived at 755 East Adams, and 16-year-old Catherine McDonald, who lived in the south duplex (113) with her parents. (RHHSFG.)

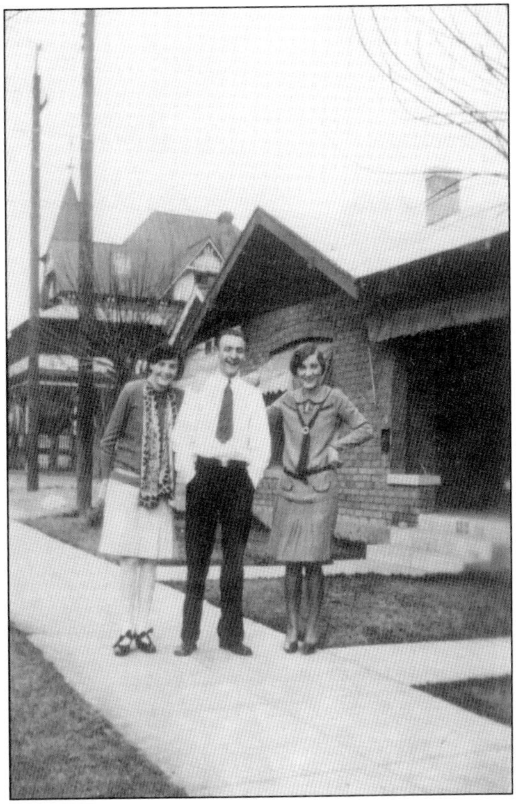

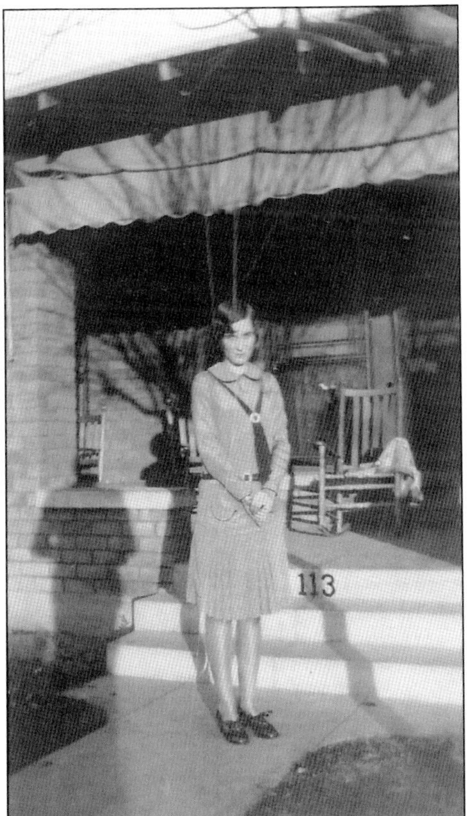

Catherine McDonald stands in front of the duplex at 113 North Sixth Street, where she lived with her parents, who rented the south half of the duplex. Catherine married John Malone and lived at 115 North Sixth Street for a short time. (RHHSFG.)

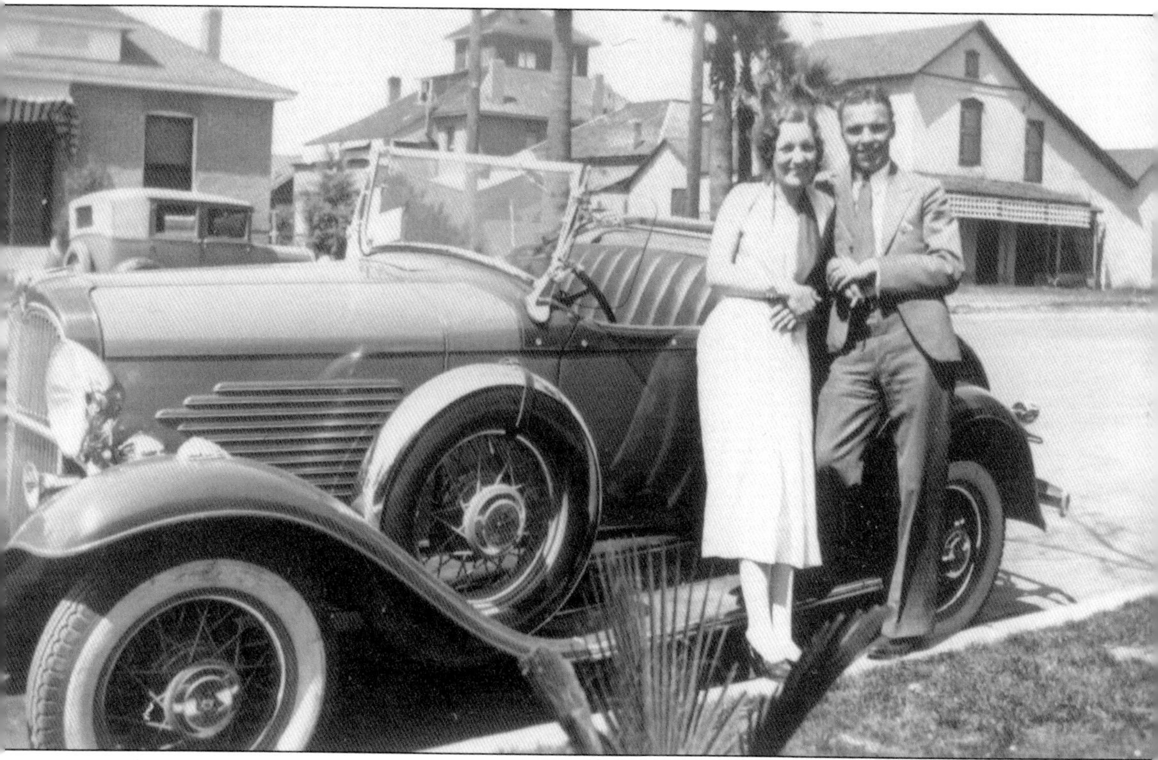

Catherine McDonald and a friend pose beside a 1932 6-90 Willys-Overland roadster, which was a joy for them to drive. This photograph may have been taken in front of her parents' home at 113 North Sixth Street. If so, the houses in the background would have been where the excavations took place during the mid-1990s park expansion (Block 13). These houses would have been the source of some of the artifacts shown in chapter one. (RHHSFG.)

Alejandro (Alex) and Maria Silva pose for this undated photograph. Alex was born in Portugal in 1860, and his wife, Maria, was born in 1868 in Mexico. Maria and Alex did not have children of their own, but helped raise several female relatives over the years. (RHHSFG.)

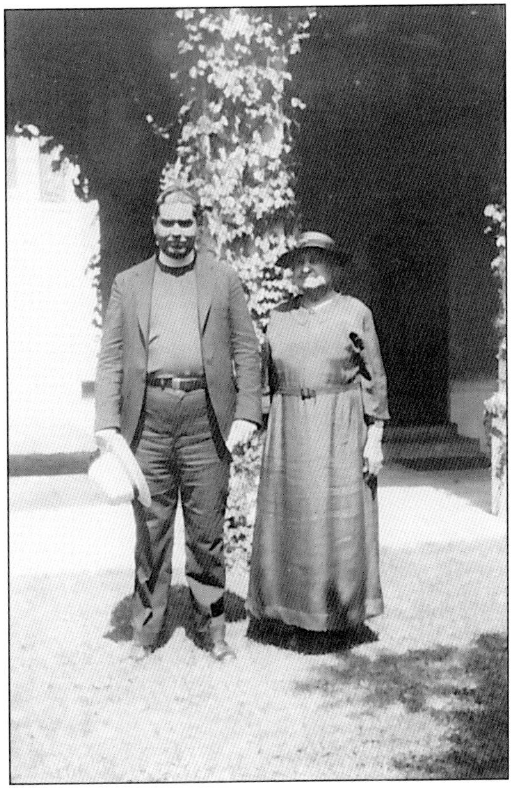

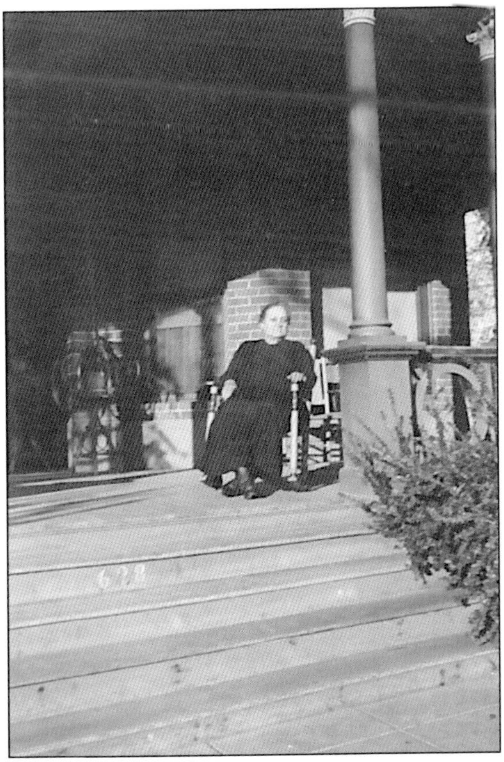

Maria Jesus Alvarez Silva, called "Tia Chu" by family members, came from a pioneer family from Hermosillo, Mexico. Maria married Alejandro in early 1895. (RHHSFG.)

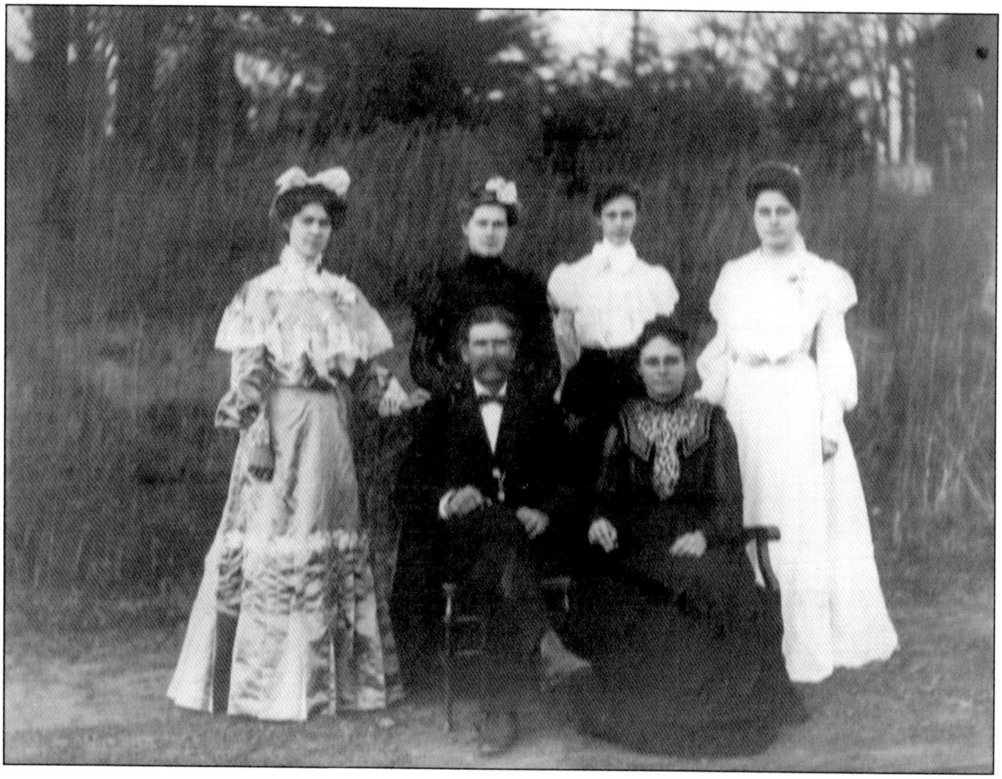

This is an undated photograph of the Silva family. Alex and Maria Silva are seated in front. In 1906, Alex Silva purchased the home at 628 East Adams Street in Historic Heritage Square that now bears his name from the widow of A.F.C. Kirchoff. (PPD.)

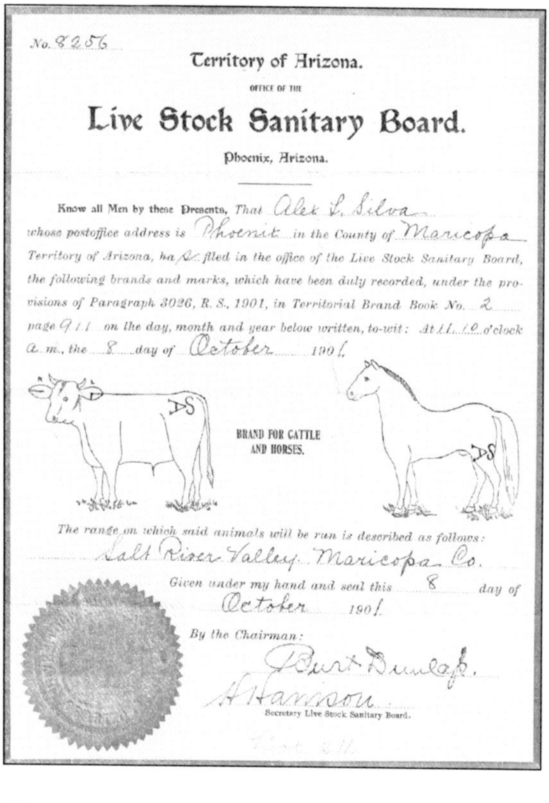

No. 8256

Territory of Arizona.

OFFICE OF THE

Live Stock Sanitary Board.

Phoenix, Arizona.

Know all Men by these Presents, That Alex L. Silva whose postoffice address is Phoenix in the County of Maricopa Territory of Arizona, has filed in the office of the Live Stock Sanitary Board, the following brands and marks, which have been duly recorded, under the provisions of Paragraph 3026, R. S., 1901, in Territorial Brand Book No. 2 page 911 on the day, month and year below written, to-wit: At 11.10 o'clock a. m., the 8 day of October 1901.

BRAND FOR CATTLE AND HORSES.

The range on which said animals will be run is described as follows: Salt River Valley Maricopa Co.

Given under my hand and seal this 8 day of October 1901.

By the Chairman:

Burt Dunlap.

H Harrison

Secretary Live Stock Sanitary Board.

Alex Silva, a consummate farmer, was one of the first to diversify his crops in the Salt River Valley. His farming success in the West Valley kept him from living in the house until 1927. He was also known for raising the best draft horses in Arizona. His simple brand, using an "A" and an "S," was recorded with the Territorial Live Stock Sanitary Board in October 1901. (PPD.)

Frances "Ponchita" Miramon (left) and Marian "Nita" Silva pose for their confirmation portrait. Frances was the daughter of Maria Silva's cousin. Frances's mother passed away, and her father remarried in 1916, sending Frances to live with Maria. Marian, the daughter of Alex's brother, lived in California with her parents. Her health caused her parents to send her to Arizona to live with her Uncle Alex and Aunt Maria in 1923. (RHHSFG.)

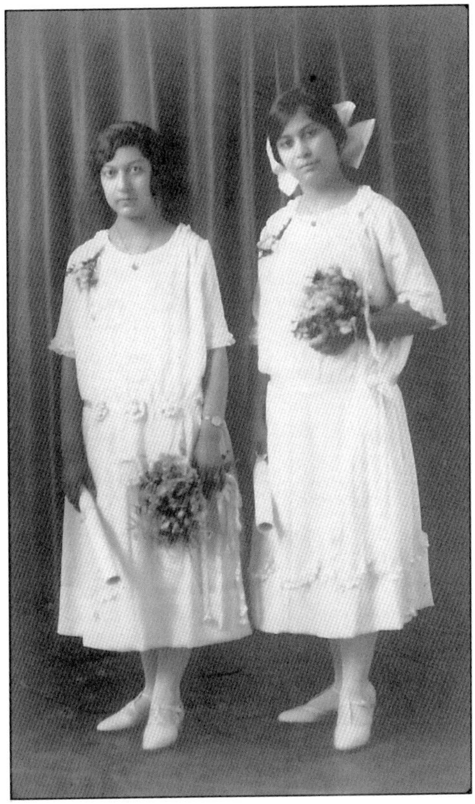

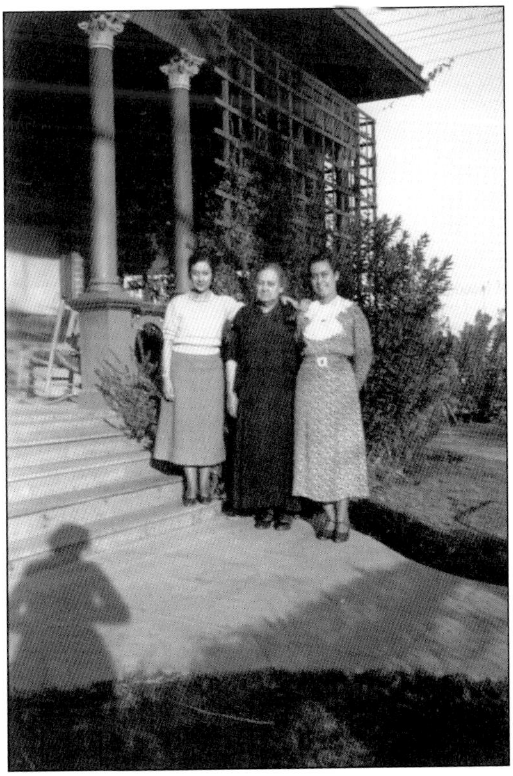

The two women on either side of Maria Silva are her second cousin Frances (left) and her niece Marian. Marian inherited the house following Maria's death in July 1948. She and Frances continued to live at 628 East Adams Street until Marian passed away in 1963. Following Marian's death, Frances lived in the house until she sold it to the City of Phoenix in 1977. (RHHSFG.)

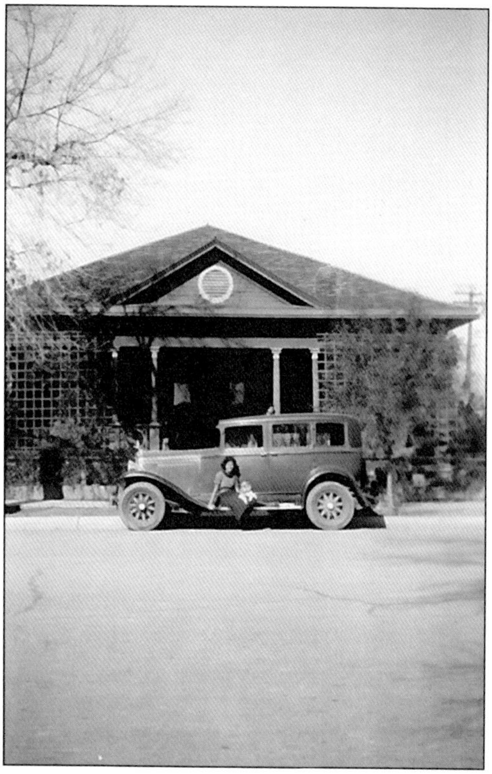

The Silva House was a rental for a number of years. E. Frank Spawr remembered living in the house in the early part of the 20th century. When he was 12, Frank and his brother rode their bikes outside the city so they could see Haley's Comet in 1910. The lattice panels added to the front of the porch provided privacy and a frame for climbing vines. (RHHSFG.)

Eliza Teeter traded some farmland near Tempe, Arizona, for this house in 1911. The original owner, Leon Bouvier, had converted the mule barn behind the house into several apartments. He lived in and rented this house and also owned another home on the 500 block of East Adams Street. (Photograph by Donna Reiner.)

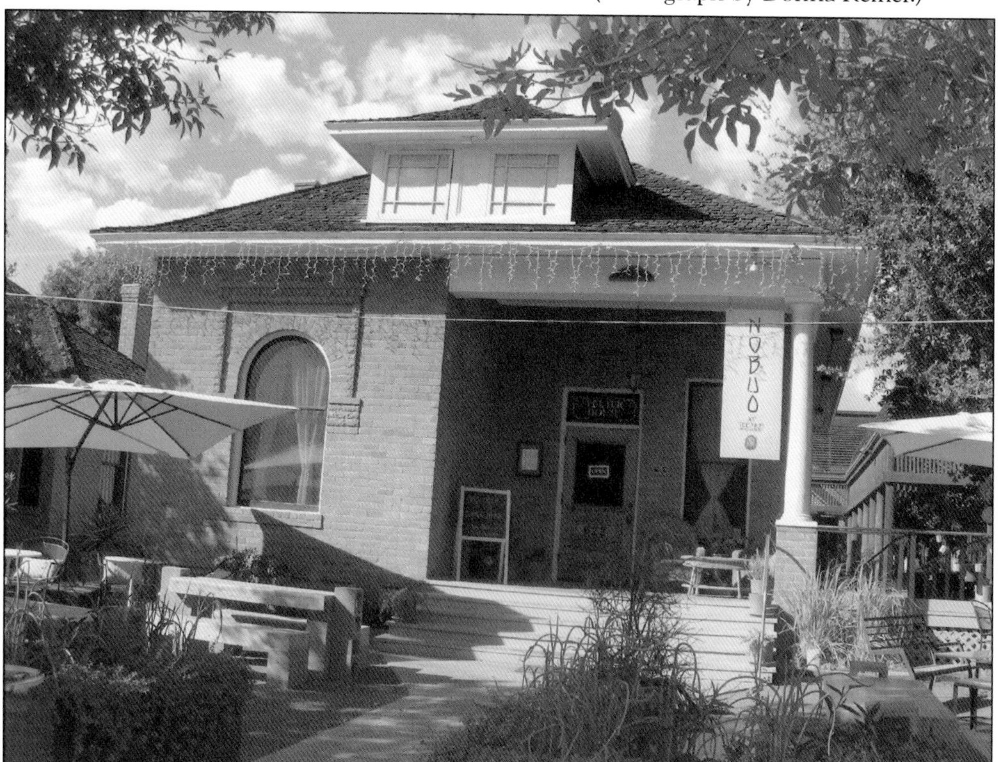

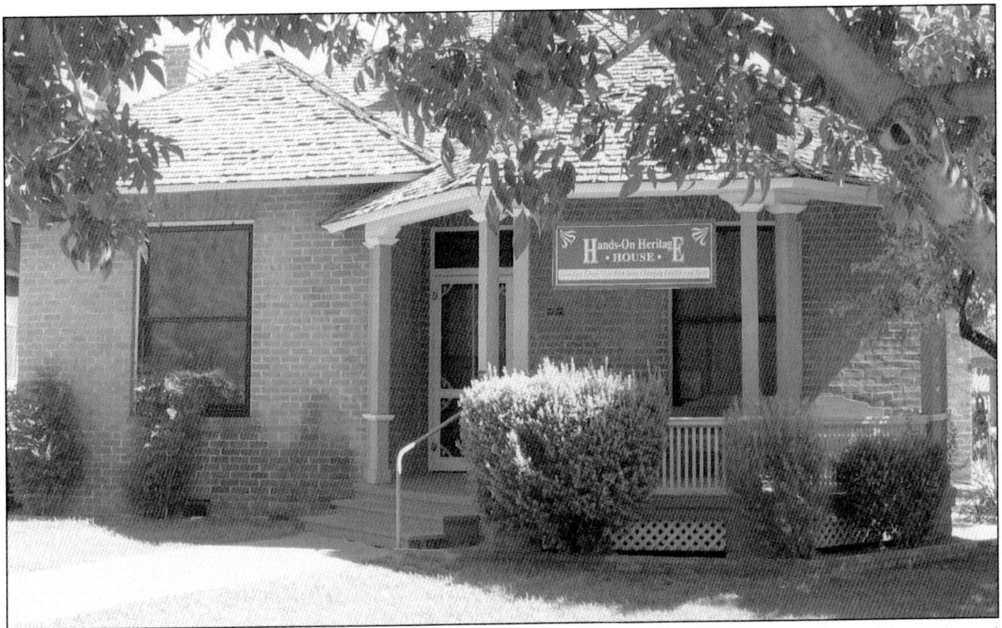

Built in 1901 for Constance Stevens as a rental property, this home was purchased by Edward Haustgen for his two sisters, Marguerite and Anna, in 1911. Following their arrival in this country from Luxembourg in 1914, they continued their dressmaking trade. Anna died in 1921, and Marguerite continued to live in this house, the Stevens House, or the duplex until her death in 1952. (Photograph by Donna Reiner.)

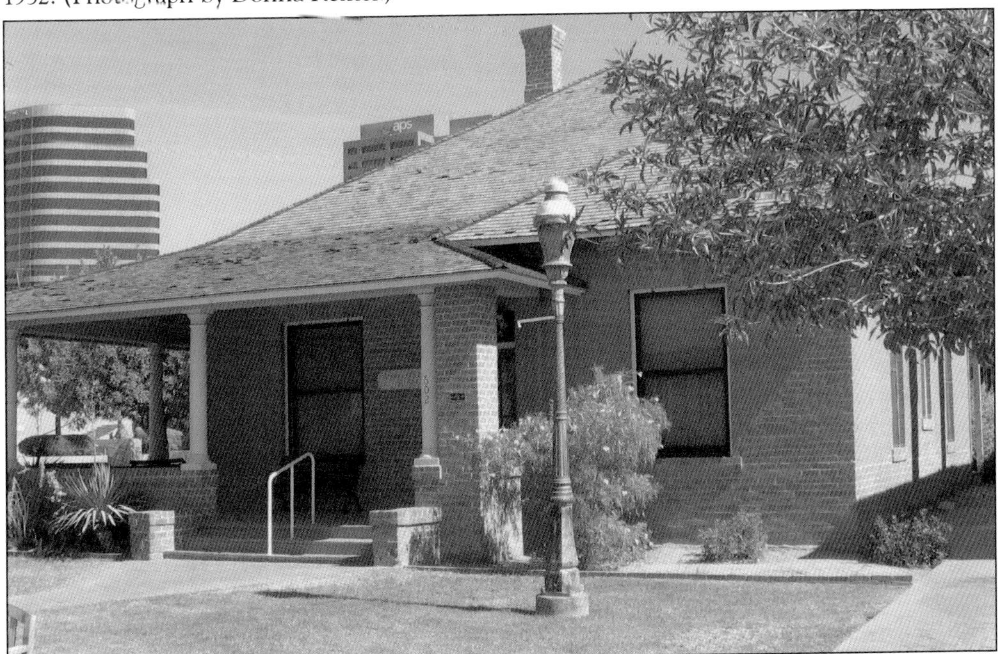

Constance Stevens, a widow, also built this house as a rental property in 1901. It does not appear that Stevens and her three children lived in either of these homes. She did, however, live for a time in the Teeter House. Stevens sold this property to Edward Haustgen. Since 1988, the Arizona Doll and Toy Museum has occupied this building. (Photograph by Donna Reiner.)

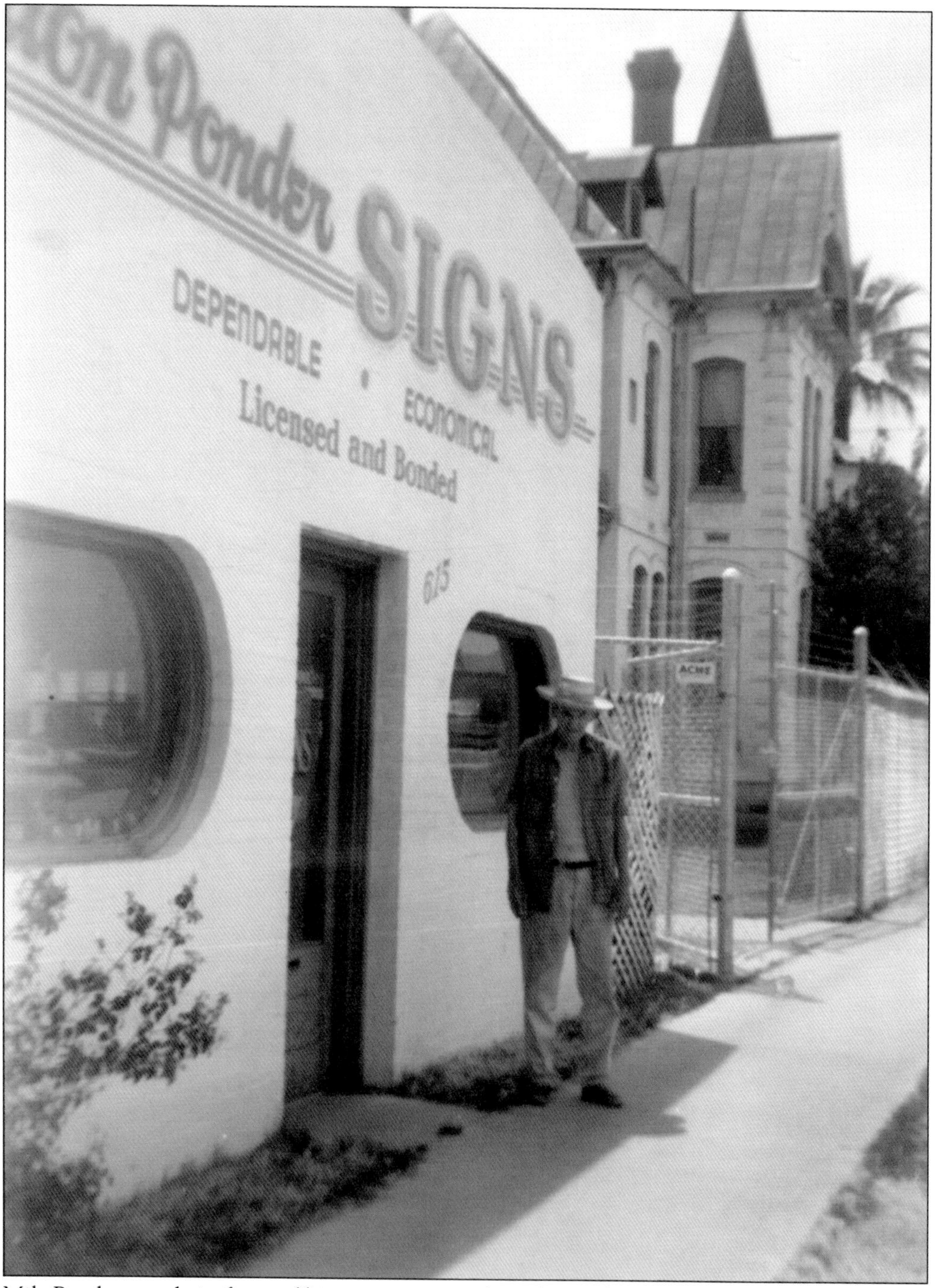

Milt Ponder stands in front of his sign-painting shop, located at 615 East Monroe Street, just east of the Rosson House. Ponder had moved to Phoenix in 1923, working as a sign painter. By 1932, he had erected this architecturally modern shop building. Ponder purchased the land from Frankie Gammel in 1939. During the creation of Historic Heritage Square, this building was torn down due to its modern style, and Milt moved his operations into the Baird Machine Shop on East Adams Street. (RHHSFG.)

Five

It's Going to Be a Park

Downtown Phoenix was long the hub of economic activity in the city. This changed after World War II, as Phoenix grew rapidly and businesses followed new residential construction into outlying neighborhoods, particularly along North Central Avenue. By the 1960s, empty storefronts were a common sight downtown, which only a few years earlier had been a bustling commercial district. Urban blight was particularly prevalent along "The Deuce," a skid row centered along Second Street. Block 14 was not immune from downtown's downward spiral. The Rosson House, with unsympathetic remodeling, had evolved into a shabby flophouse.

Urban renewal initiatives were proposed in the early 1970s to reinvigorate downtown Phoenix, including one that would raze the buildings on Block 14 to create a parking lot for the new Phoenix Convention Center. The plan proved controversial and was abandoned. The Rosson House, which had been listed in the National Register of Historic Places in 1971, had an influential ally in Phoenix mayor John Driggs as well as public sentiment favoring preservation.

Eventually, the city established a history-oriented park on Block 14 to provide an urban oasis and an attraction downtown. Mayor Driggs was the project's major driving force, using his connections with the Nixon administration to assist the city in obtaining a Housing and Urban Development grant to acquire Block 14 in 1974. The park, designed by local architect Robert Frankeberger, was named Historic Heritage Square.

Rehabilitation of the park's aging structures began in 1976, when the Rosson House was designated Arizona's Bicentennial Meeting House by the state's bicentennial commission. Funding was provided by major local companies and service organizations, and area construction firms provided in-kind services to upgrade the historic buildings that composed the park. A museum was created in the Rosson House with assistance from the Junior League. After four years of work, including the construction of the Lath House for open-air functions, Historic Heritage Square opened in May 1980. The park expanded in 1996 with the addition of the Arizona Science Center, the Phoenix Museum of History, and a multistory parking garage. The park was then renamed Heritage and Science Park.

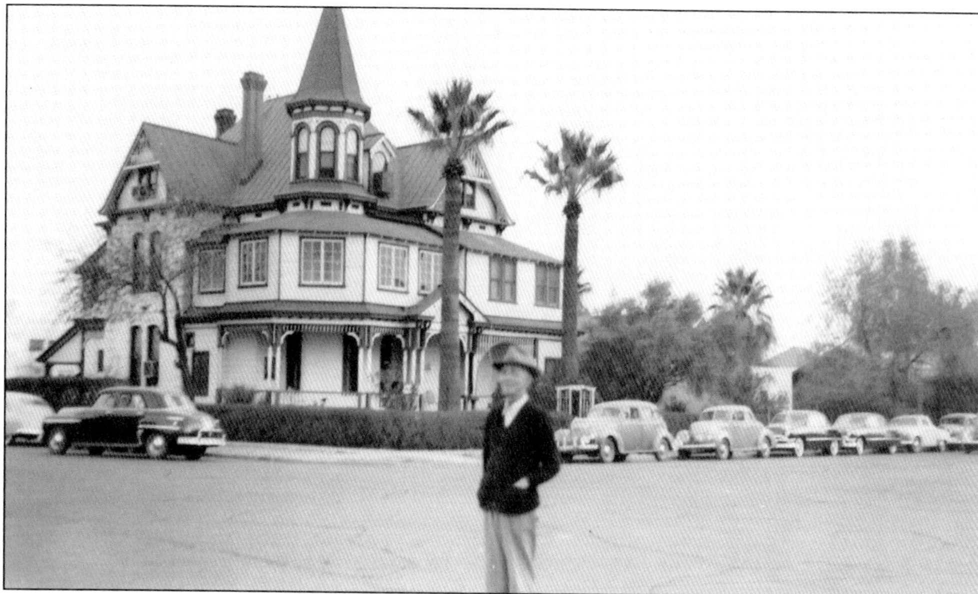

This photograph of the Rosson House was taken in the early 1950s from the north side of Monroe and Sixth Streets. The beautiful red brick has been painted white, and the front and back upstairs porches are enclosed. A boxwood hedge has replaced the picket fence. The house had 19 rooms for rent, but only two full bathrooms when it was listed for sale. (RHHSFG.)

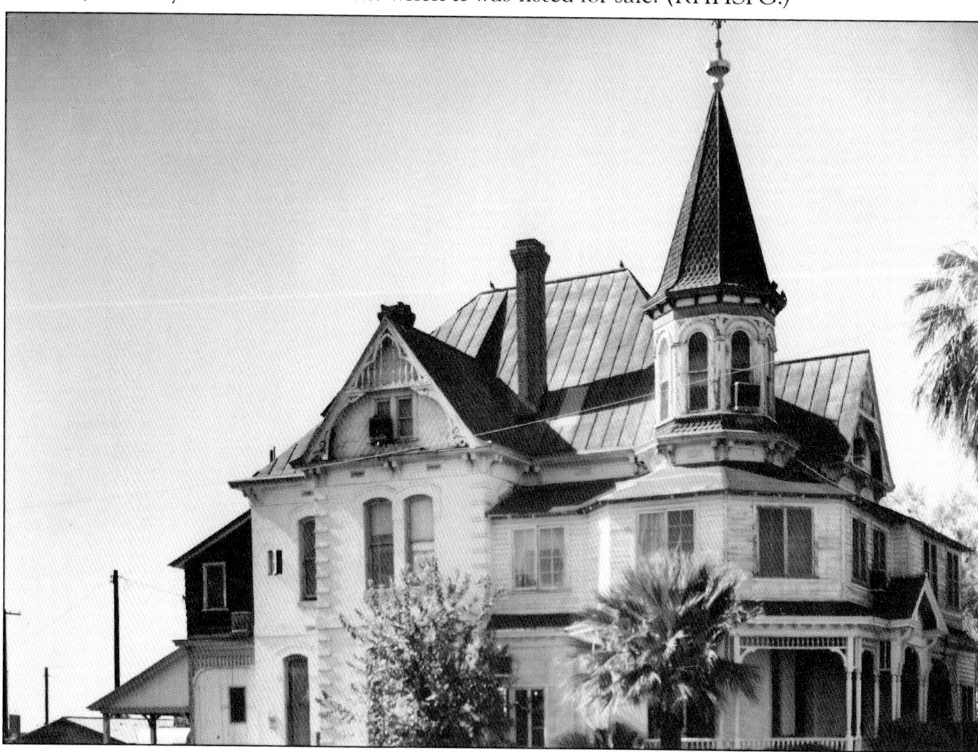

The condition of the Rosson House had declined when the city purchased the property in 1974. Peeling paint, enclosed porches, and an extended back porch altered the home's original beauty, and air conditioners protruded from several attic windows. (RHHSFG.)

This aerial photograph shows the large number of surface parking lots that surrounded Block 14; it is surprising that it, too, was not razed. Phoenix Union High School, at the top of the photograph, has had three of its buildings survive; they now house part of the University of Arizona School of Medicine. (RHHSFG.)

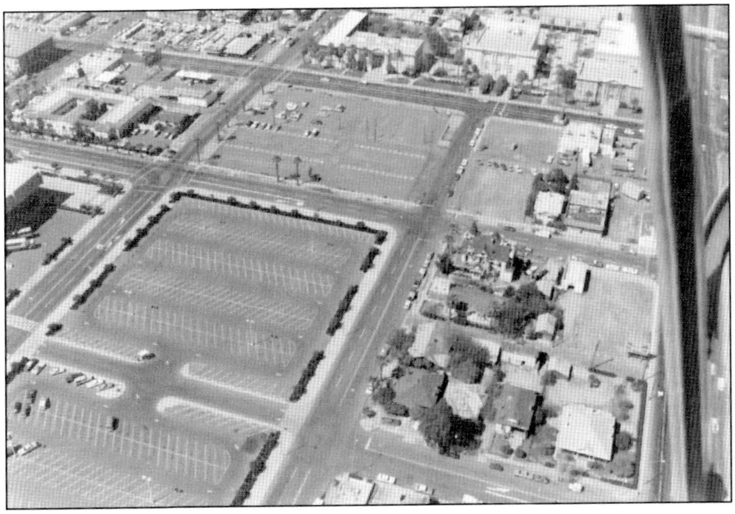

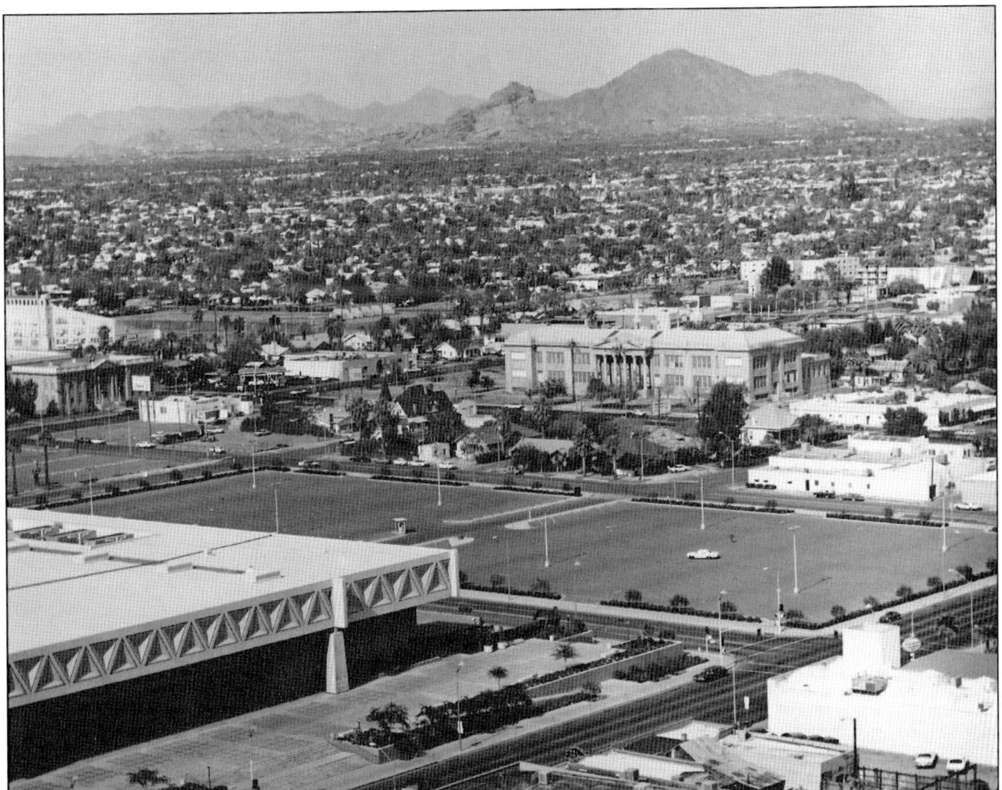

This northeast-facing photograph was taken before renovation had begun on what would become Historic Heritage Square. Monroe Elementary School is across the street to the east. The building in the foreground is the Phoenix Convention Center. In the background is one of the city's iconic landmarks, Camelback Mountain. (RHHSFG.)

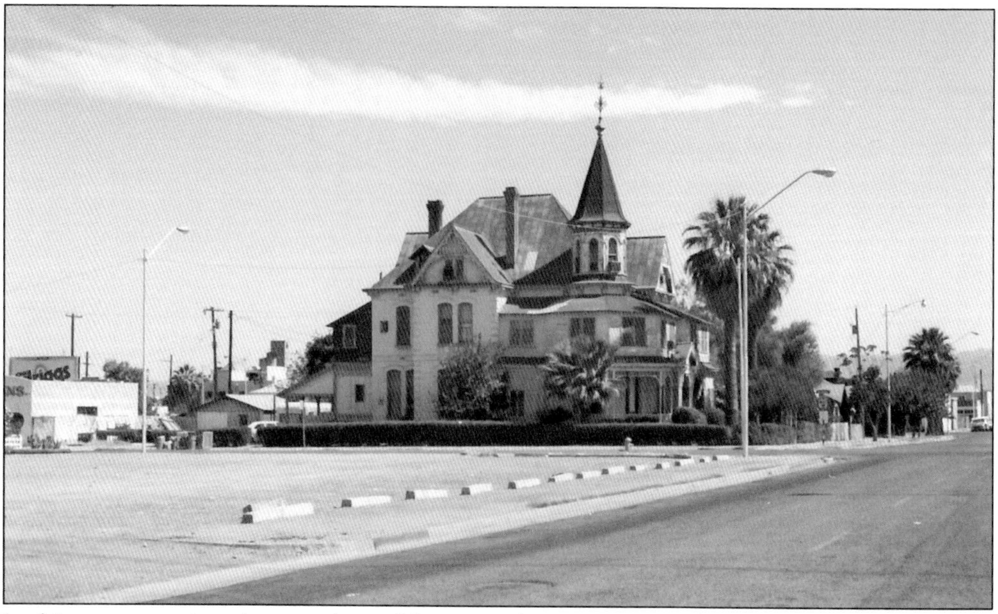

In this pre-restoration photograph, work has yet to begin to remove the palm trees, strip the white paint, and remove the porch enclosures and the back porch additions. After the restoration, the original Victorian mansion would reveal itself. (RHHSFG.)

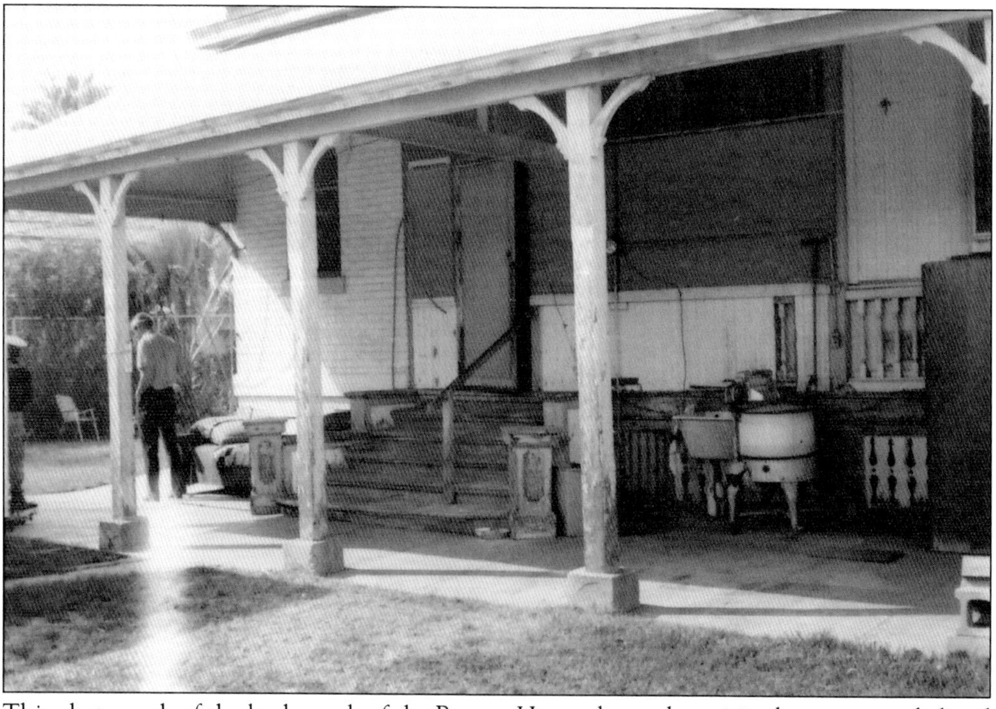

This photograph of the back porch of the Rosson House shows the original steps, extended and filled in by renovations. The steps come off from the original back porch that leads to the kitchen. The original railing of the back porch has been partially encased in wood, which protected it over the years. (RHHSFG.)

The porch on the south side of the house was also filled in, along with the small porch on the second story over this side door. In some Victorian homes, this might have been the carriage entrance. The Rosson family did not have a carriage house, however, so that type of entrance was not necessary. (RHHSFG.)

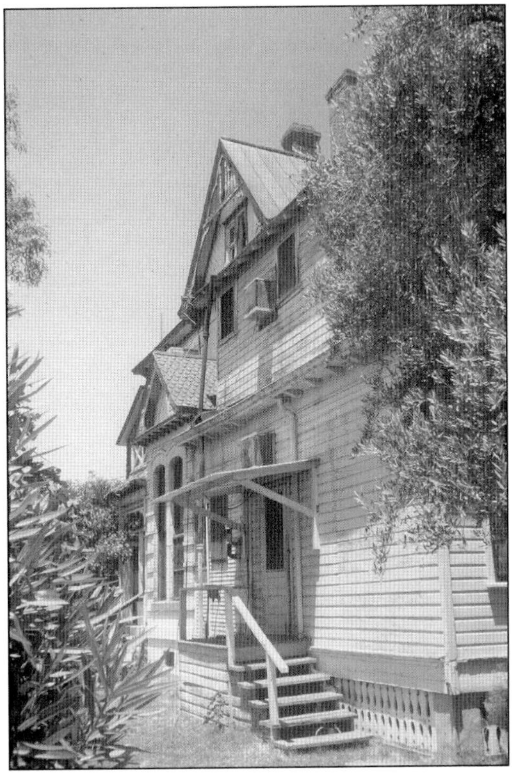

The upstairs back porch and the downstairs back porch were enclosed on the Rosson House. In addition, the back porch was extended. The Gammel family kept its refrigerator on this back porch, as the original kitchen was too small for the appliance. Georgia Gammel Valliere's second husband, George, did many of the alterations. (RHHSFG.)

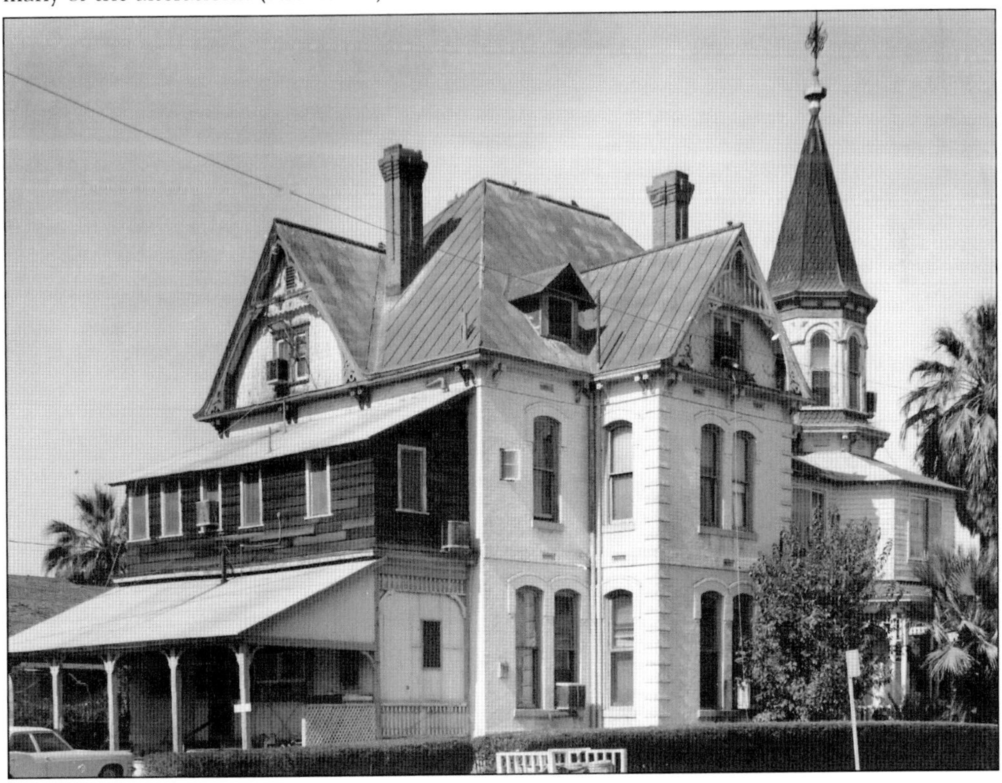

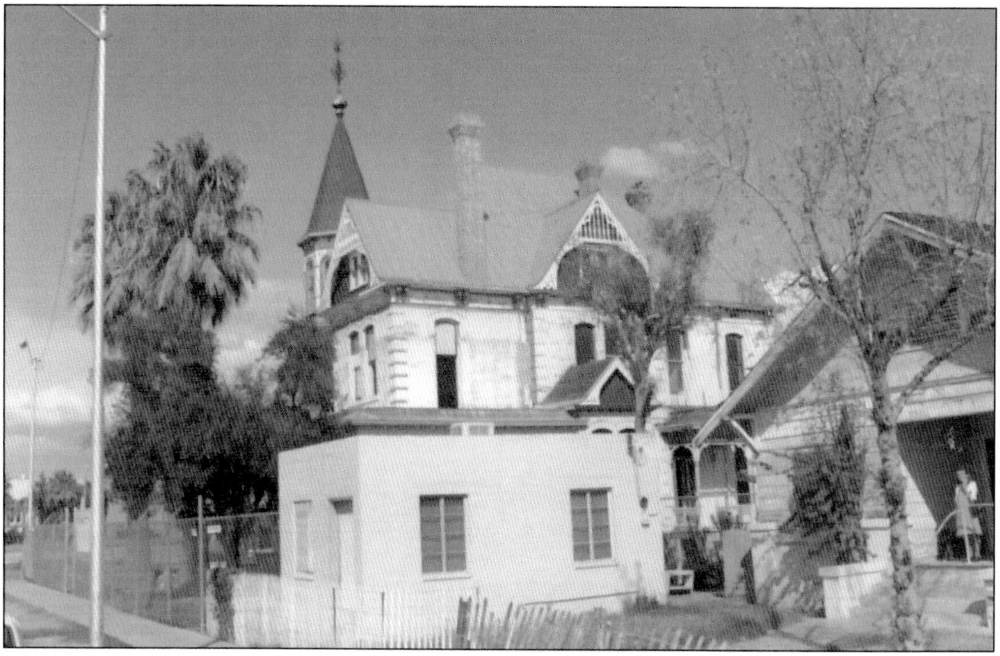

The Historic Heritage Square Restoration Committee debated what to do with buildings that were inappropriate to the concept of a block of early-20th-century homes. The committee eventually decided to raze the small block building in the foreground and the four-apartment bungalow on the right. (RHHSFG.)

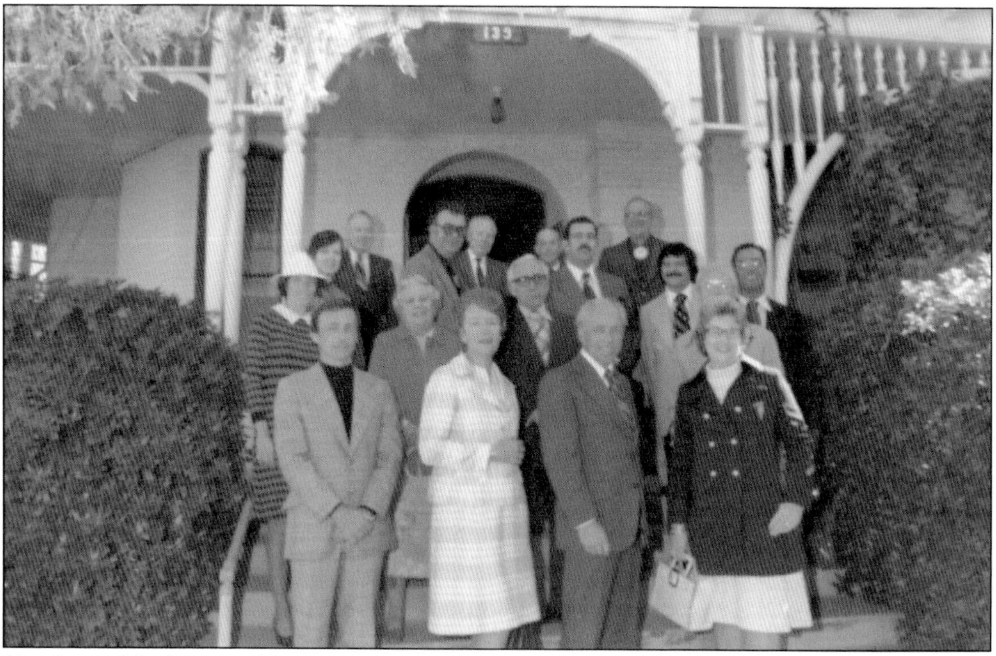

Members of the Historic Heritage Square Restoration Committee, created by former mayor John Driggs, stand on the steps of the Rosson House before the start of restoration work. Driggs is in the first row, second from right, and Mayor Margaret Hance is second from the left. Adam Diaz, Phoenix's first Latino councilman, is standing in the second row, at center. (RHHSFG.)

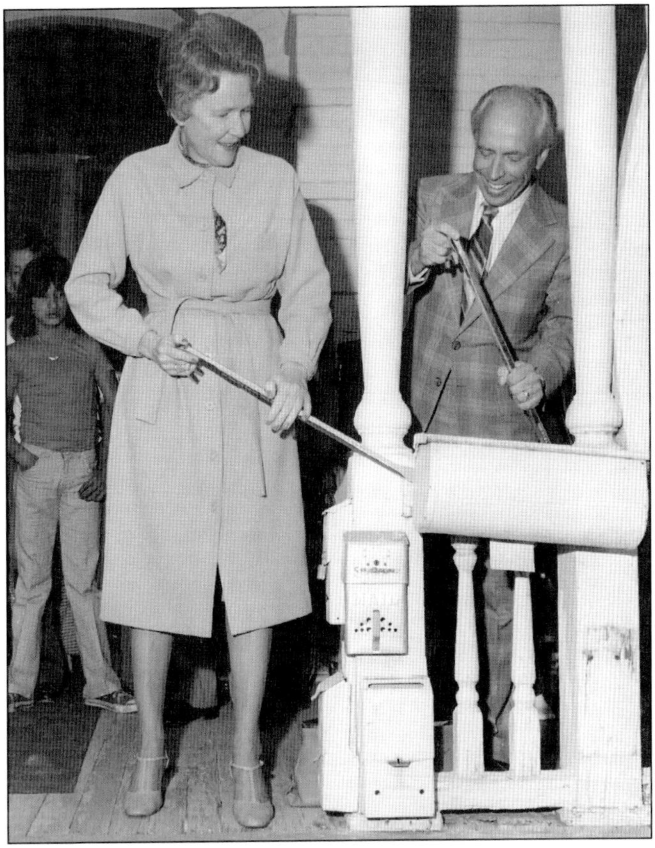

The restoration of the Rosson House officially began with a nail-pulling ceremony (right) featuring Phoenix mayor Margaret Hance and former mayor John Driggs. Below, Driggs speaks to the crowd attending the official start of restoration work. (Right, photograph by Al Ruland, RHHSFG; below, RHHSFG.)

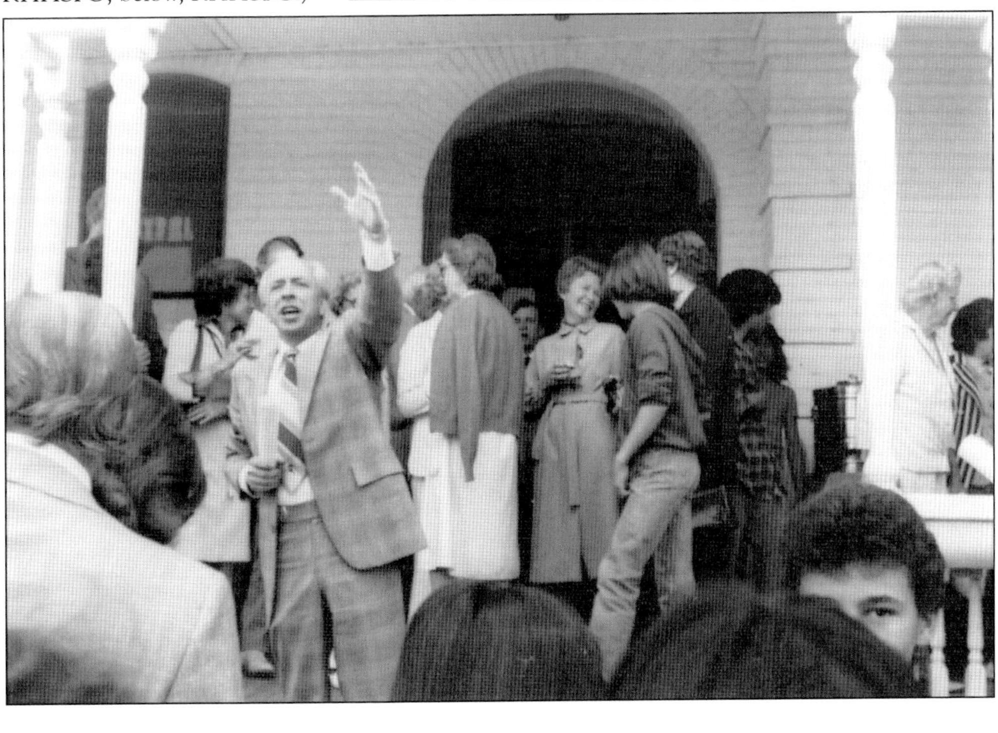

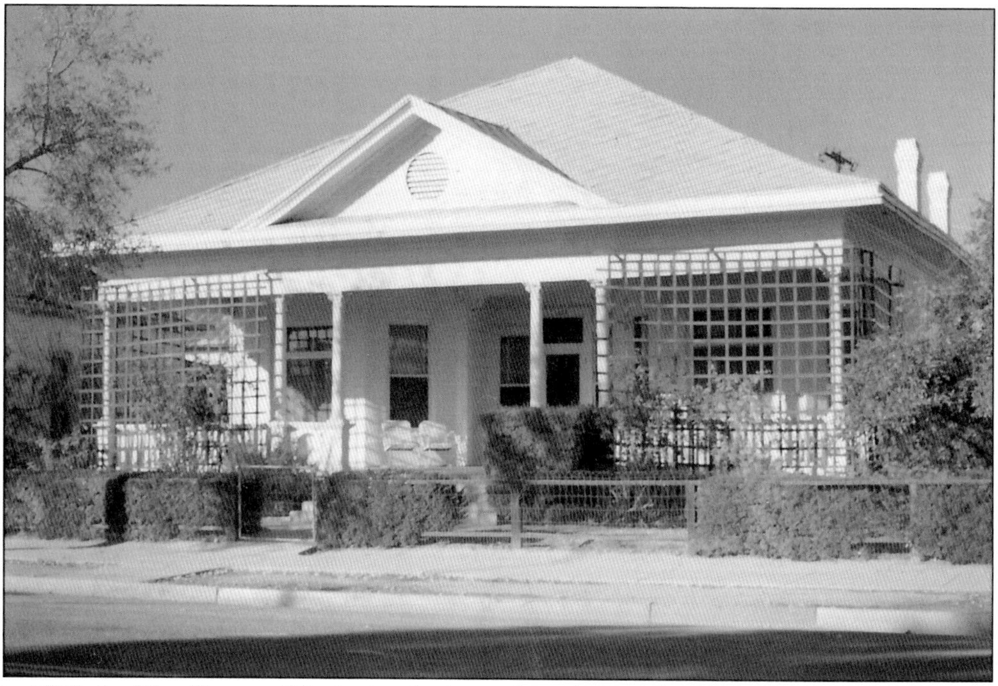

In 1976, the Silva House still looked in fairly good condition. The white paint would have to be removed from the brick surface in order to restore the home to its original state. It was the house on the block that had been in the same family for the longest time, 70 years. (RHHSFG.)

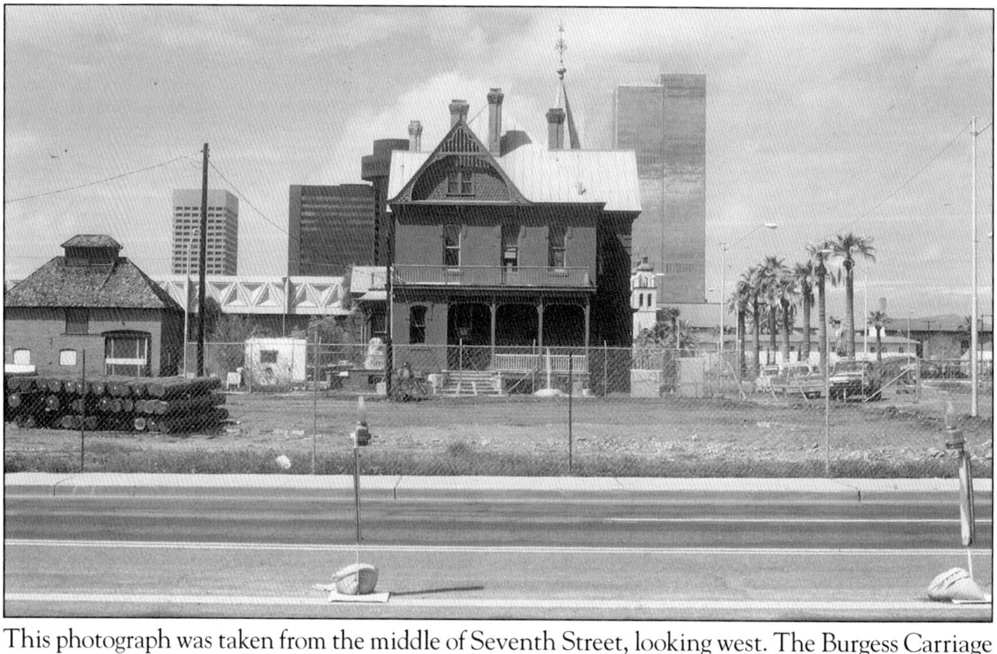

This photograph was taken from the middle of Seventh Street, looking west. The Burgess Carriage House has been relocated, and the wood pillars for the Lath House are stacked in the foreground. Behind the Rosson House are, from left to right, the First Interstate Bank Tower (now Wells Fargo Bank), the Hyatt Regency Hotel, and the Valley National Bank Tower (now Chase Bank). The older twin towers of St. Mary's Basilica also are visible. (RHHSFG.)

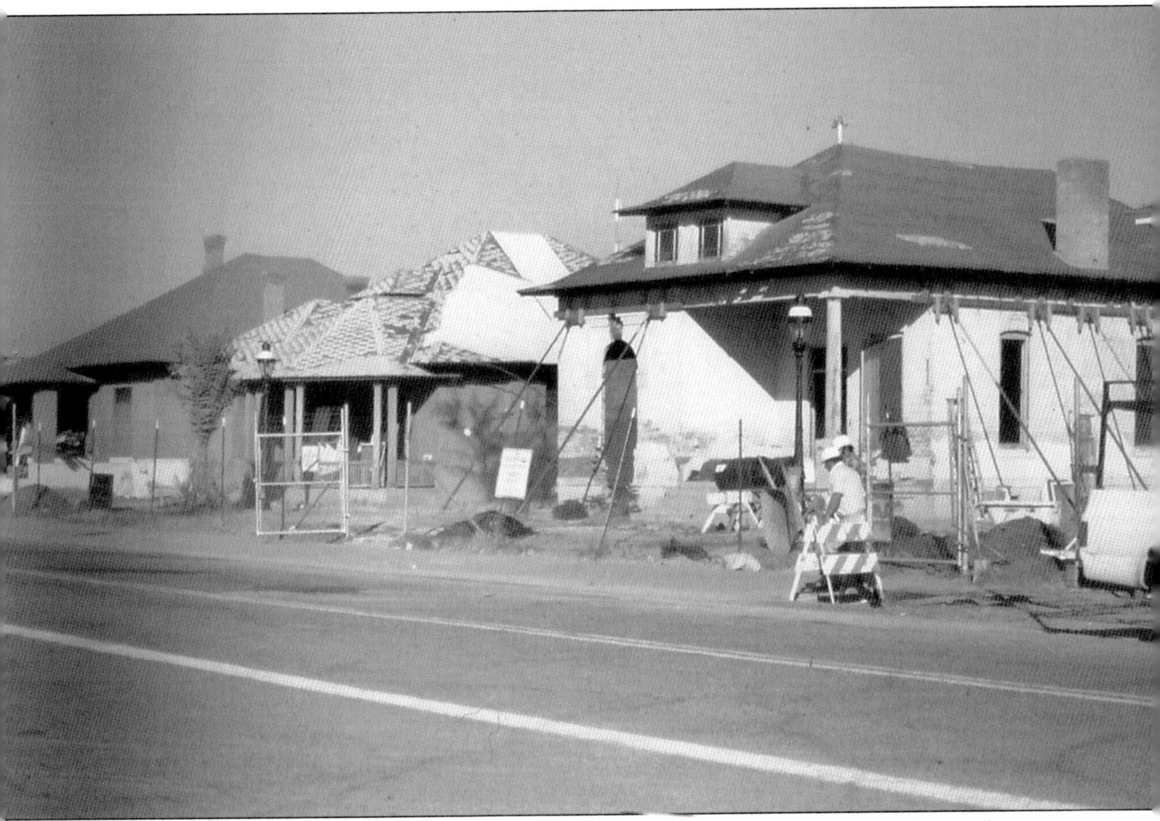

The roof of the Stevens-Haustgen House is being reconstructed, and the Teeter House features braced supports. The Teeter House was one of the most structurally unstable buildings on the square when the city acquired the land. Like the Rosson House, the Teeter House has a small basement. An interesting connection exists between the Stevens-Haustgen House and the Teeter House. Constance Stevens, who had the Stevens-Haustgen House built in 1901, had previously rented the Teeter House. (RHHSFG.)

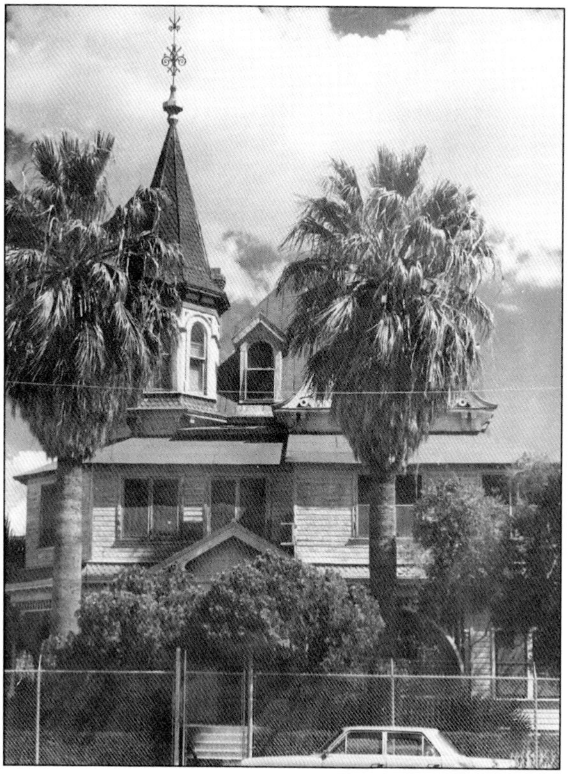

The left photograph shows a window air-conditioning unit in the enclosed portion of the second-story wraparound porch. A portion of the ground-floor wraparound porch was also enclosed, as seen on the right. From this perspective, it is not apparent that the house is brick. In the below photograph, taken months later, the enclosed portions have been removed, as has the vegetation directly in front of the entrance. The home's exterior Victorian design is now apparent and reveals a beautiful structure. (RHHSFG.)

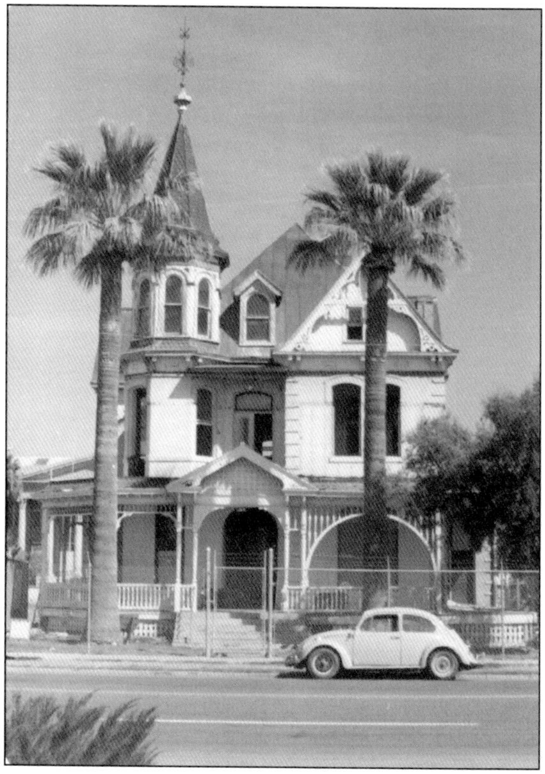

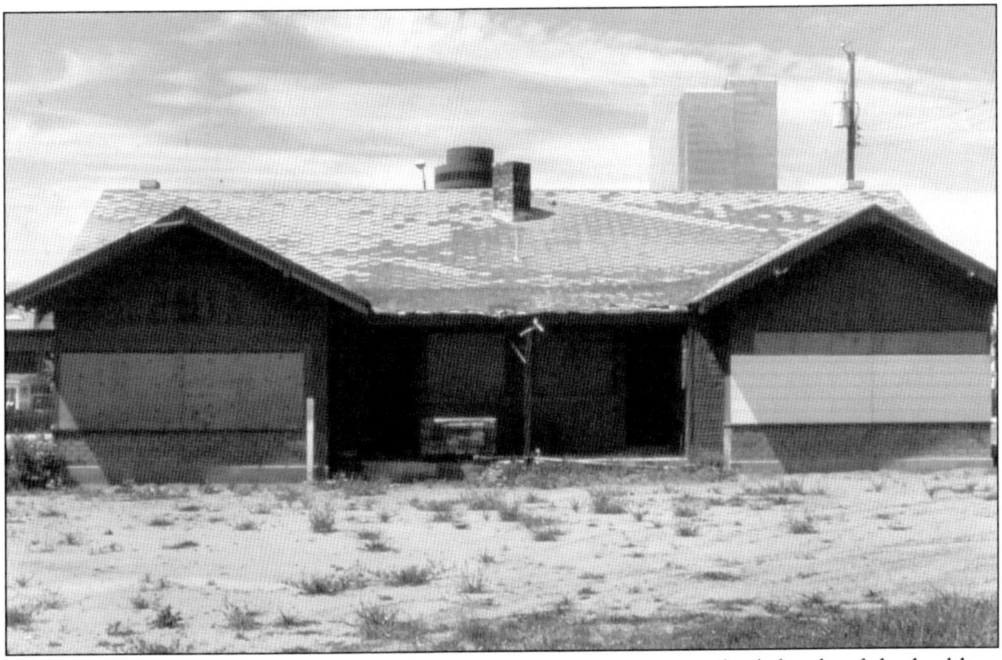

The rear of the duplex is seen here before the start of restoration. The left side of the building currently houses the Rosson House–Heritage Square Foundation and Guild office, and the right side houses the City of Phoenix Parks office. The tall building in the background is the Valley National Bank Tower, now Chase Bank. At 40 stories, it is the tallest building in Arizona and was completed in 1972. (RHHSFG.)

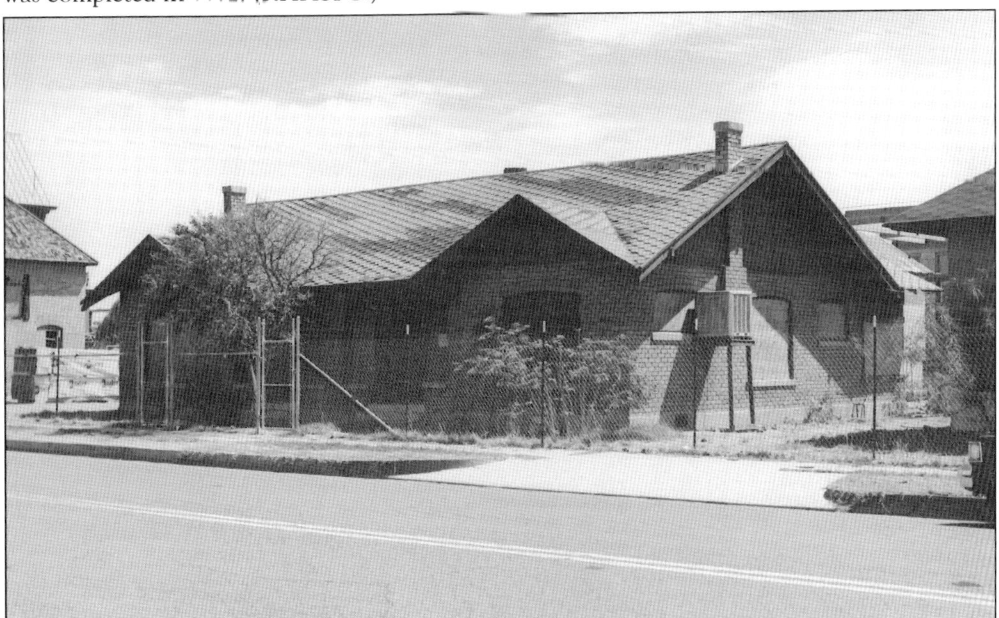

This is the front of the 1923 duplex, looking east from Sixth Street. At left, a portion of the south side of the Burgess Carriage House is visible, as is the steep roof of the Rosson House. Today, it may be difficult to imagine that this lot sat empty for nearly 30 years after the Rosson House was completed in 1895. (RHHSFG.)

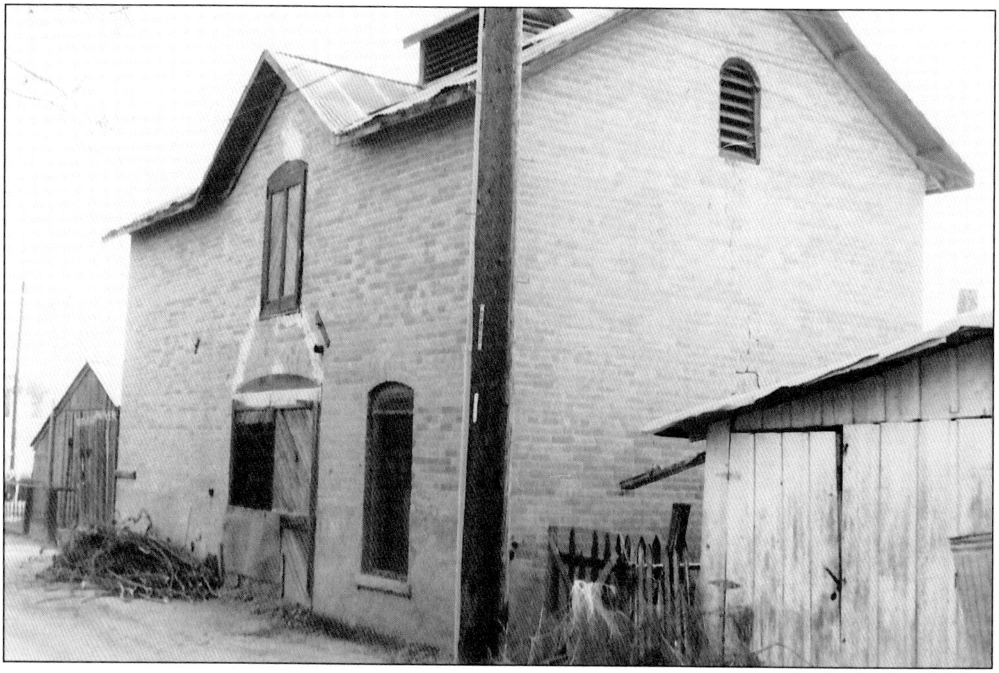

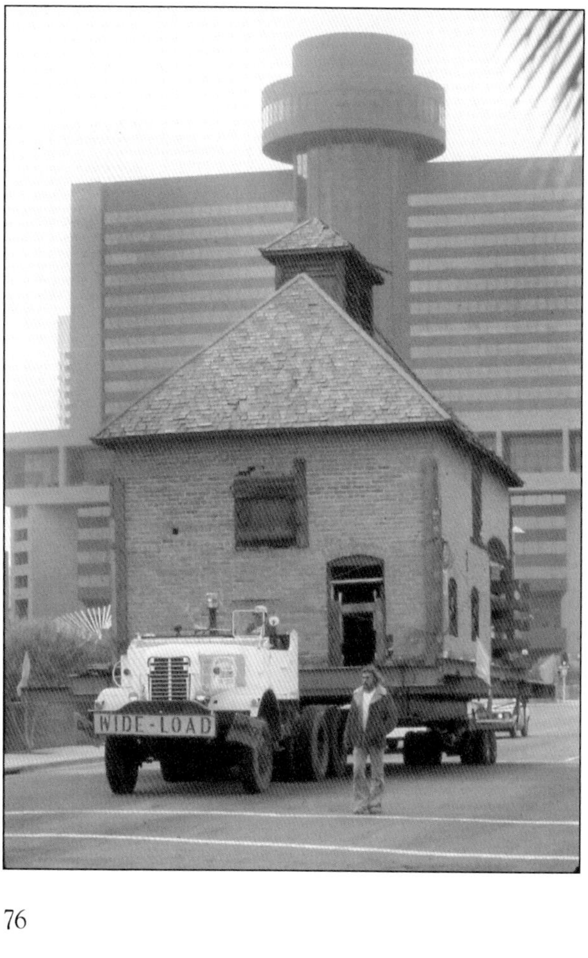

The Teeter Carriage House was originally located off the alley that ran east-west through the center of Block 14. It was one of the few carriage houses built at the same time as its accompanying home. The surrounding wood auxiliary buildings were removed in the restoration process. (RHHSFG.)

The Burgess Carriage House travels east on Monroe Street en route from 130 East Taylor to its new home at the square. While the structure's original location was only a half-dozen blocks northwest of the park, it was a slow and methodical process to safely move the brick building. In the background is the Hyatt Regency Hotel. (RHHSFG.)

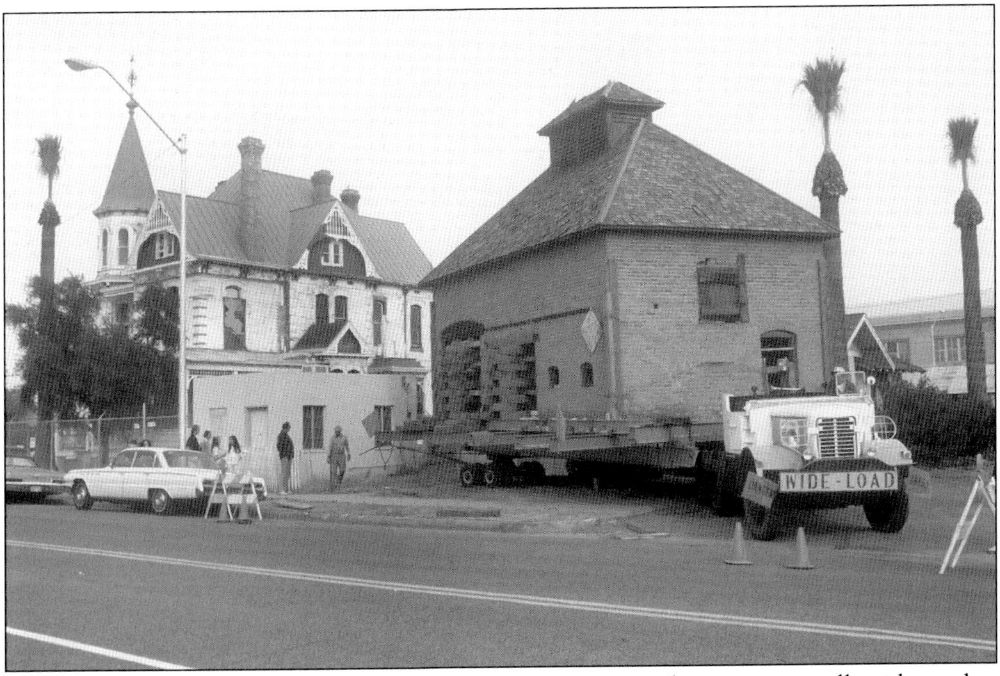

It proved difficult to back the Burgess Carriage House into its new location, especially with another structure directly behind this site. For those who had the opportunity to witness the building's transportation, it must have been quite a show. (RHHSFG.)

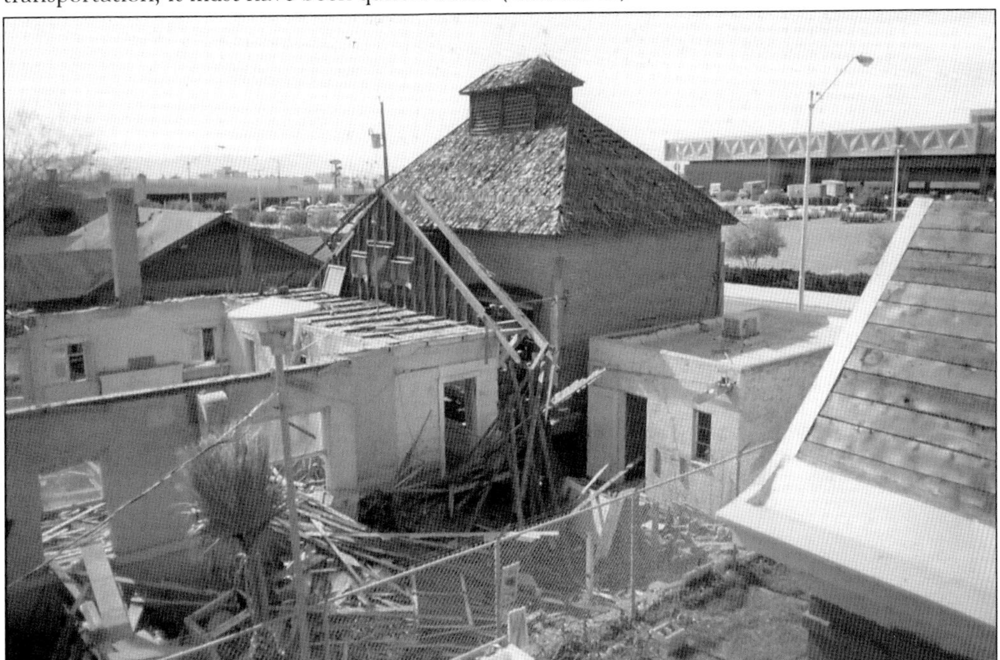

This image shows the limited space the movers had to work with when relocating the Burgess Carriage House to the square. The small building to its right and the larger one to its left would eventually be removed, as their architectural styles were not compatible with the original brick homes of Block 14. The parking lot in the background is Block 13. (RHHSFG.)

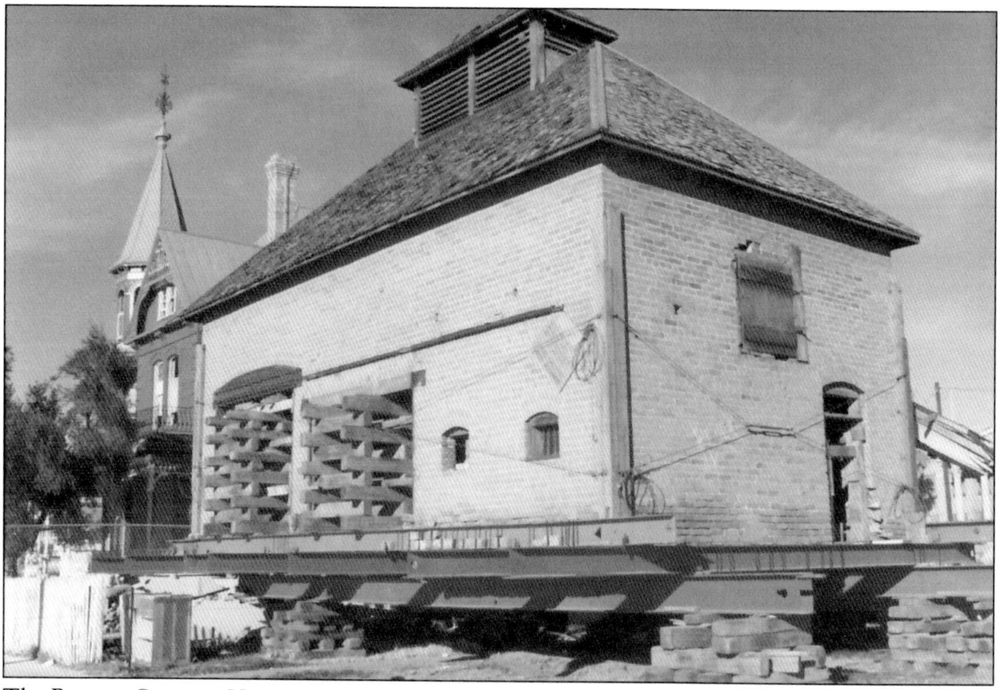

The Burgess Carriage House is raised over its permanent site in Historic Heritage Square (above). Once the foundation slab was poured, the house was lowered and secured to its new location. The Rosson House in the background was painted red to cover up the old white paint. Below, the Burgess Carriage House sits on its new foundation. The buildings formerly abutting the house have been razed. The framework of the Lath Pavilion is in the background. (RHHSFG.)

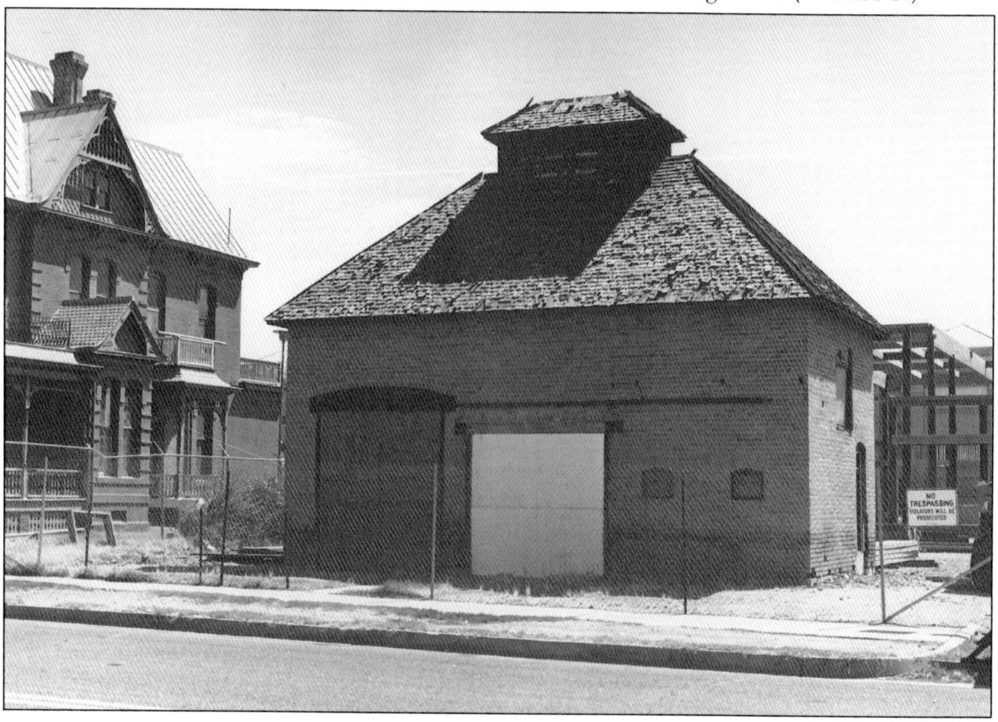

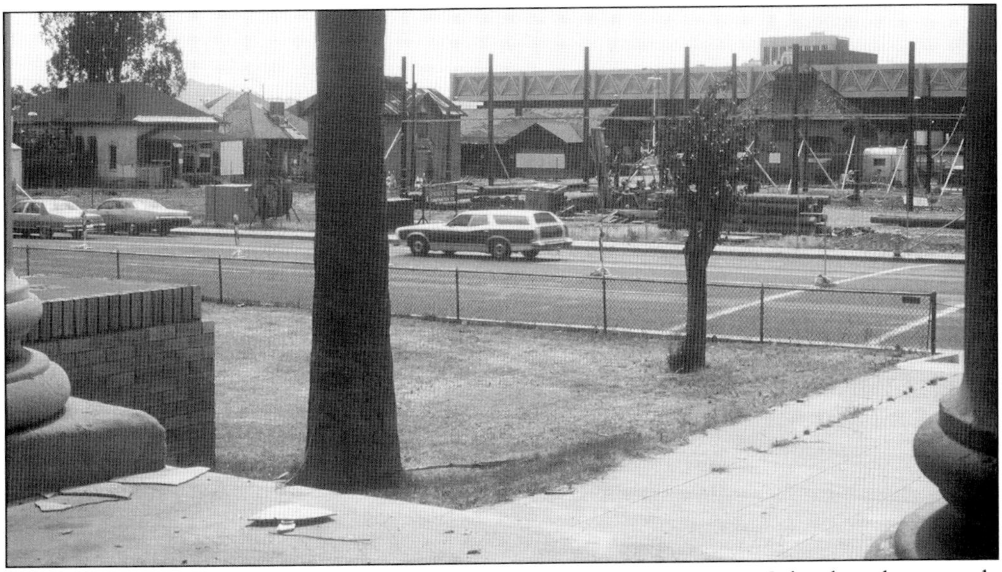

This west-facing photograph, taken from the steps of Monroe Elementary School on the east side of Seventh Street, shows the wood pillars for the Lath Pavilion. The Phoenix Convention Center is in the background. Viewed from the rear, the other buildings on the square demonstrate their rough condition, which necessitated extensive restoration. (RHHSFG.)

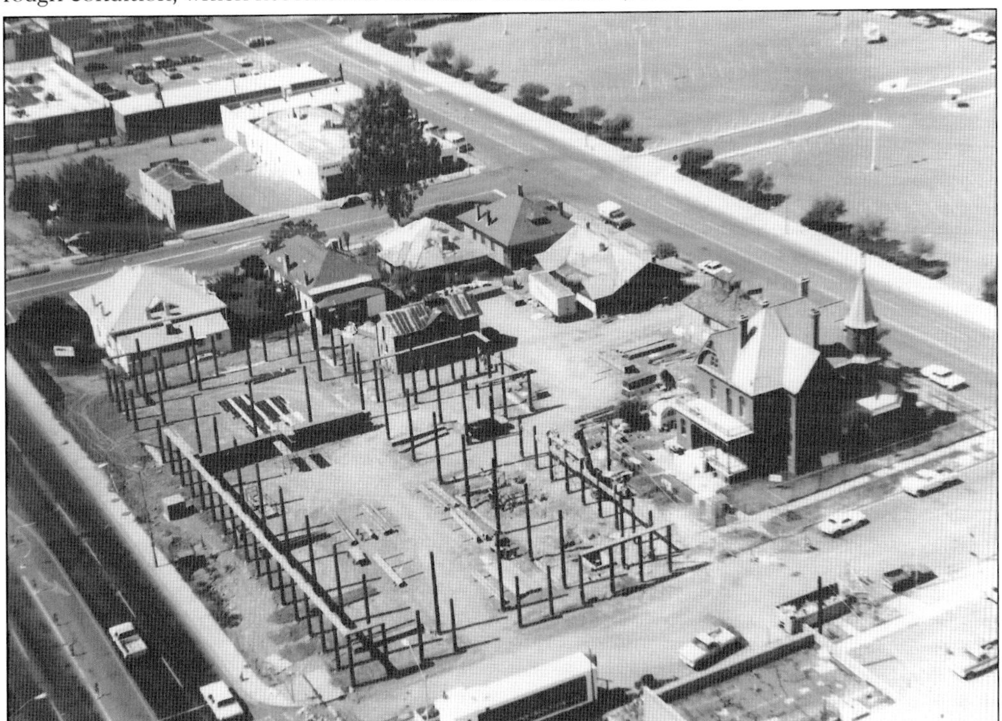

This aerial photograph of Historic Heritage Square looks southwest. The Lath Pavilion is under construction, the exterior of the Rosson House more closely resembles its original state, and the duplex, the Stevens-Haustgen House, and the Teeter Carriage House are in various stages of restoration. (RHHSFG.)

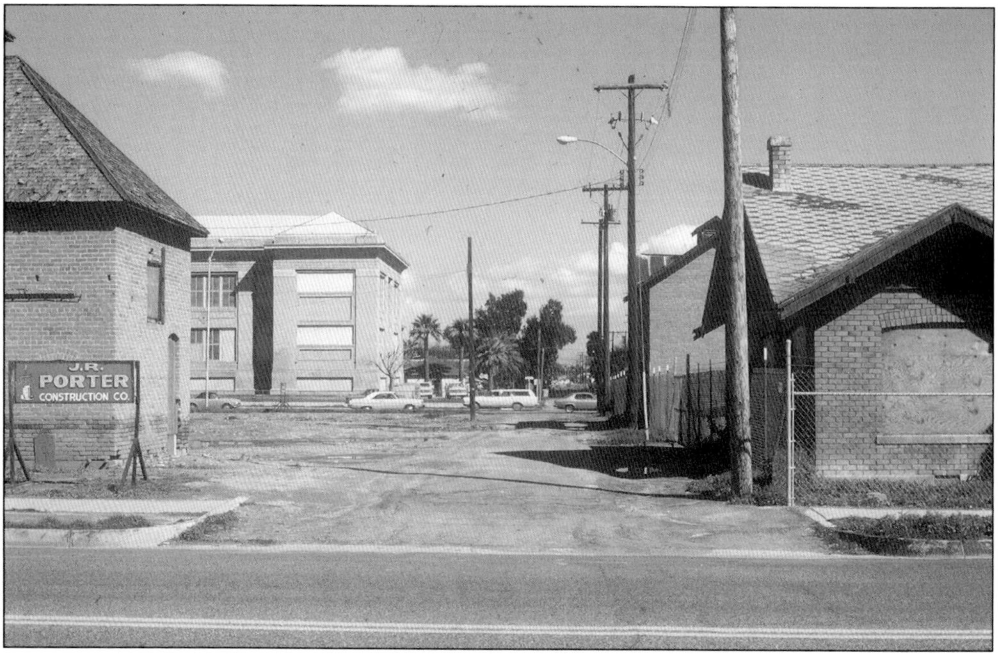

In the original Phoenix townsite, many of the blocks had alleys, such as this one through Block 14. On the right is a portion of the duplex, with the Teeter Carriage House just behind it. Typically, carriage houses would have access to the alley for easier maneuvering of horses, carriages, and, later, automobiles. (RHHSFG.)

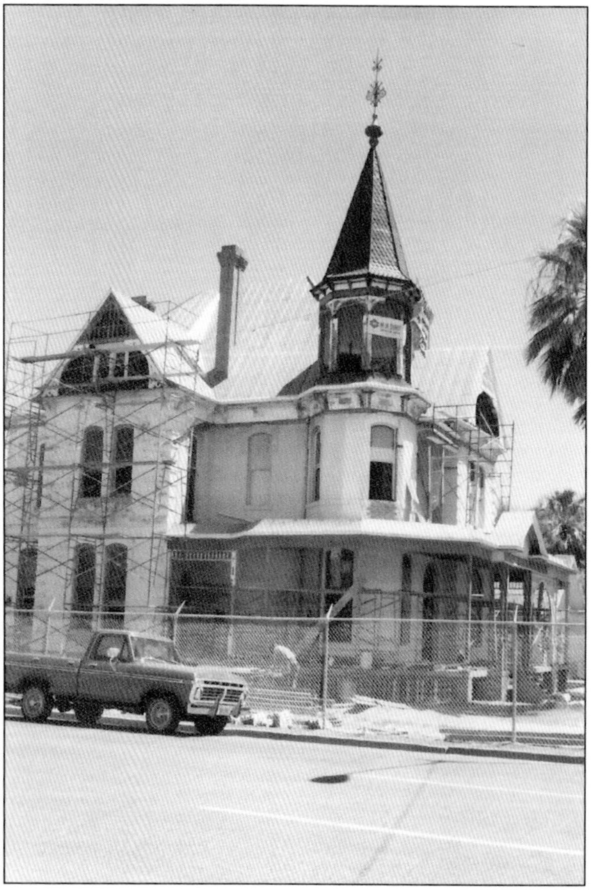

Scaffolding supports parts of the Rosson House's front porch, allowing crews to work. Slowly, the house's original structure was revealed. The wraparound porch on the second floor has yet to be constructed. To the sidewalk foreman, the restoration scene may have looked chaotic. (RHHSFG.)

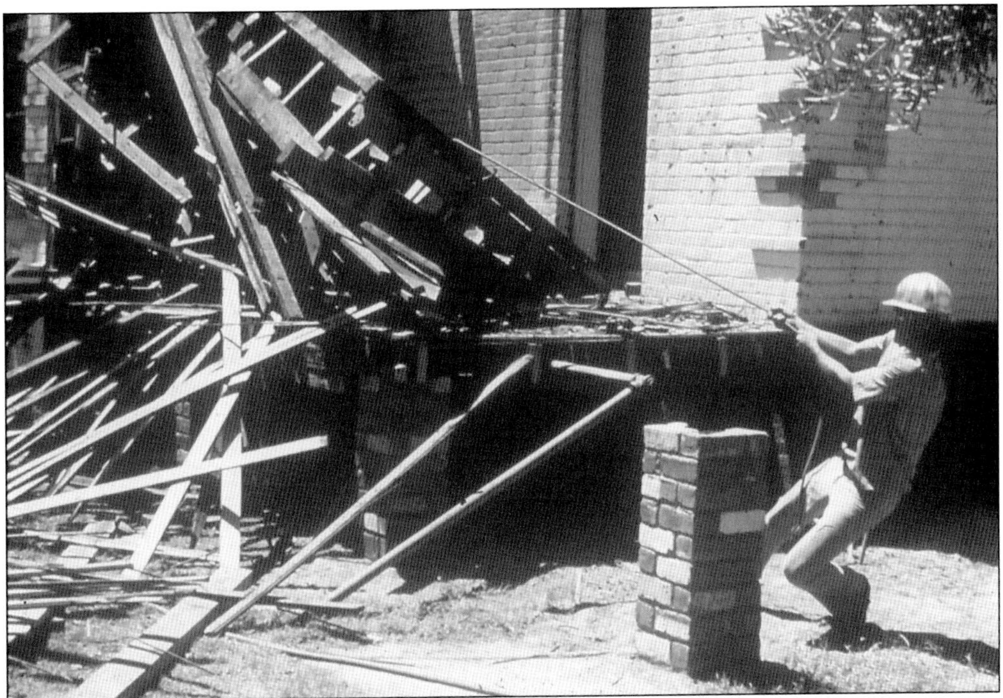

This worker is not trying to prevent a portion of the porch from collapsing, but, instead, is helping to remove additions made to the Rosson House over the years. (RHHSFG.)

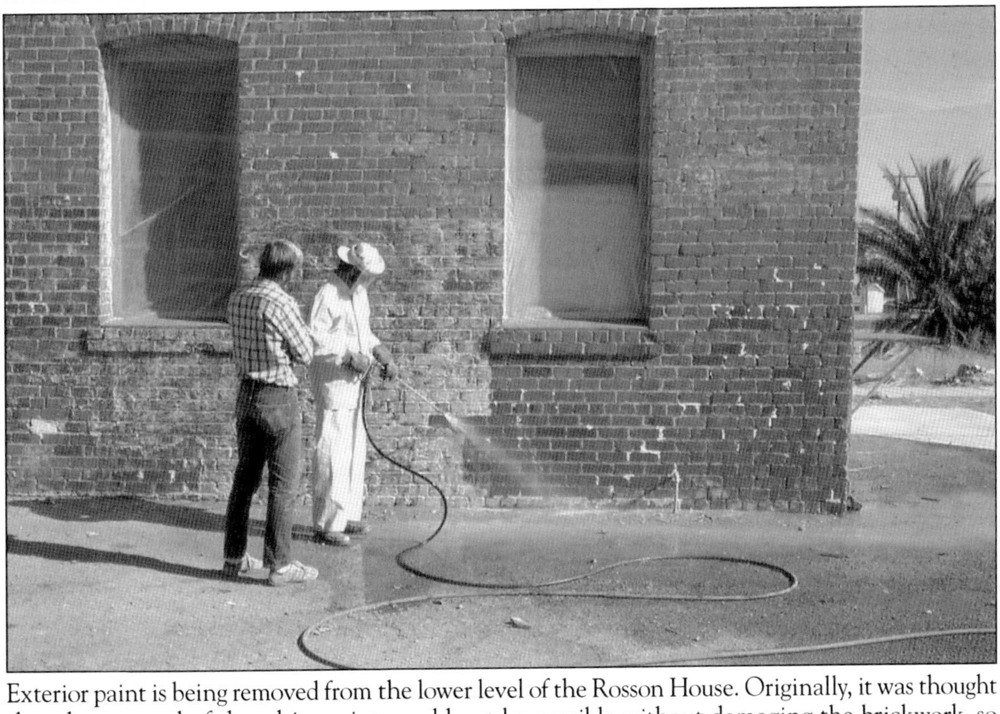

Exterior paint is being removed from the lower level of the Rosson House. Originally, it was thought that the removal of the white paint would not be possible without damaging the brickwork, so the house was repainted a brick-red color. Later, however, a new process proved successful in removing the paint. (RHHSFG.)

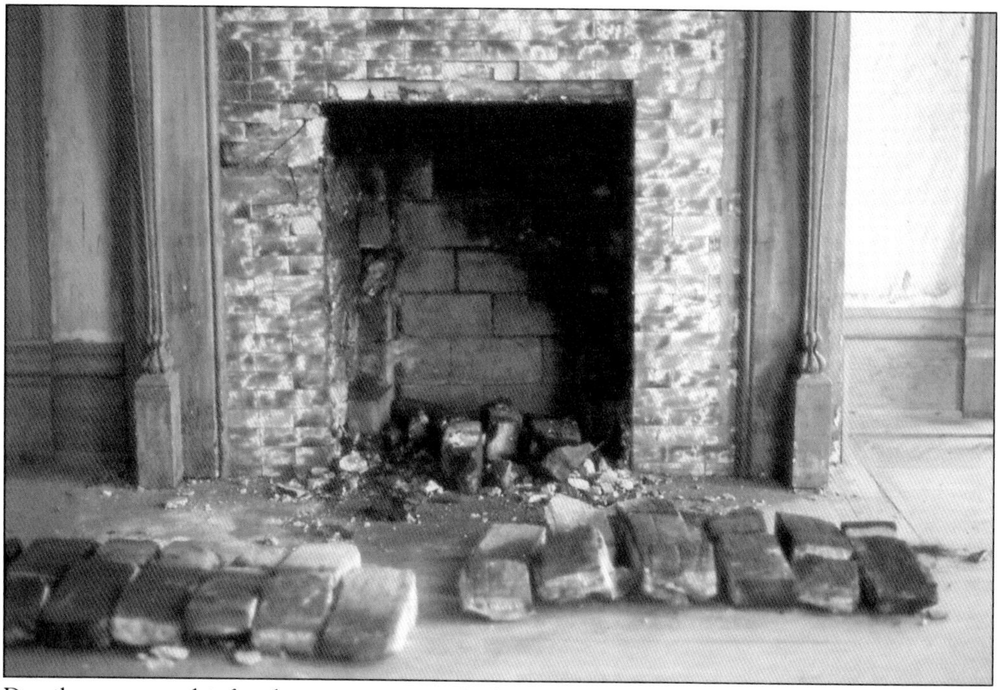

Details appear on this fireplace in an upstairs bedroom. During renovation, it was determined that the house had coal-burning fireplaces, though a coal chute was never discovered in the house's small basement. The incongruity still has not been solved. (RHHSFG.)

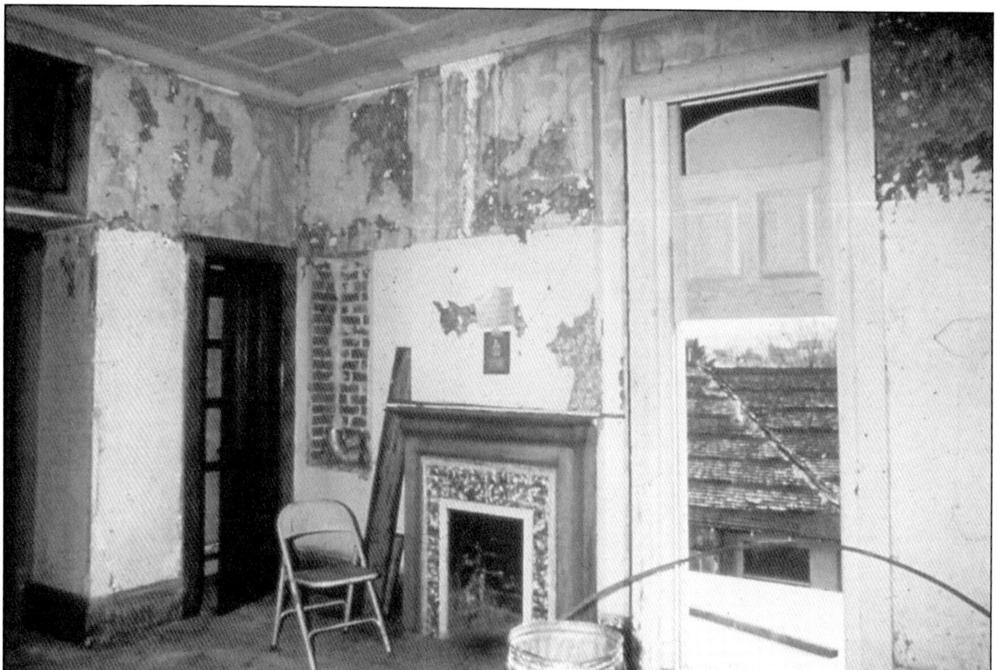

The master bedroom is seen here during restoration. A closet is to the left of the fireplace. The window on the right is a gib, or double-hung window door. Paint and old wallpaper have been removed in places to reveal what was originally on the walls. (RHHSFG.)

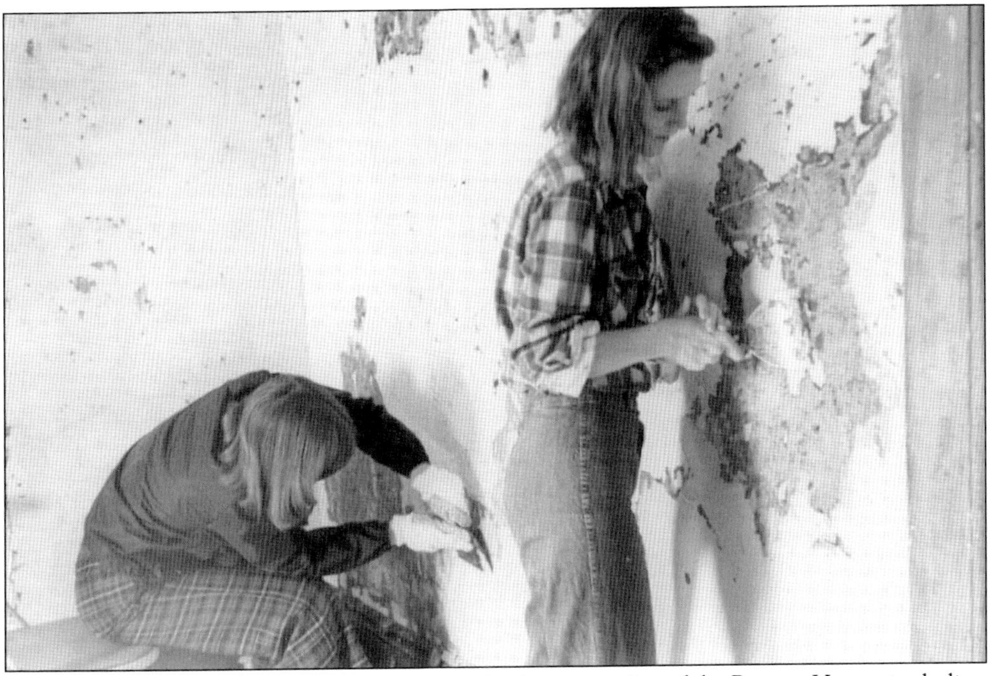

The Junior League of Phoenix was quite active in the restoration of the Rosson House, including Vicki Beaver (above, left). League members and their spouses helped in scraping away over 80 years of history before discovering the first layer. A keg of beer was provided to encourage participation. Below, Junior League members who had been working on the Rosson House examine the scraps of wallpaper discovered during the interior restoration. Based on their research, the wallpaper currently on the walls of the Rosson House matches what was originally there in 1895. (RHHSFG.)

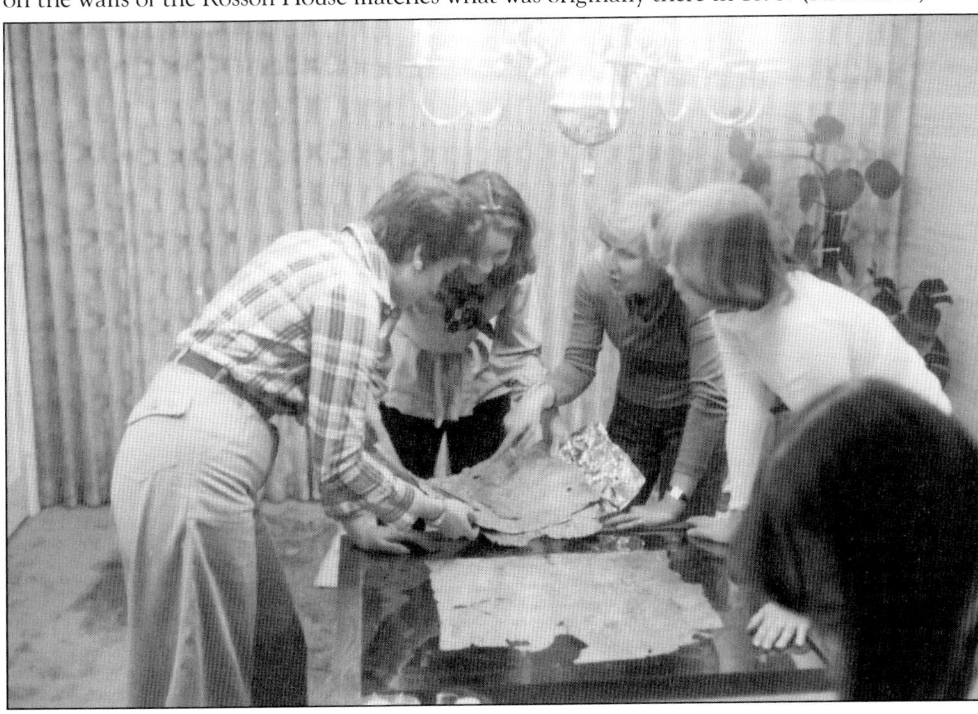

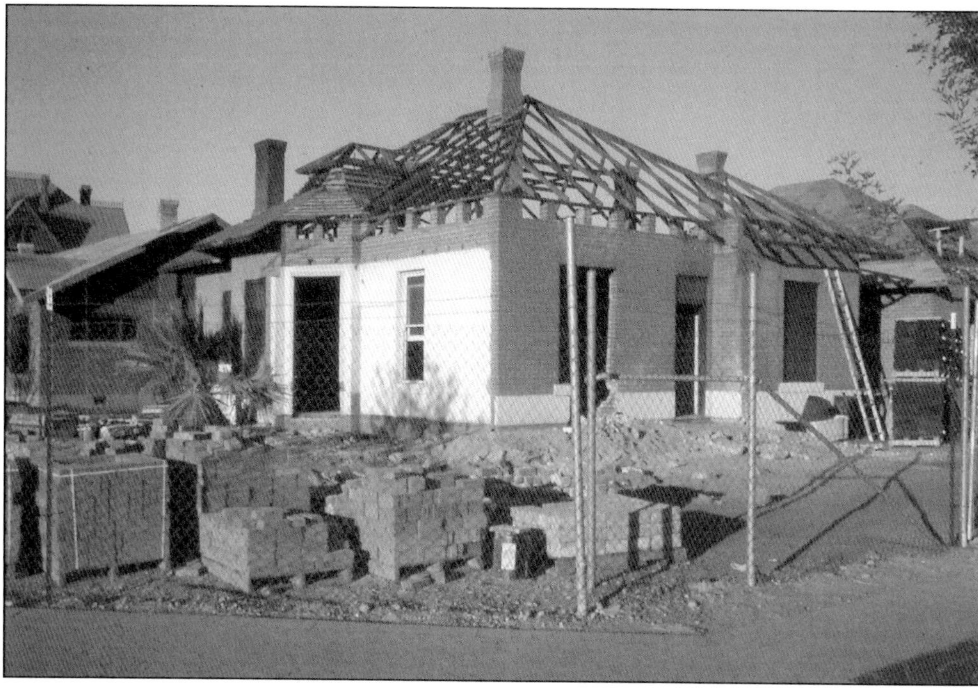

Each house on Block 14 required extensive renovation and restoration. Above, the Stevens House stands on the corner of Sixth and Adams Streets. The white paint will be removed from the exterior brick, a new roof will be installed, and, eventually, the front wraparound porch will be reconstructed. Below, the sheathing to support the new cedar-shingle roof is nearly complete. When the white paint was removed, workers repointed the bricks. (RHHSFG.)

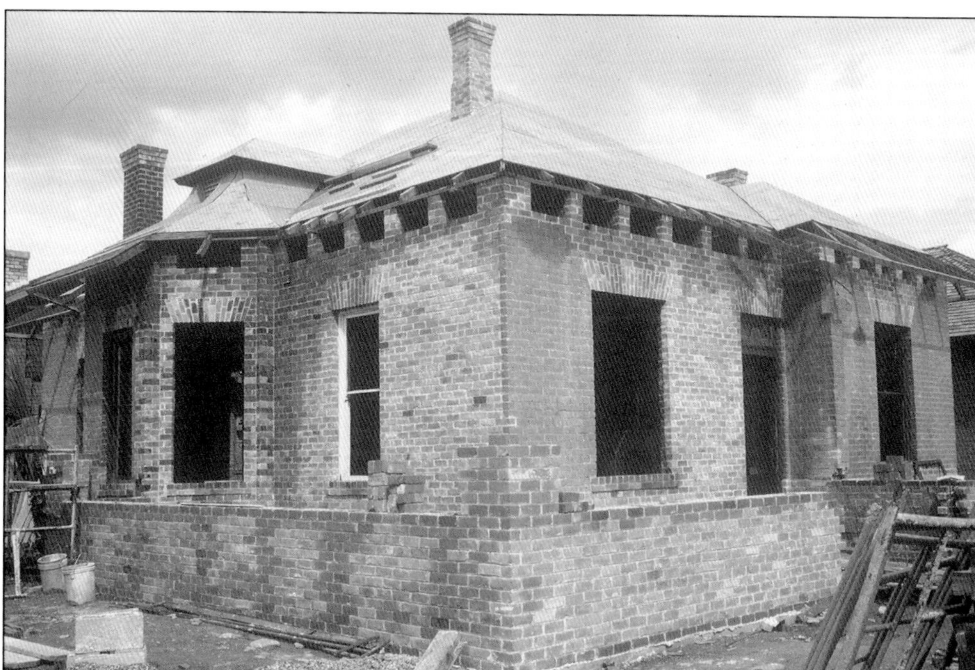

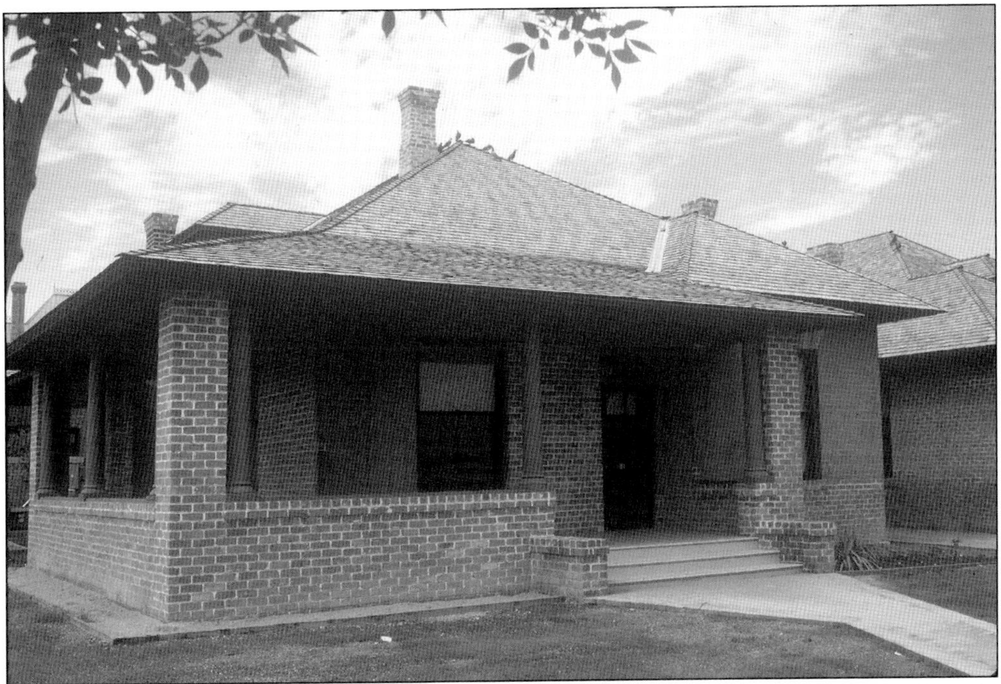

Unlike the other homes along Adams Street, the Stevens House had a brick wraparound porch. During the restoration process, the porch was rebuilt. The building is now home to the Arizona Doll and Toy Museum. (RHHSFG.)

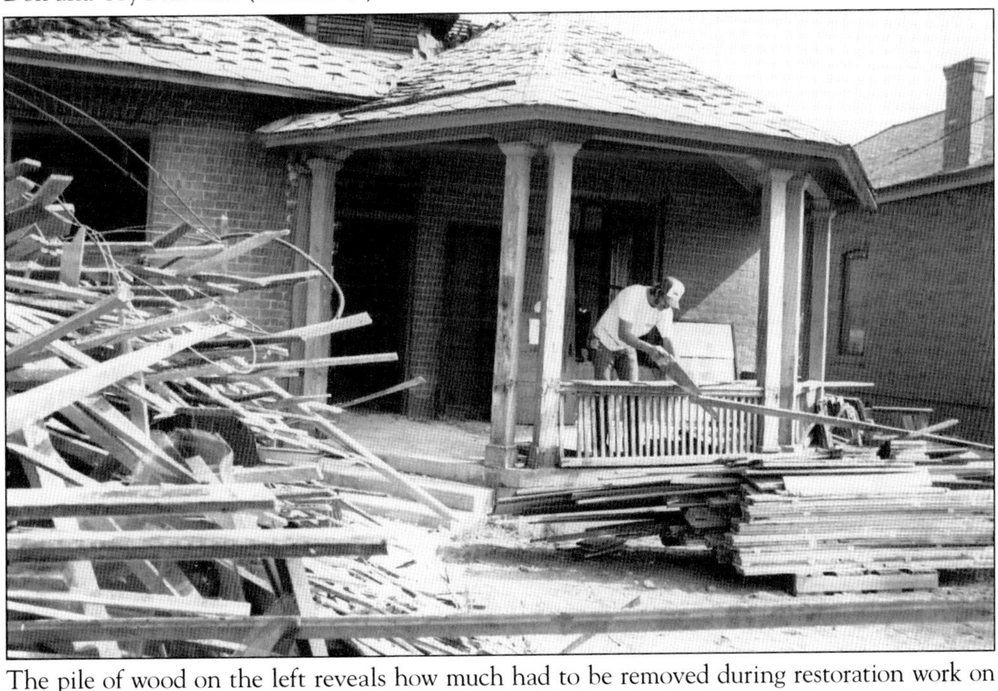

The pile of wood on the left reveals how much had to be removed during restoration work on the square. The workman is using the dilapidated railing on the Stevens-Haustgen House as a support as he renovates the interior. The photograph was taken before the house's roof was replaced. (RHHSFG.)

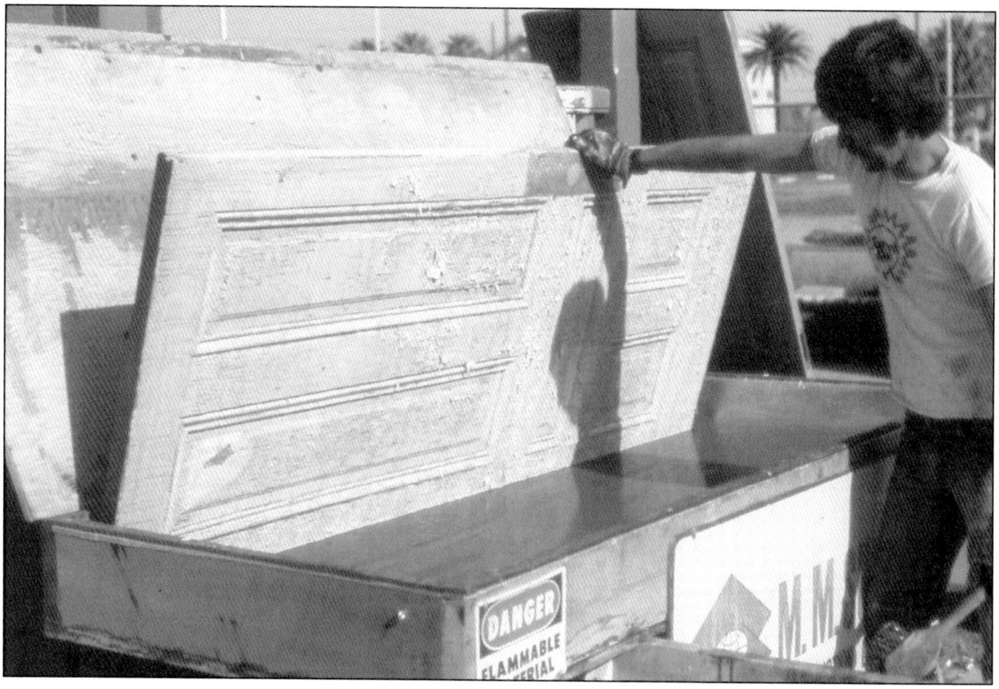

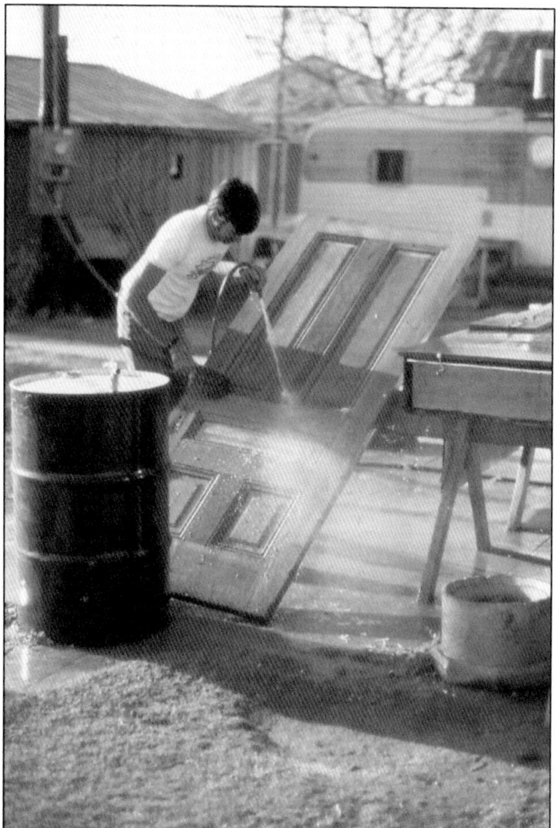

House interiors can change dramatically over the years. Above, a workman dips wood doors into a solvent to remove decades of paint and varnish. Another step in the process (left) is to reveal bare wood. Once the original color was determined, craftsmen began to restore the doors to their original splendor. Final confirmation of the wood color occurred with the discovery of unpainted pocket doors between the parlor and dining room. (RHHSFG.)

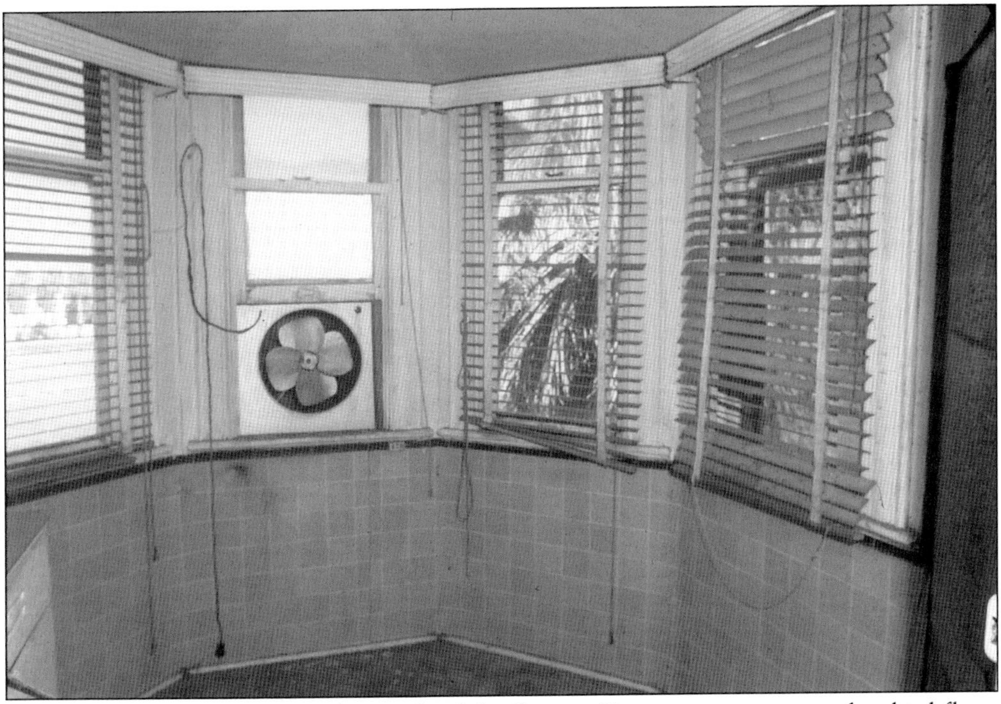

The above photograph shows the inside of the Rosson House tower room on the third floor, including a window air conditioner, venetian blinds, and tile below the windows. These features are not characteristic of the Victorian era. Below, another room has a small heater using the flue of the former coal-burning fireplace. A window fan and sink have been added to this room. All of the beautiful wood has been painted white. (RHHSFG.)

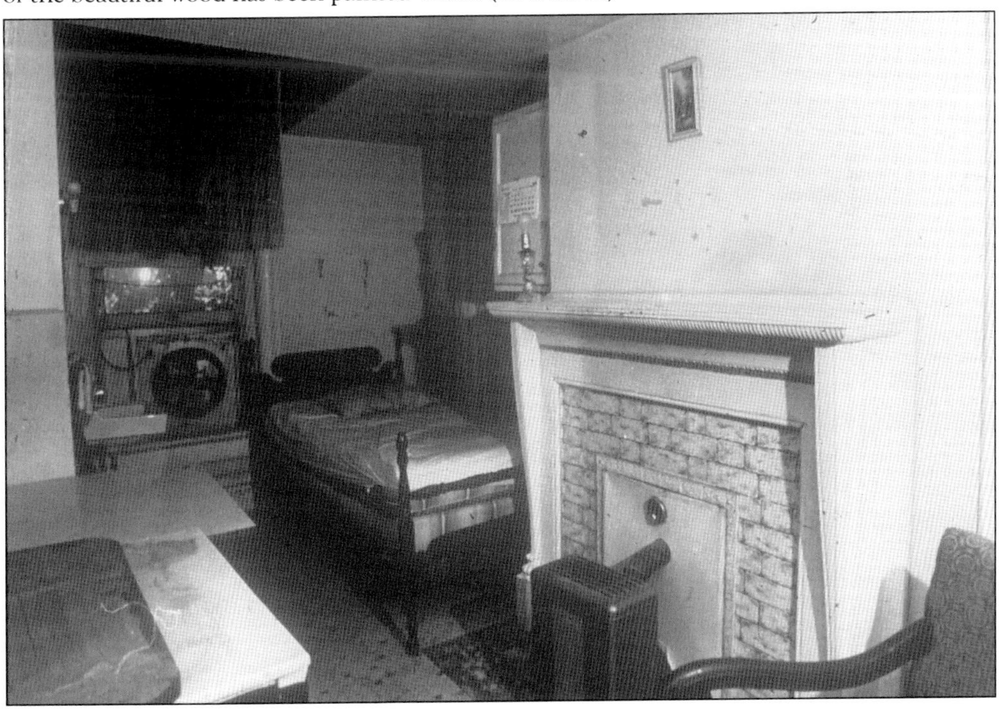

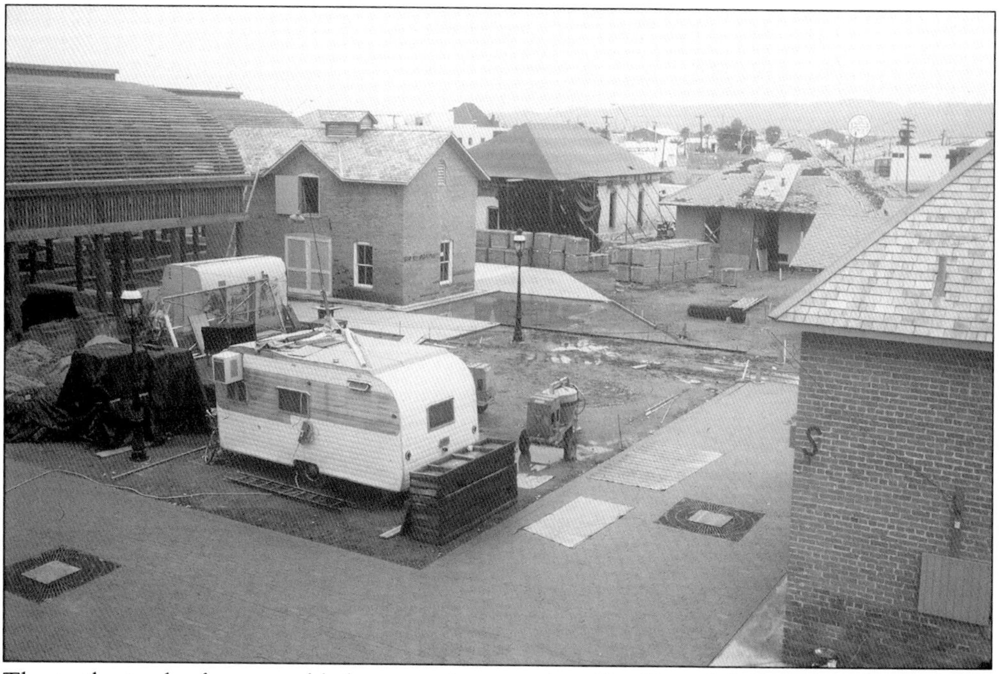

The trailer in the foreground belongs to the caretaker, Kai "Speedy" Skounborg. The Teeter House, with braces holding the walls in place, and the roof of the Stevens-Haustgen House, still in disrepair, are in the background. (RHHSFG.)

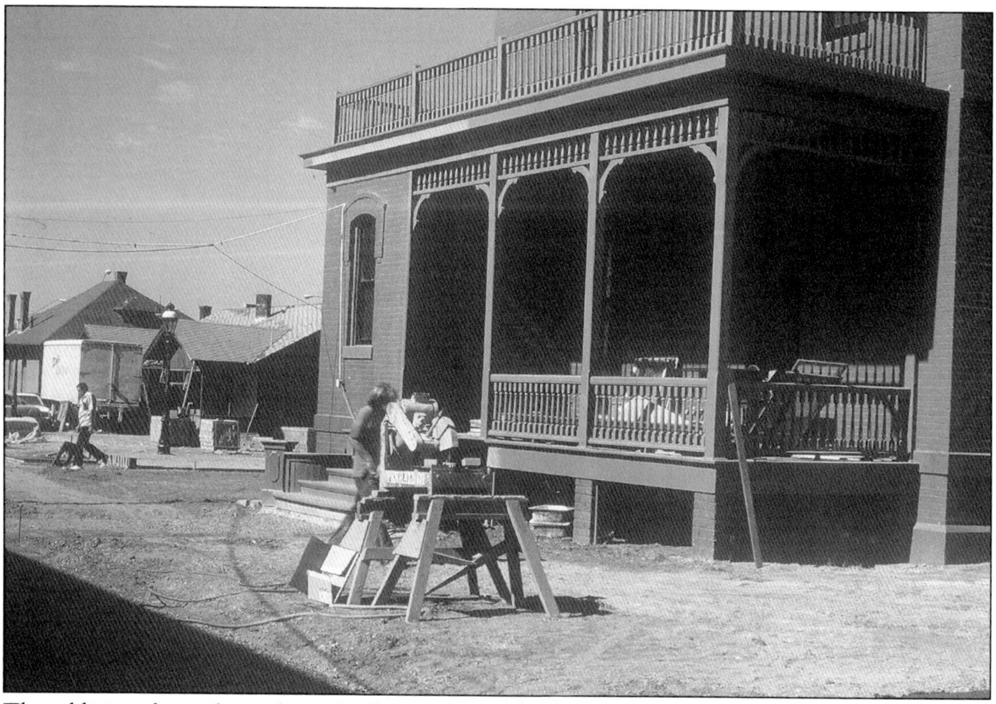

The additions formerly masking the Rosson House back porch have been removed, and the porch has been painted a brick-red color. The new paint would later be stripped to reveal the original brickwork. (RHHSFG.)

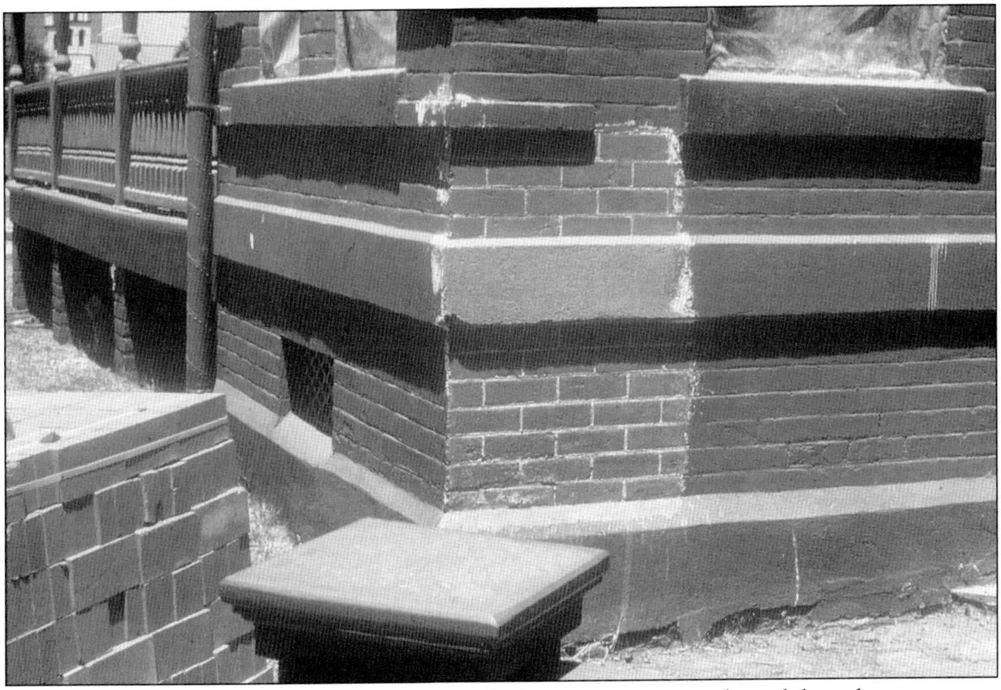

The exterior of the Rosson House was painted white, as were a number of the other structures on Block 14. This created a dilemma, for the removal could damage the brick. A man suggested a method to the restoration committee that proved successful in removing now two paint layers. (RHHSFG.)

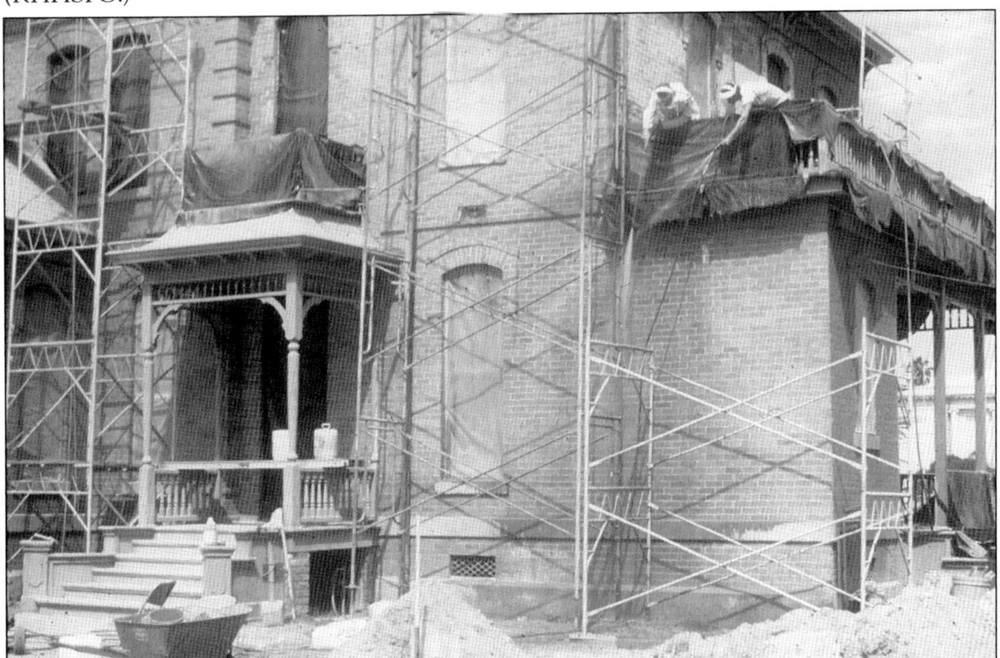

The crew power-washes the brick from the second-story back porch. This was a very time-consuming but vital process to remove the paint. (RHHSFG.)

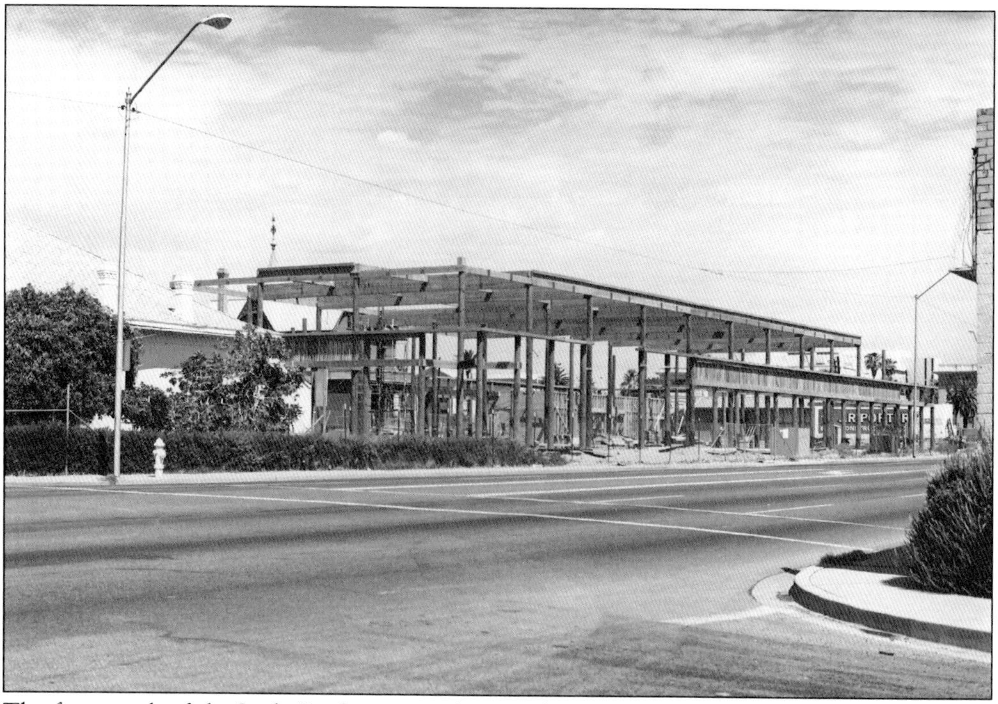

The framework of the Lath Pavilion is in place in this photograph taken from the east side of Seventh and Monroe Streets. Looking northwest, the white building on the left is the Silva House. The spire of the Rosson House is just visible in the background. (RHHSFG.)

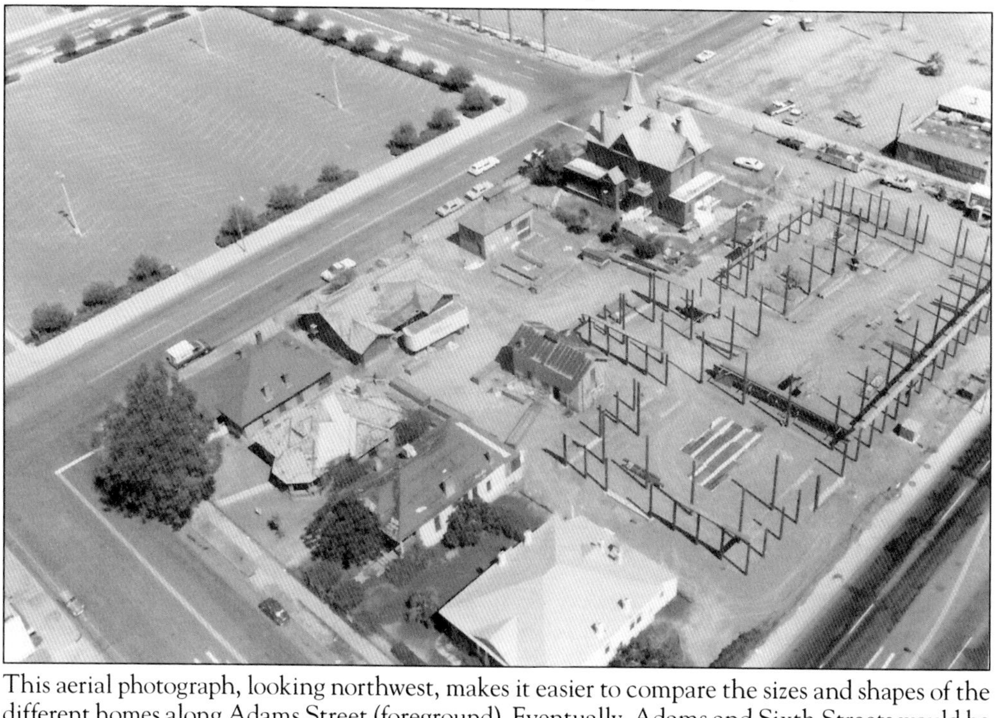

This aerial photograph, looking northwest, makes it easier to compare the sizes and shapes of the different homes along Adams Street (foreground). Eventually, Adams and Sixth Streets would be closed to vehicular traffic. (RHHSFG.)

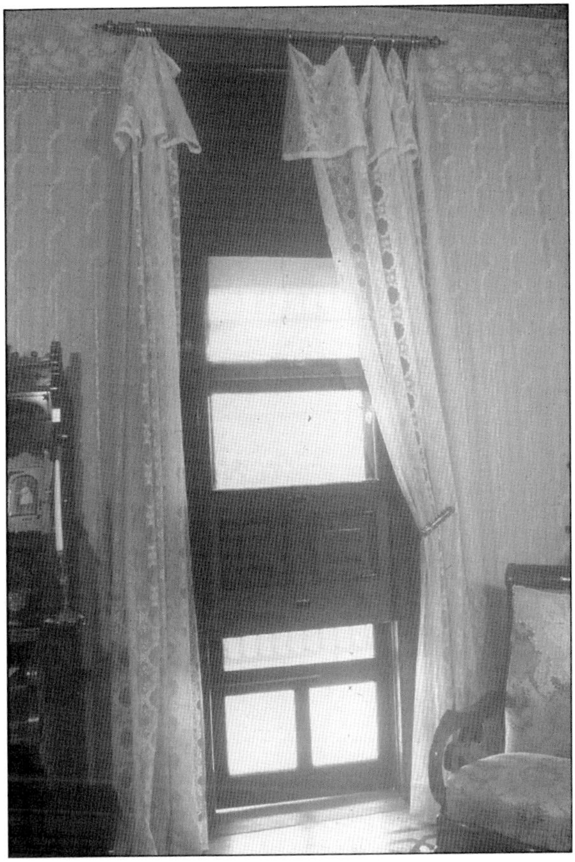

Perhaps the most unusual features of the Rosson House are the nine gib doors, one of which is shown at right. No other house in Phoenix, or in Arizona, is known to have gib doors. The gib doors are double-hung like windows, but, when raised, the opening is nearly as tall as a standard door. The gib doors enhanced air flow in the house. A close-up photograph of the parquet flooring on the first floor of the Rosson House (below) does not adequately illuminate the different pieces of oak, cherry, and walnut. Miraculously, it was not ruined or destroyed over the years. Each room on the first floor has a different pattern. (RHHSFG.)

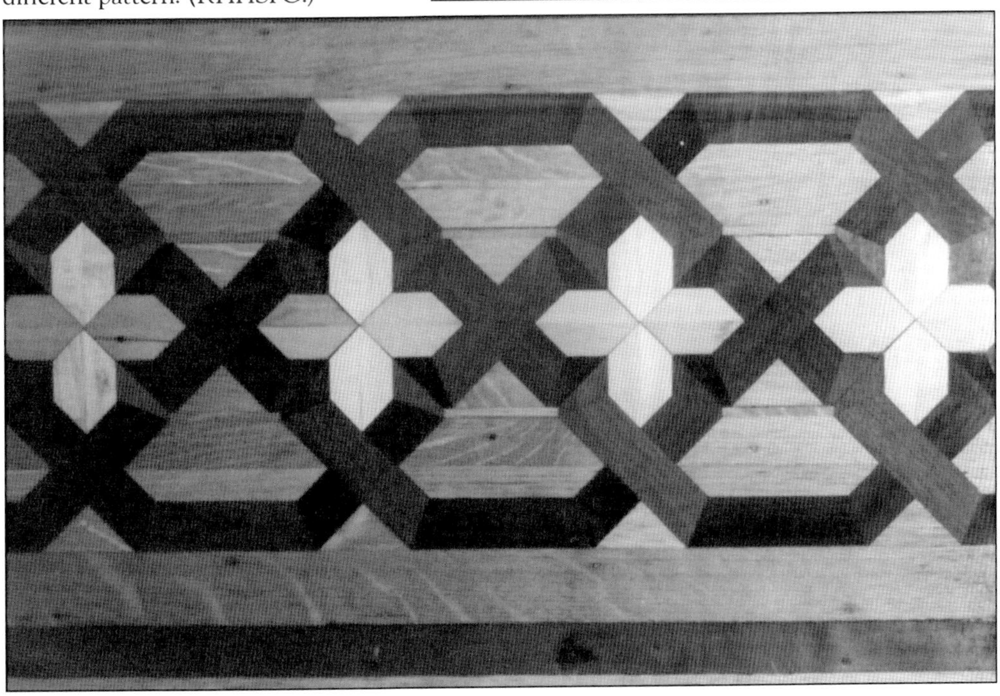

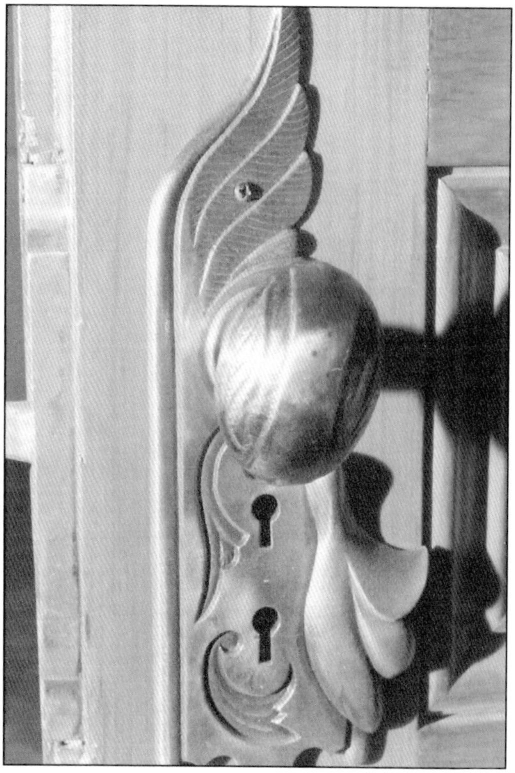

The Rosson House door handles (left) are quite detailed. Over 75 percent of them are original. The upstairs flooring is composed of simple fir strips, as that section of the house was not considered a public area. The door handles upstairs, however, are the same as those found downstairs. It was necessary to replicate many of the smaller pieces of hardware, such as those pictured below. At this stage, it was easy to differentiate between the old and the new hardware. Once the new pieces were installed using the original nail holes as guides and began to age, it became more difficult. (RHHSFG.)

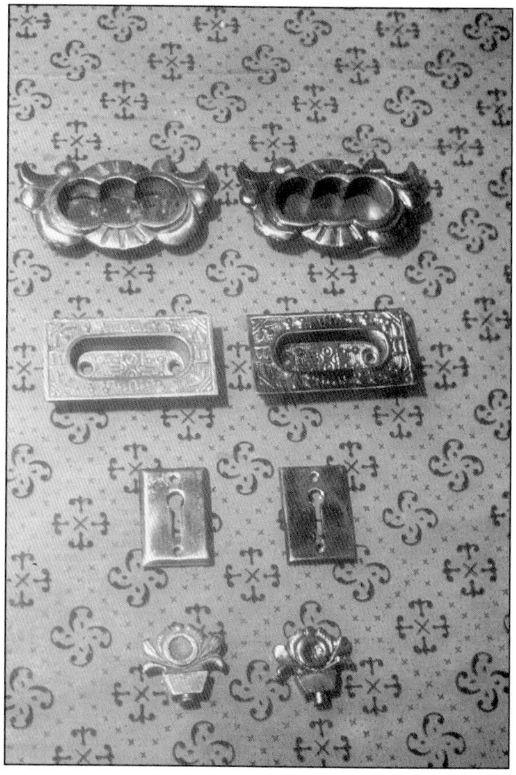

This is a promotional image of Mayor John Driggs posing by the speaking tube in the Rosson House. Discovered during the restoration, the tube is located in the second floor hallway and by the downstairs back staircase. The communication device functions much like the tubes found on a ship. Blowing into it causes a whistling sound, signaling to the opposite floor that someone is "calling." The tube still works, although one must be fairly close to clearly understand what is being said. (RHHSFG.)

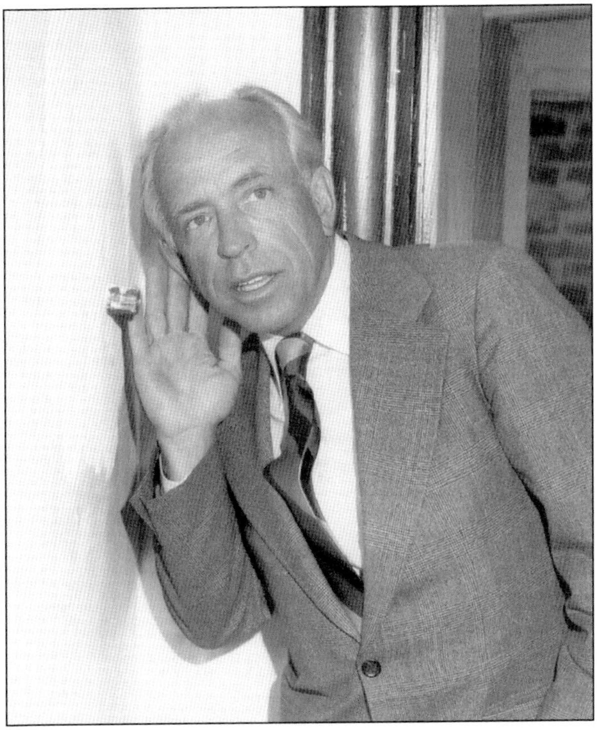

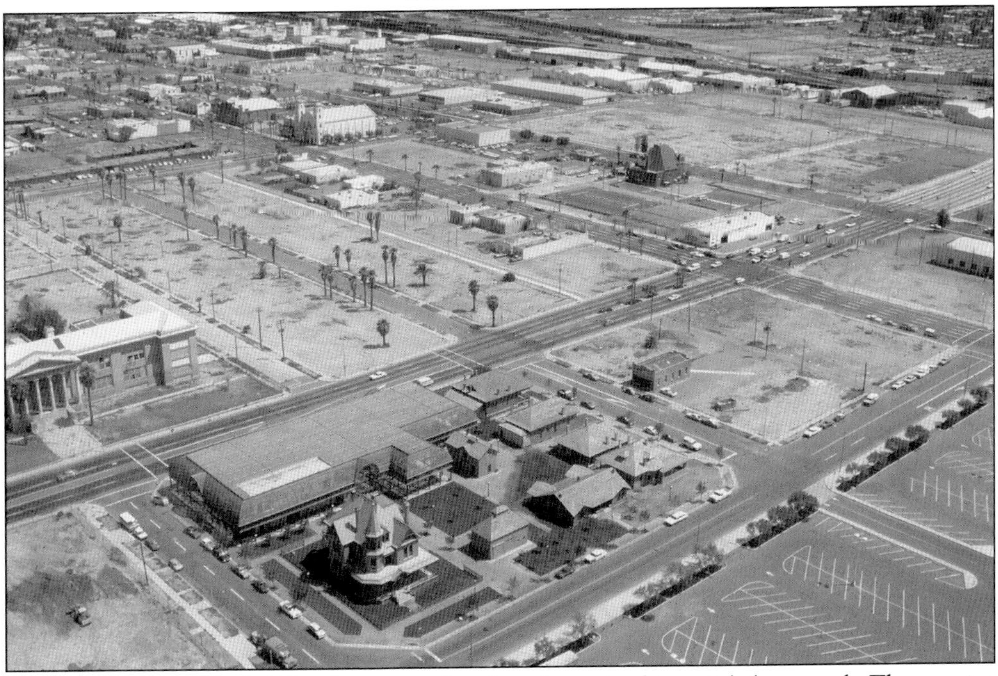

The restoration of Block 14 has been completed, as shown in this aerial photograph. The massive clearing of blocks to its east and south is also visible. Development of these blocks would be critical to the success and survival of this part of downtown. Apartments were added on the east side of Seventh Street; three blocks south, Chase Field, home of the Arizona Diamondbacks, was constructed. Today, nearly all of these empty lots are filled. (RHHSFG.)

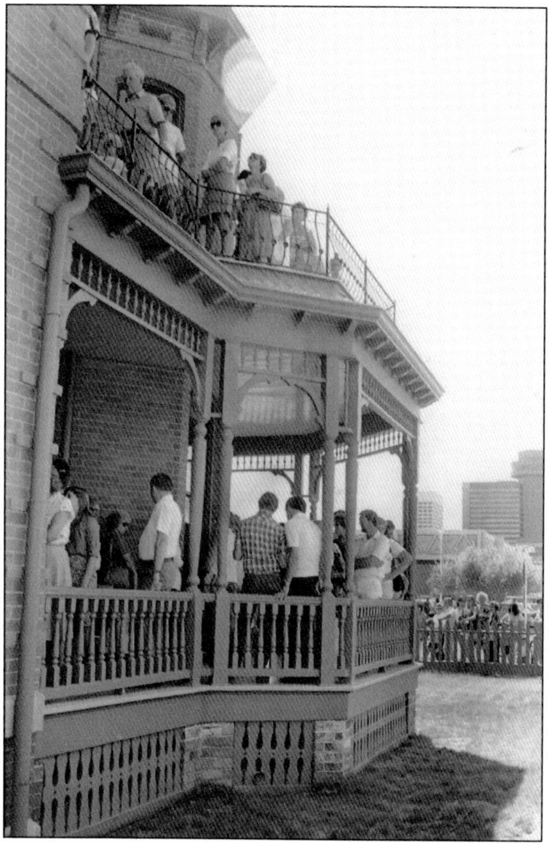

Years of anticipation culminated on opening day, May 4, 1980, as crowds of people patiently stood in line to visit the Rosson House (left). Lines wound inside and around the house, even though no formal tour was provided. In the below photograph, people are seen on the upstairs porch, which is no longer open to the public. Group tours are limited to 15 people, allowing visitors to readily examine the details of this lovingly restored Victorian home. (Left, photograph by Bob Rink, RHHSFG; below, RHHSFG.)

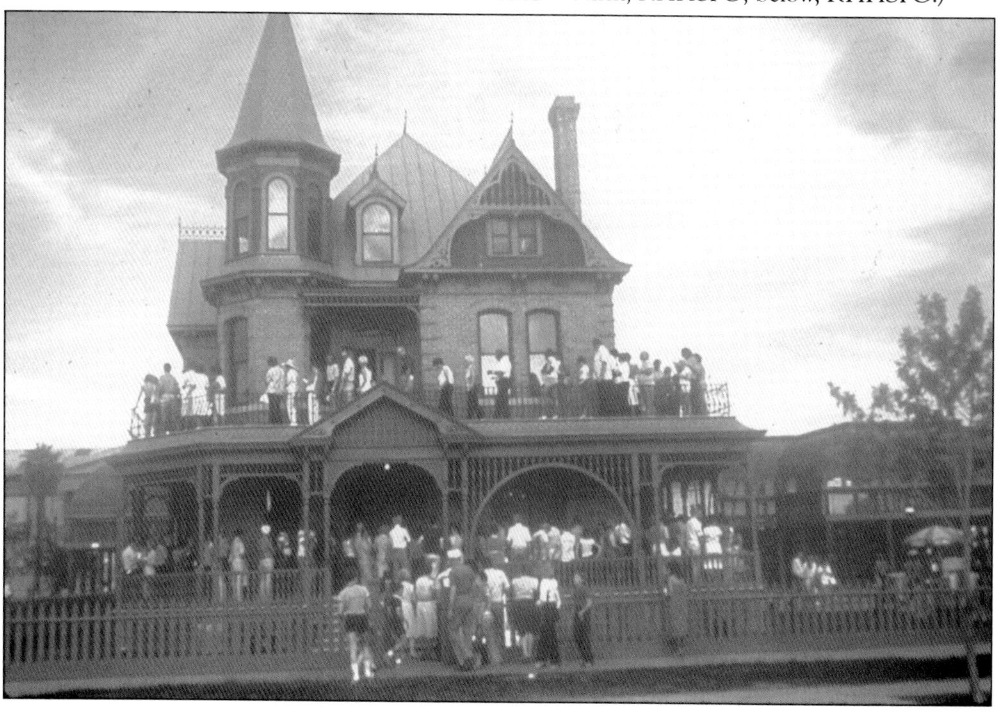

Over the years, the Rosson House has been honored by various renditions in gingerbread, drawings, needlepoint, photographs, and paintings by both professional and amateur artists. This replica was made not long after the restoration was completed. (RHHSFG.)

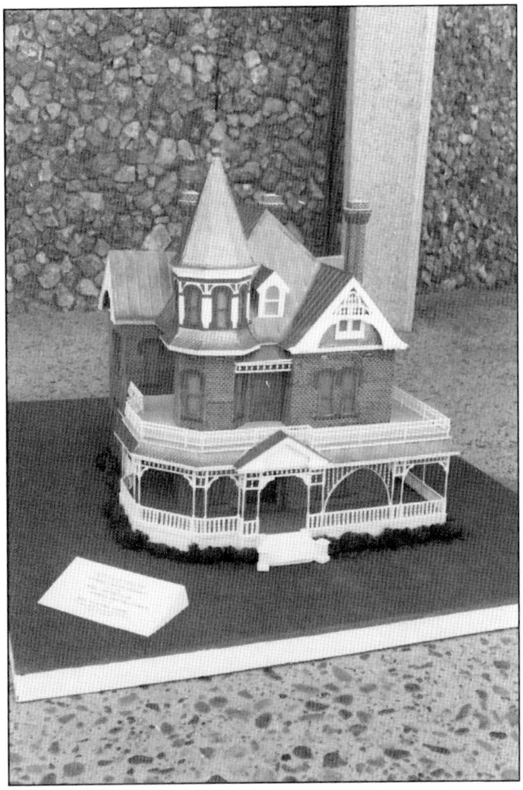

On the south side of Adams Street was the Baird Machine Shop, now the home of Pizzeria Bianco. Katherine Baird used funds she received from a lawsuit involving the wrongful death of her husband to have this building erected in 1929. She and her son, Arthur, operated the business for several years. (RHHSFG.)

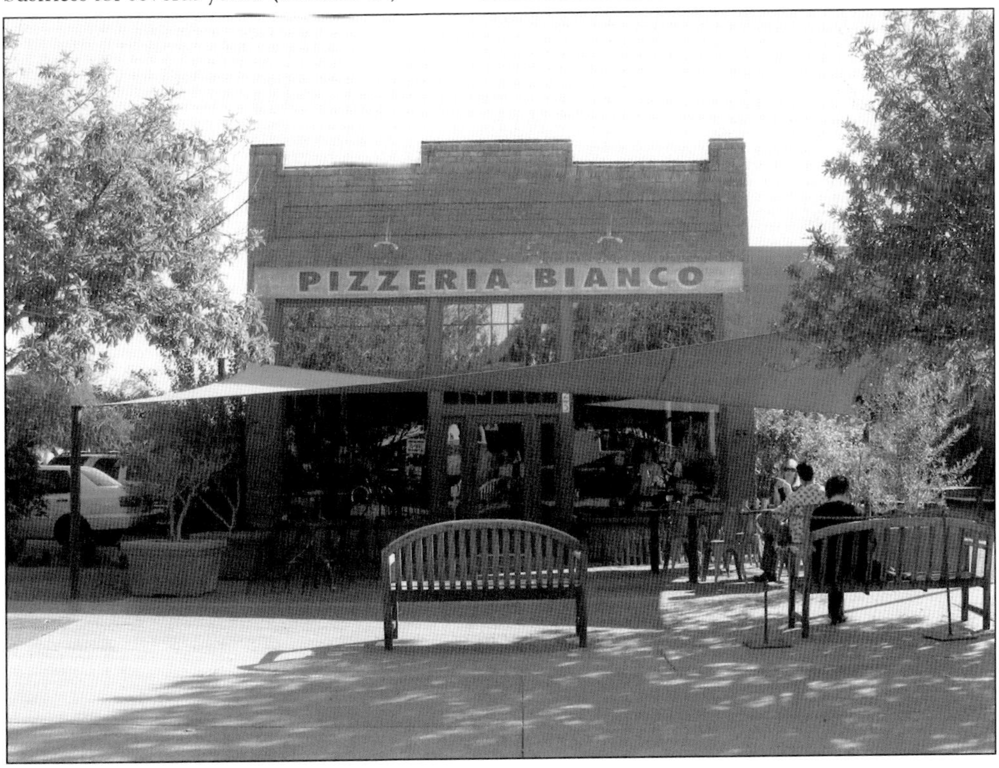

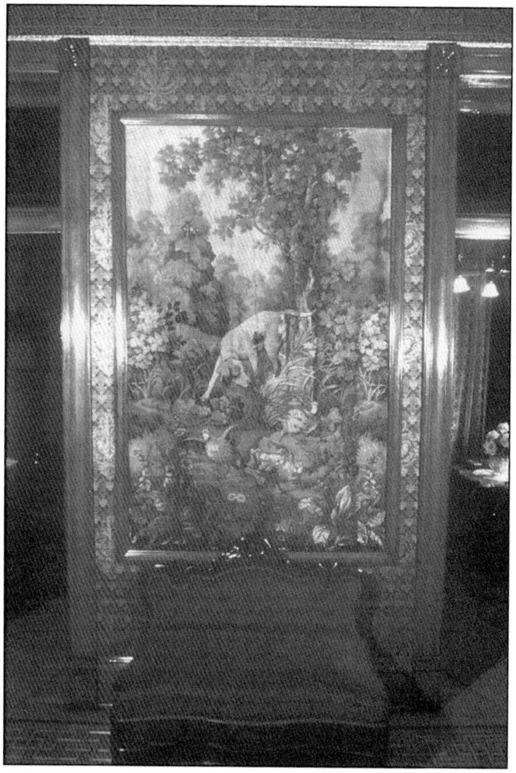

This tapestry hangs in the foyer of the Rosson House. The textile is known as the Higley tapestry, since it was purchased by Stephen Higley, possibly at the St. Louis Exposition of 1904. Apparently, the Gammel family insisted that the tapestry be part of the acquisition when they purchased the house from the Higleys in 1914. Museum staff later discovered that Mills College in California owns the same tapestry. (RHHSFG.)

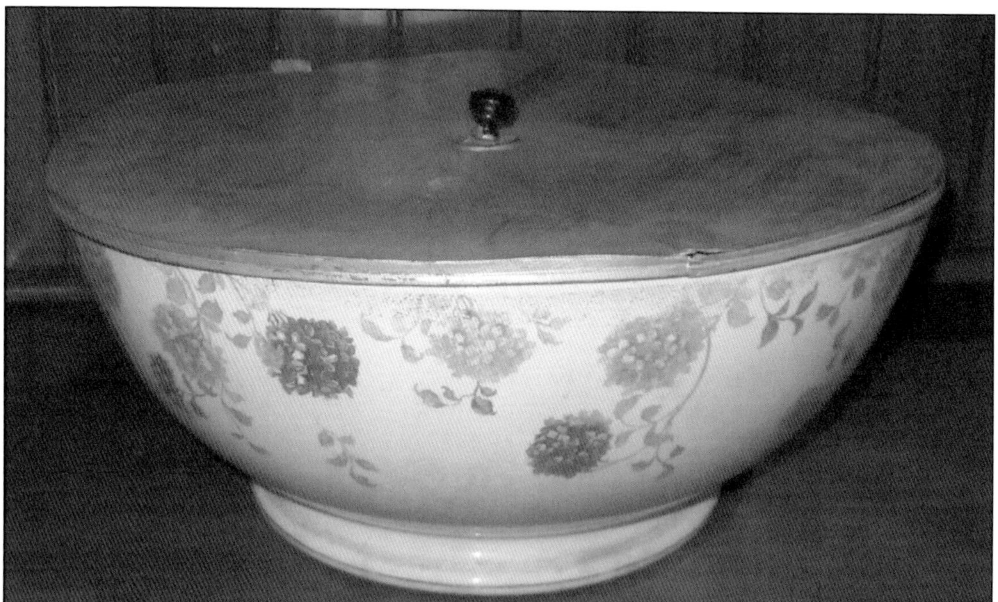

This large ceramic punch bowl painted with flowers was owned by the Gammel family and was donated to the Rosson House Museum. Georgia Gammel Valliere told the Rosson House Restoration Committee in the late 1970s that it had a metal lid to keep insects out of the punch, because the family often used it at outdoor parties. It was filled with eggnog for visitors on New Year's Day before Prohibition. (RHHSFG.)

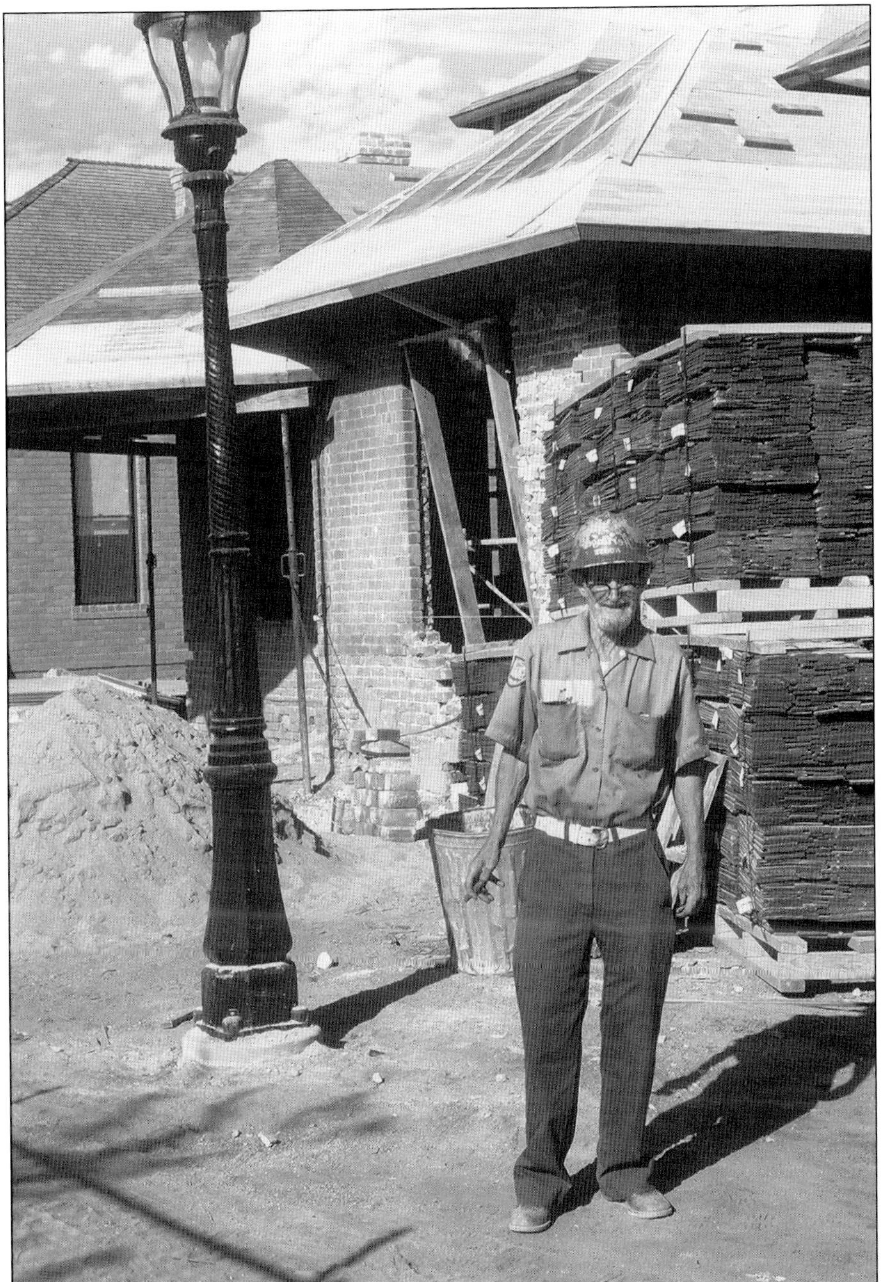

Kai "Speedy" Skounborg was a resident of the Rosson House from 1962 until the City of Phoenix purchased the building in 1974. Speedy then lived onsite in a trailer and acted as the caretaker of Historic Heritage Square while the buildings were undergoing restoration. Afterward, Speedy continued to assist with activities at the Rosson House, such as opening and closing the museum. One of the museum's docents related that it was difficult to tell Speedy not to touch items in the house, as he had formerly lived there. On the evening of Saturday, January 24, 1981, he was murdered in his trailer at the age of 71. Speedy may have interrupted a robbery. To date, the crime has never been solved. (RHHSFG.)

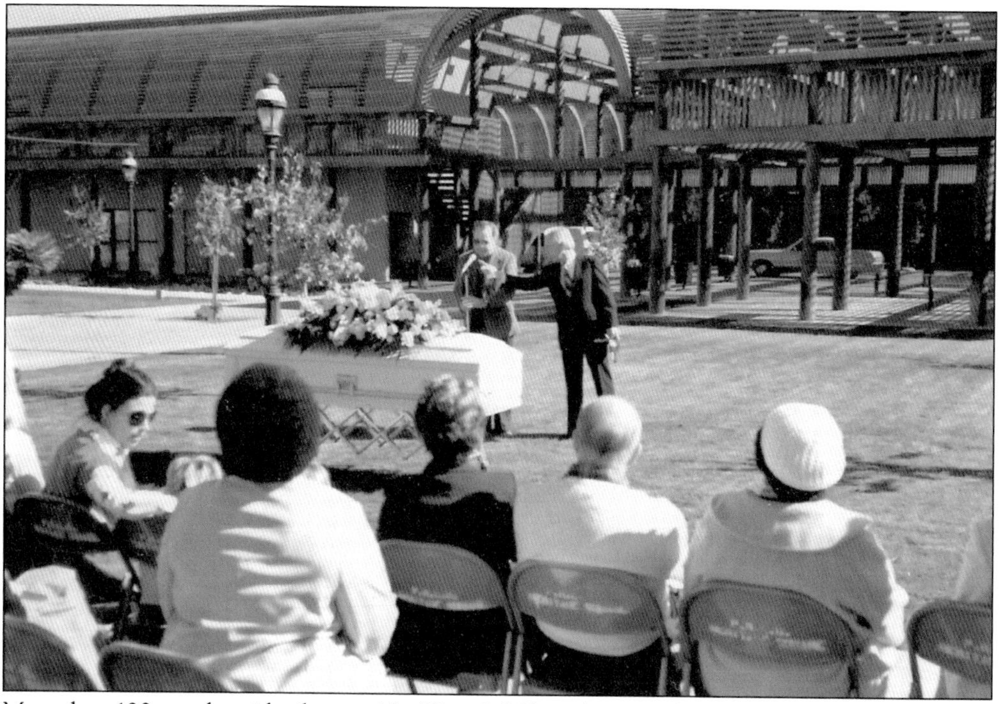

More than 100 people paid tribute to Kai "Speedy" Skounborg on the grass adjacent to the Rosson House. Standing by the casket are his brother Carl (left) and former mayor John Driggs. The Rosson House was home to Speedy after he had spent most of his life on the road. (RHHSFG.)

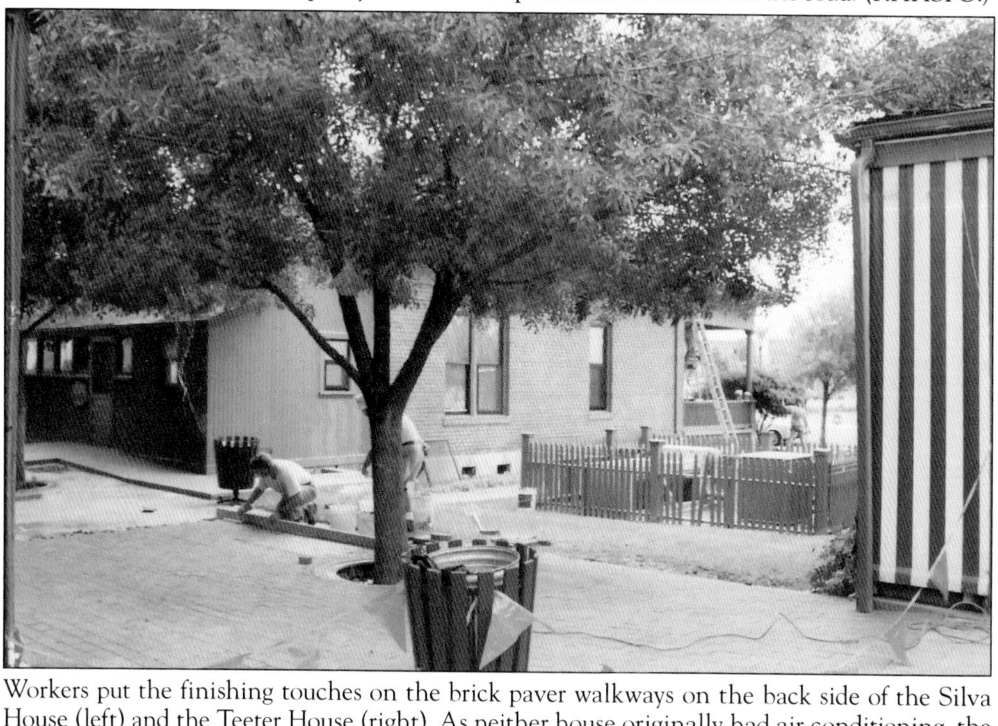

Workers put the finishing touches on the brick paver walkways on the back side of the Silva House (left) and the Teeter House (right). As neither house originally had air-conditioning, the units were removed and set on the ground between the two buildings. (RHHSFG.)

Frank Thomas moved to Arizona in 1895 with his family. He was appointed city recorder in 1904, elected to that position in 1905, and was also a police judge. Thomas was appointed the first Phoenix city clerk in 1914 and later became the first city magistrate. Extremely active in the Republican Party and the Masons, Thomas resigned his city positions in 1922 to become secretary of the Masonic Bodies of Phoenix. He served in that position until his death in 1926 at the age of 71. (Courtesy of Dean Isaac.)

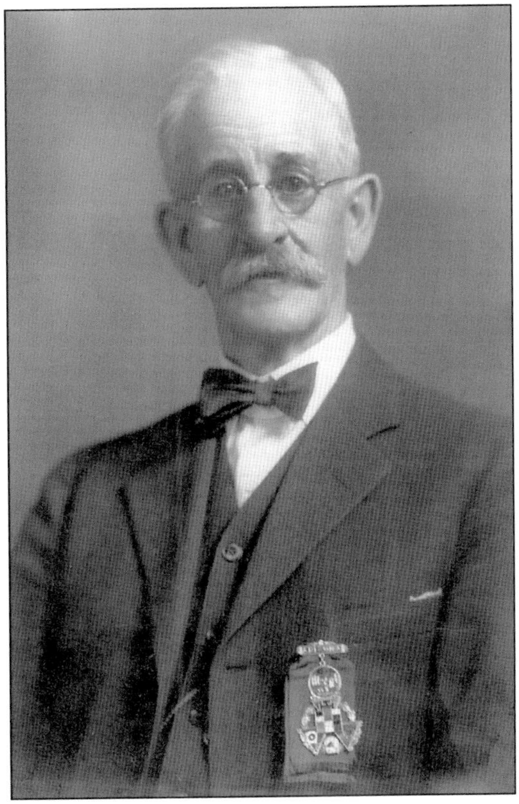

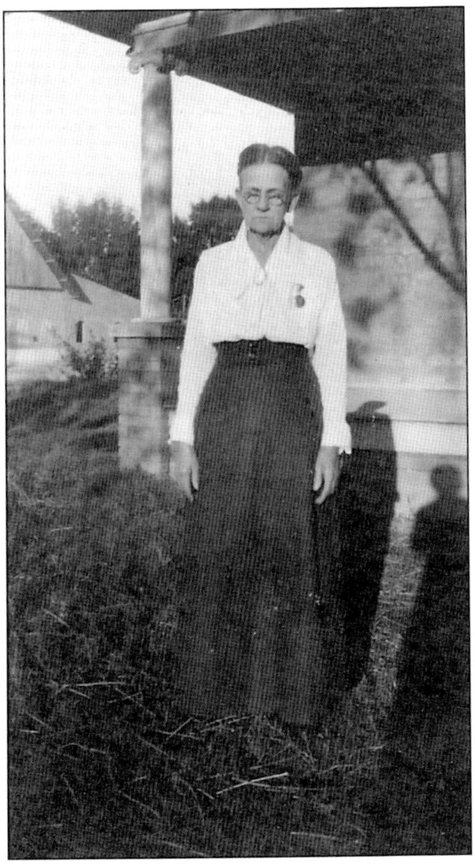

Julia Etta Thomas, wife of Frank Thomas, stands at the side of the family home at 723 South First Avenue. The Thomas family came to Phoenix from Minnesota after living in several other states. The two youngest of the family's five children were born in Phoenix. (Courtesy of Dean Isaac.)

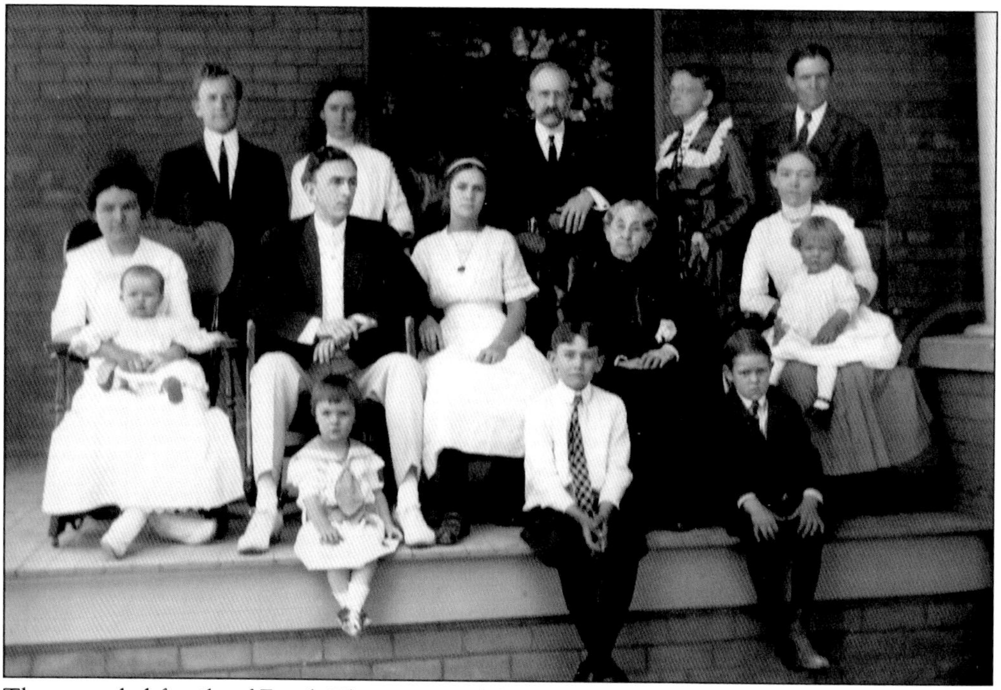

The extended family of Frank Thomas posed for a picture in 1913 on the front porch of the Thomas House. In the back row, Judge Thomas is at center, and his wife, Julia, is second from right. The Sanderhoff and Grijalva families also lived in this house. The Sanderhoffs were related to the Thomas family; Pauline Sanderhoff was the daughter of Frank and Julia Thomas. (Courtesy of Dean Isaac.)

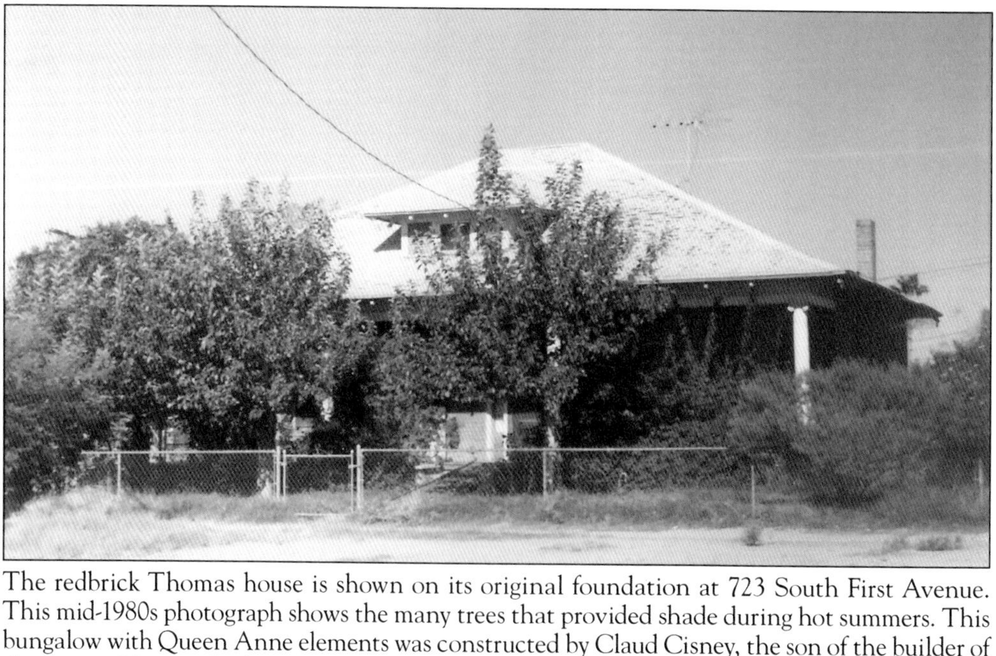

The redbrick Thomas house is shown on its original foundation at 723 South First Avenue. This mid-1980s photograph shows the many trees that provided shade during hot summers. This bungalow with Queen Anne elements was constructed by Claud Cisney, the son of the builder of the Rosson House. The house shows the transition from Queen Anne cottage to bungalow home, making it an ideal fit with the original homes of Block 14. (Courtesy of Dean Isaac.)

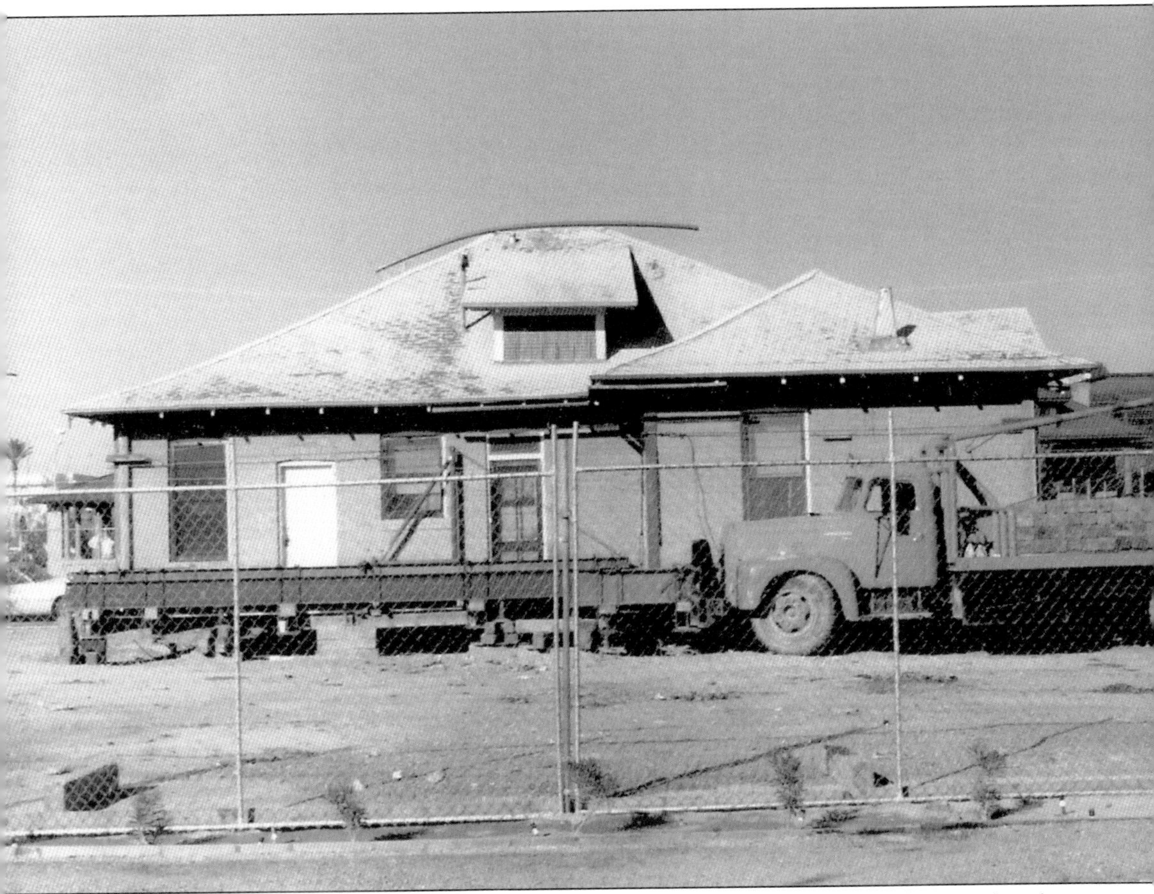

The City of Phoenix elected to move the Thomas House onto Historic Heritage Square after the first phase of the park development was completed. Preparations took approximately six weeks, as the Thomas House first needed to be lifted off its foundation in order for steel girder supports to be inserted beneath it without any structural damage. The house became a makeshift trailer with the addition of wheels, allowing a truck to pull it on its slow journey to its new home in December 1985. It was a relatively easy trip in those days, as impediments such as the light rail system did not yet exist. (Courtesy of Dean Isaac.)

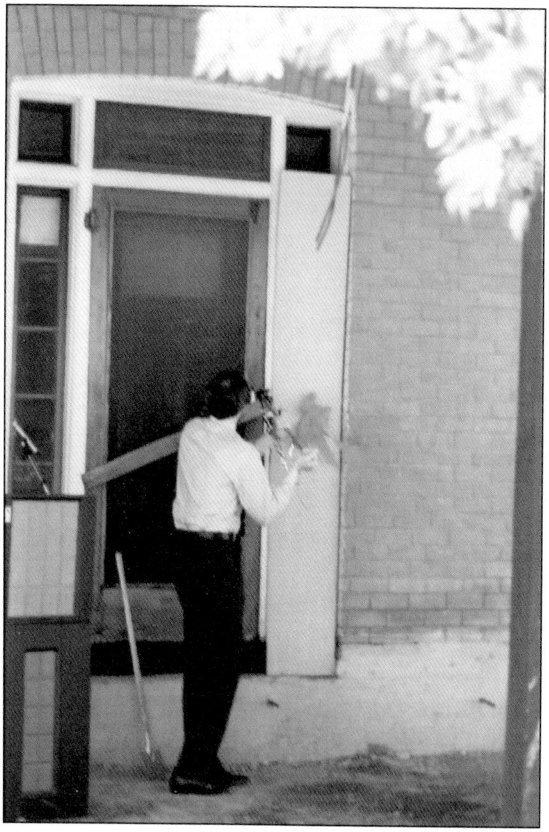

After the Thomas House was placed on its new foundation, there was a ceremonial removal of some of the support braces (left). Restoration of the Thomas House transformed the structure into the home of Bar Bianco. Guests can view the detailed interior of this former home. (Left, RHHSFG; below, photograph by Donna Reiner.)

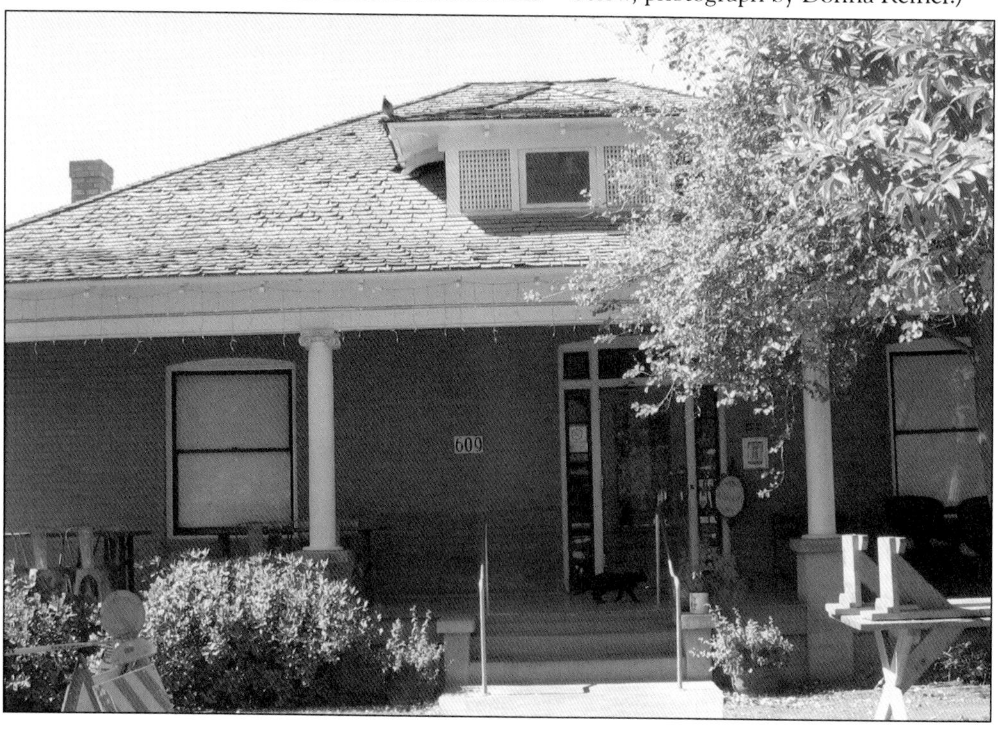

Six

"Modern" Historic Heritage Square

Historic Heritage Square was opened as a park by the City of Phoenix in 1980 and quickly became a vital component of downtown's cultural landscape. Juxtaposed against the city's modern skyline, the square's historic ambiance provides a unique urban setting. In accord with its mission, "where the past and present ignite imagination," the park annually attracts thousands of visitors drawn to its historic buildings, educational opportunities, beautiful landscaping, and memorable events. The square's historic structures contain an interesting mix of museums, showing how residents lived during Arizona's territorial period (pre-1912), and award-winning restaurants offering culinary delights. The park was honored as one of 30 unique places in the city when selected as a "Phoenix Point of Pride" by Valley residents in 1992.

In addition to the Rosson House Museum, there are nine other historic buildings at the park. These include three museum-associated buildings: the Rosson House Ticket Office and Museum Store (originally the Burgess Carriage House); the Hands-On Heritage House at the Stevens-Haustgen House; and the duplex, which houses the offices of Phoenix Parks & Recreation and the Rosson House–Heritage Square Foundation and Guild. Another educational building is the Arizona Doll and Toy Museum at the Stevens House. The other five buildings are notable purveyors of fare, including Nobuo at Teeter House, Pizzeria Bianco, Bar Bianco, the Rose and Crown Pub at the Silva House, and Royal Coffee at the Carriage House.

In 1978, the Lath House, designed by noted architect Robert Frankeberger, was built adjacent to the Rosson House. The partial open-air structure is the focus for many events and has become a popular setting for weddings. Historic Heritage Square became part of Heritage and Science Park in the late 1990s with the addition of three new buildings: the Arizona Science Center, the Phoenix Museum of History (now the Arizona Science Center annex), and the Heritage and Science Parking Garage. Since opening, Historic Heritage Square has hosted numerous cultural, ethnic, and culinary festivals, such as Matsuri—A Festival of Japan, Zombie Walk, Victorian Holiday, Rainbow Festival, Diwali Festival of Lights, Aloha Festival, and Motoring Thru Time.

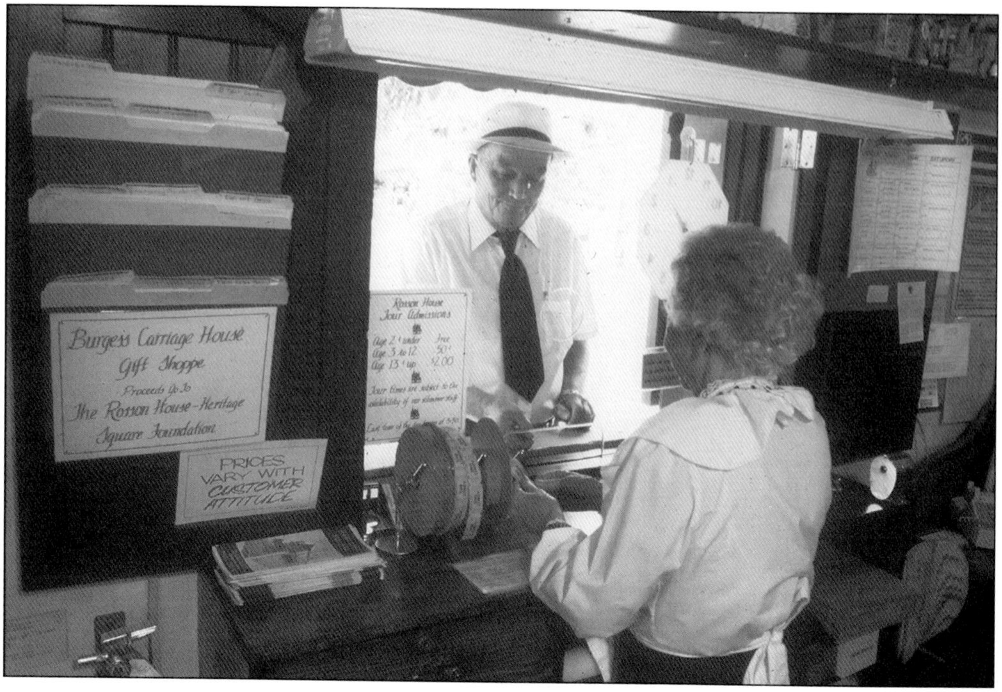

The Burgess Carriage House includes the ticket office (above) for tours of the Rosson House. Based on the posted admission prices, this photograph is probably from the 1980s. Today, visitors still purchase tickets at the carriage house, which also serves as a gift shop. To start their tour, visitors are greeted by a docent in period clothing at the front door of the Rosson House. Below, Linda Messenger, first president of the Heritage Square Guild, is on the doorstep. (RHHSFG.)

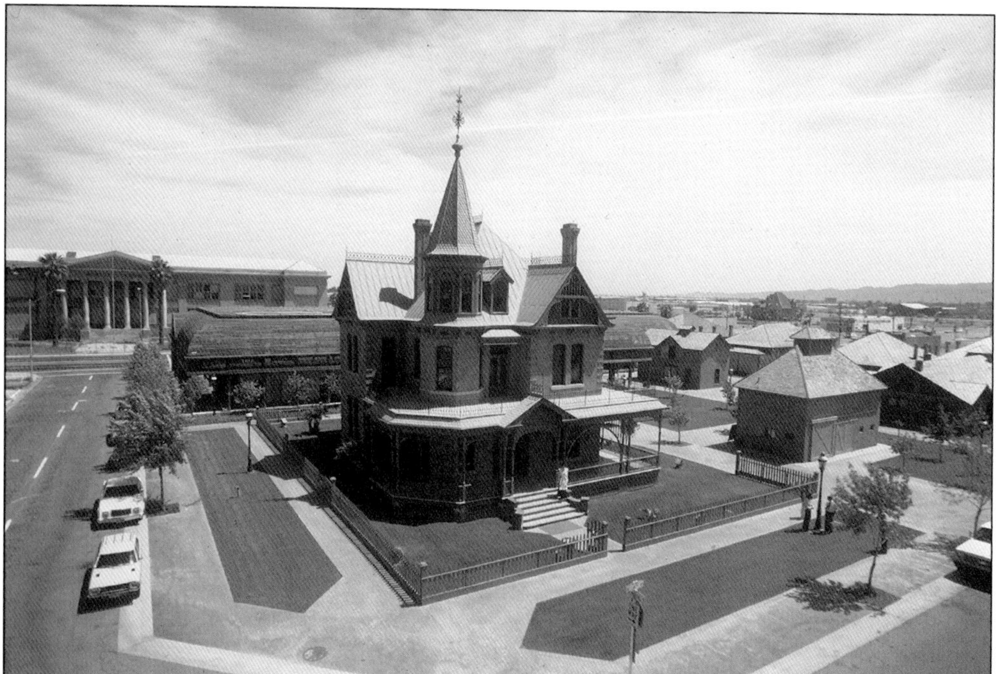

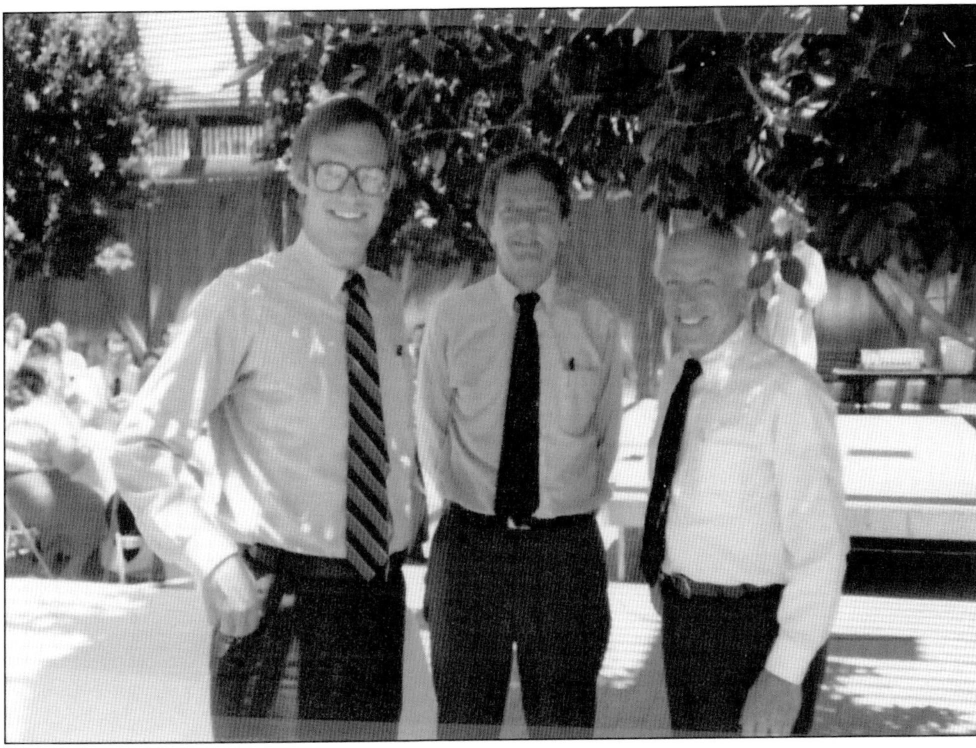

Dignitaries frequent Historic Heritage Square. In the above photograph, from left to right, Phoenix mayor Terry Goddard, Arizona governor Bruce Babbitt, and former mayor John Driggs gather in 1984. Babbitt was later appointed US secretary of the interior by Pres. Bill Clinton. Dignitaries of a previous era have also visited the square. At right, Whitelaw Reid (left, as portrayed by Thomas Walsh, former executive director of the Rosson House) and Pres. Theodore Roosevelt (Joe Wiegand, famed "T.R." impersonator who has performed at the White House) reminisce. Reid resided in the Rosson House over two winters, and President Roosevelt visited Phoenix in 1911 to dedicate a dam that was subsequently named after him. (Above, RHHSFG; right, courtesy of Douglas C. Towne.)

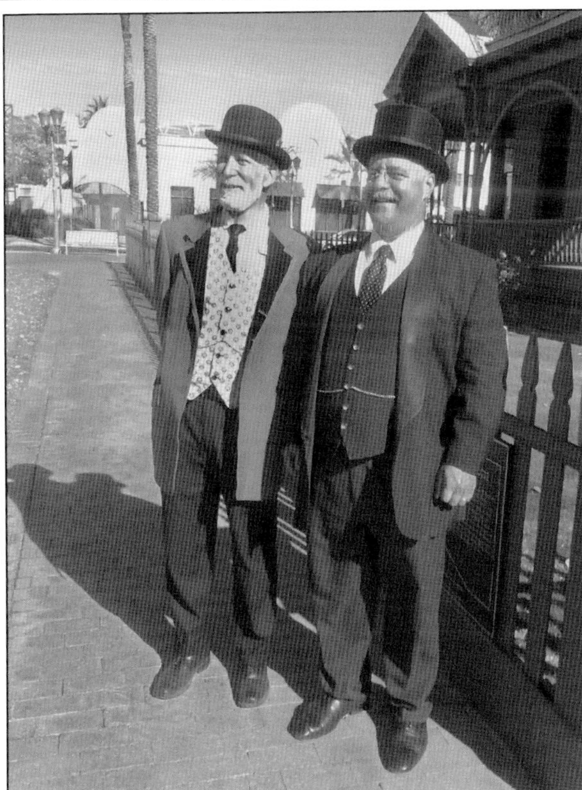

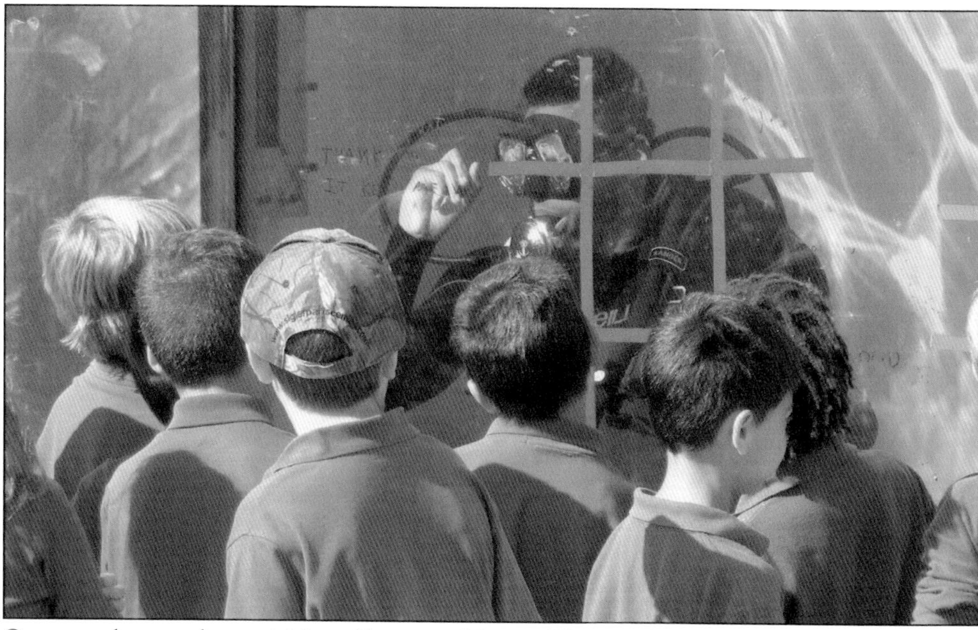

One never knows what activities will occur in Historic Heritage Square. On this day, a diving tank was set up near the Arizona Science Center. Children on a school field trip had the opportunity to communicate with US Navy divers performing inside. Those who came for lunch at one of the nearby restaurants were also intrigued by the unusual exhibition. (Photograph by Marilyn Sklar; RHHSFG.)

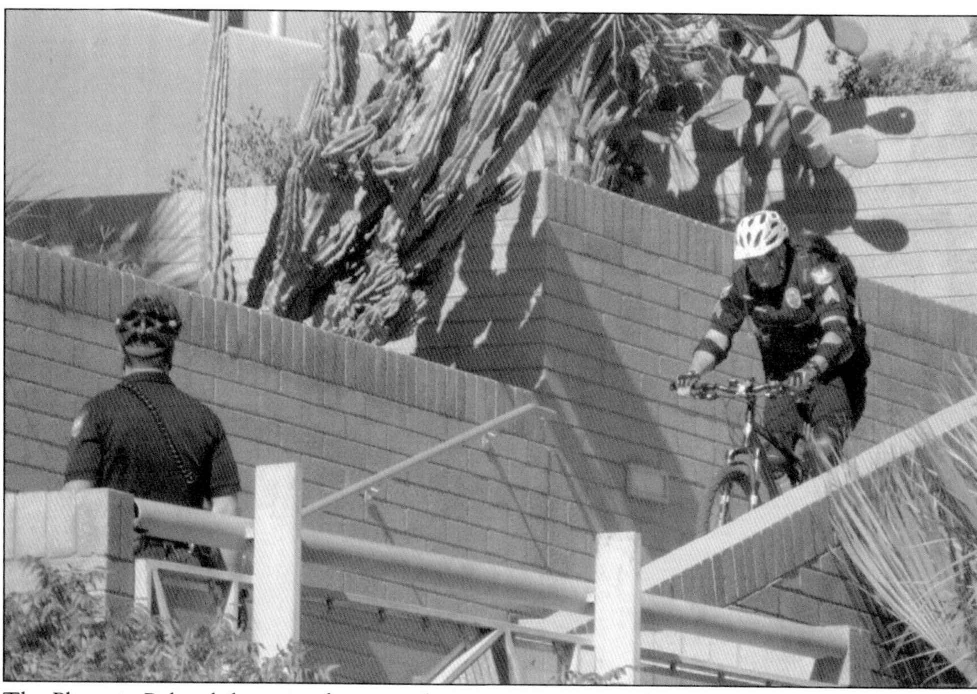

The Phoenix Police bike unit often uses the exterior stairs on the square's parking garage as part of its training program. The public, however, is not allowed to have the same fun. (Photograph by Marilyn Sklar; RHHSFG.)

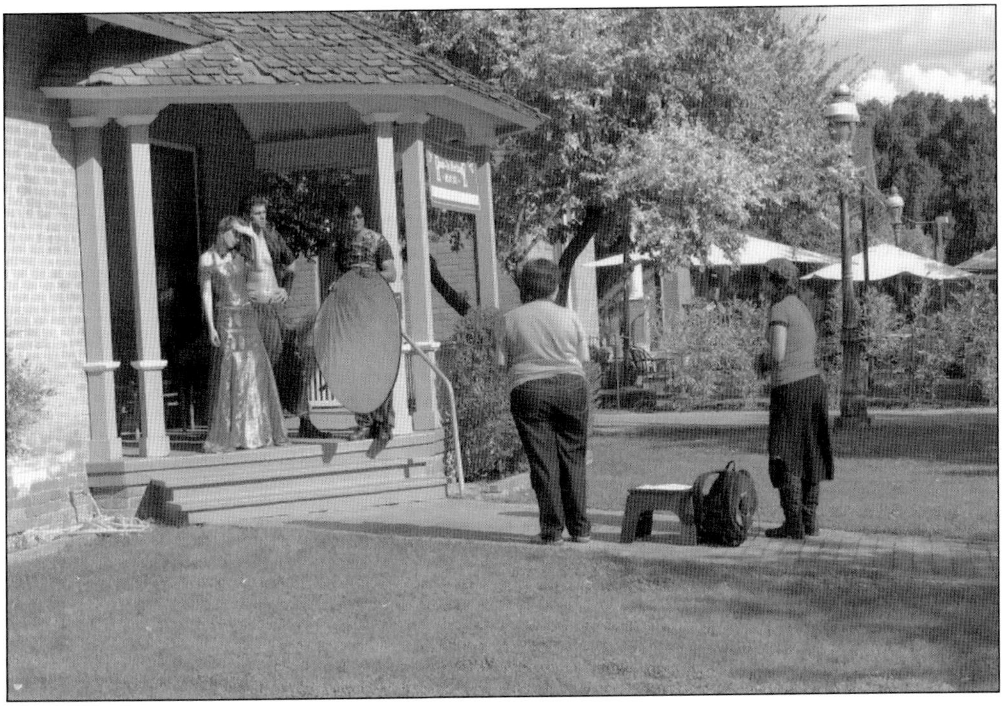

Historic Heritage Square is a popular backdrop for photographers both professional and amateur. Several photographers may concurrently use the historic buildings as a backdrop. On this day, the Stevens-Haustgen House was the site of a fashion shoot. (Photograph by Marilyn Sklar; RHHSFG.)

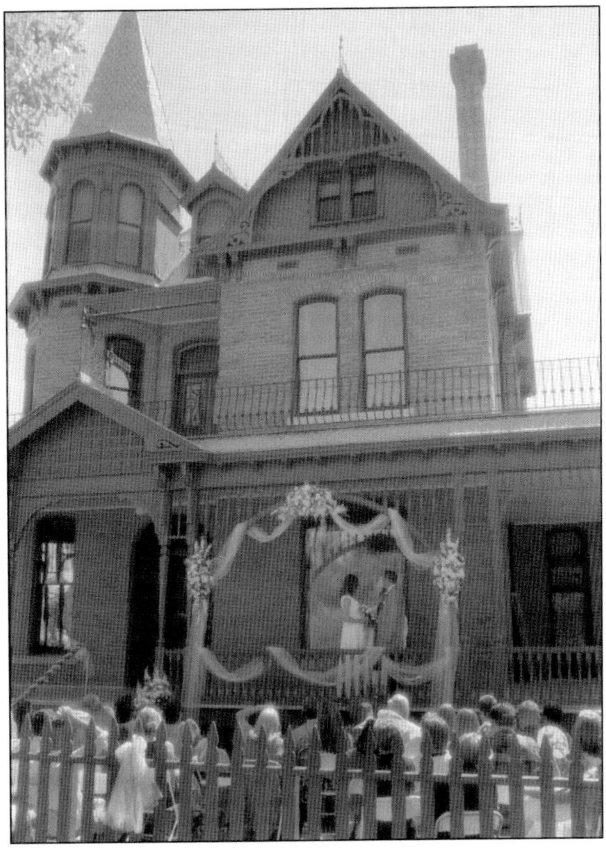

Matt and Rebecca Fritz, a couple who still reside in Phoenix, were married in May 2004 on the porch of the Rosson House. A favorite site for weddings, couples often return to the house to celebrate anniversaries of their joyous event. Larger groups opt for the spaciousness of the nearby Lath Pavilion for their ceremonies. (Courtesy of Matt Fritz.)

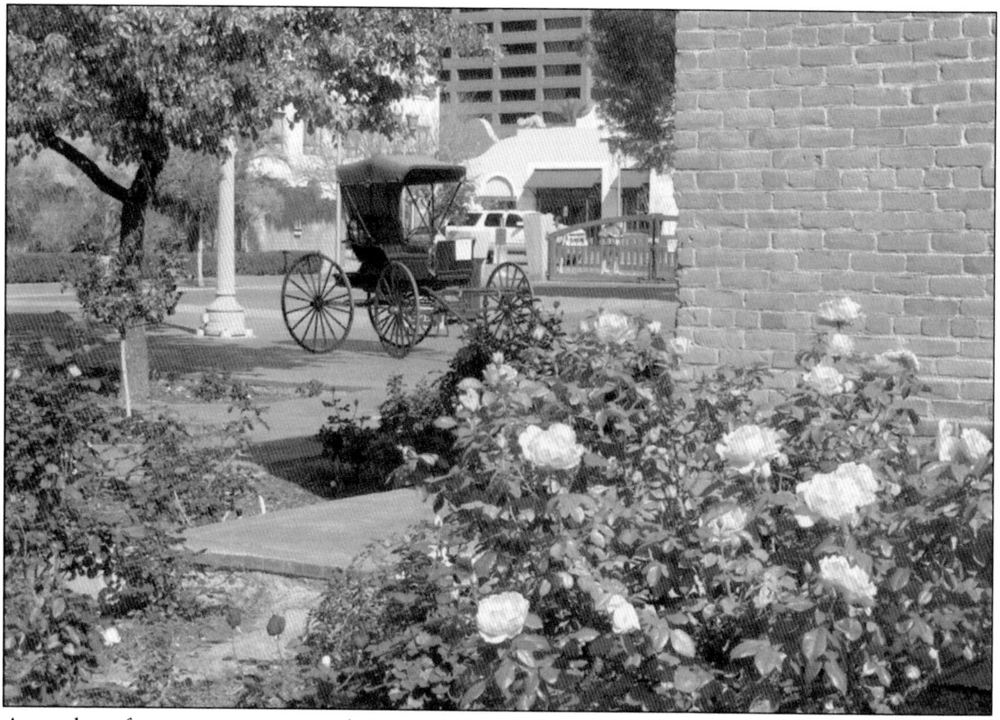

A number of years ago, a memorial rose garden was planted near the carriage house. A prominent sign beside the garden lists the names of the roses and those who are honored. Tended by dedicated volunteers, the roses burst forth with a rainbow of colors in early spring and continue to bloom sporadically through December. (Photograph by Marilyn Sklar; RHHSFG.)

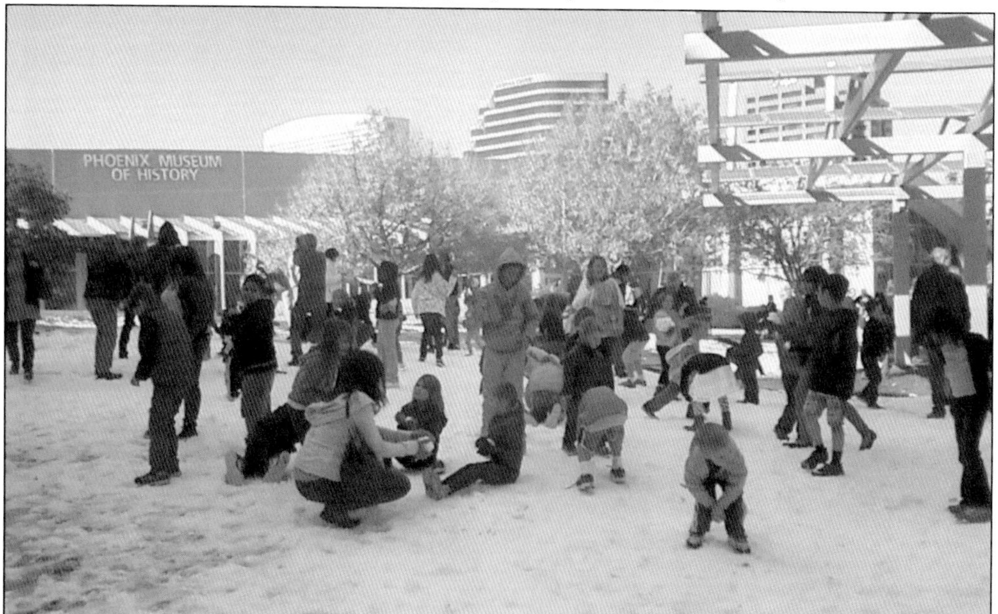

Although winters are mild in Phoenix, that does not mean people should miss out on one of the basic elements of that time of year: snow. Here, the Arizona Science Center has placed tons of manufactured snow in the square, to the delight of the crowd. (RHHSFG.)

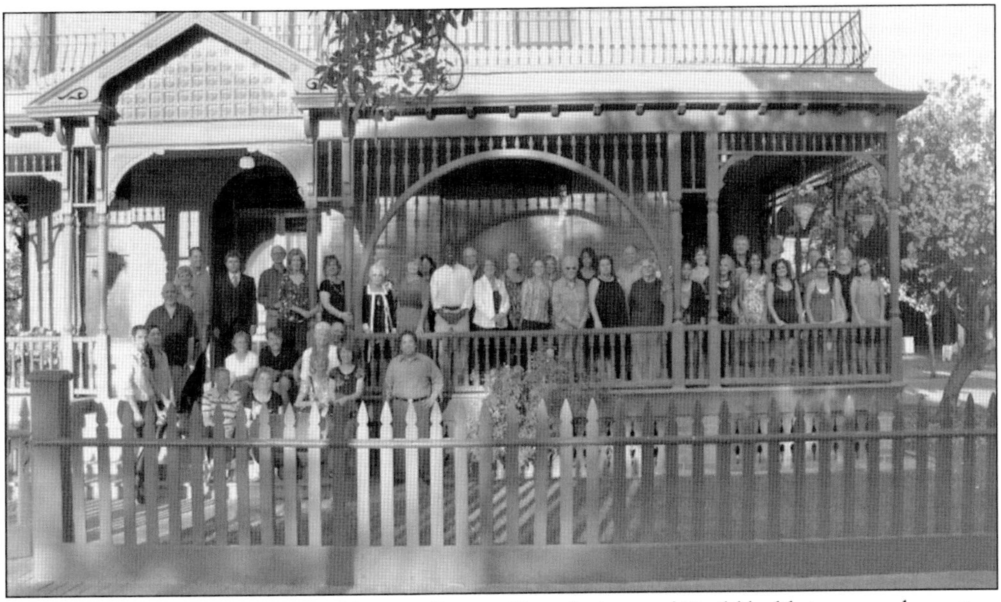

Each spring, the Rosson House–Heritage Square Foundation and Guild holds its annual meeting in the Lath Pavilion to honor volunteers and elect new board members. In recent years, the attendees have posed on the steps of the Rosson House for a group photograph, such as this one in 2012. (Photograph by Marilyn Sklar; RHHSFG.)

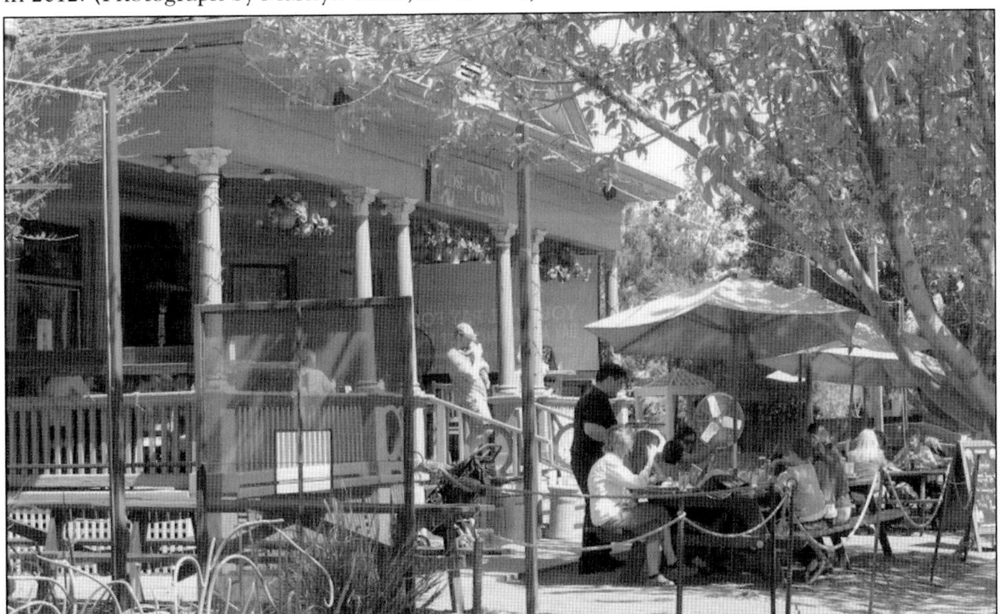

A lunch at the Rose and Crown Pub, located in the Silva House, can be enjoyed indoors or out. The establishment features British hospitality and atmosphere, beer, grub, an eclectic jukebox with a selection of vintage punk, new wave, and ska tunes, and interactive trivia competitions. Over the years, a number of restaurants have occupied this structure. (Photograph by Marilyn Sklar; RHHSFG.)

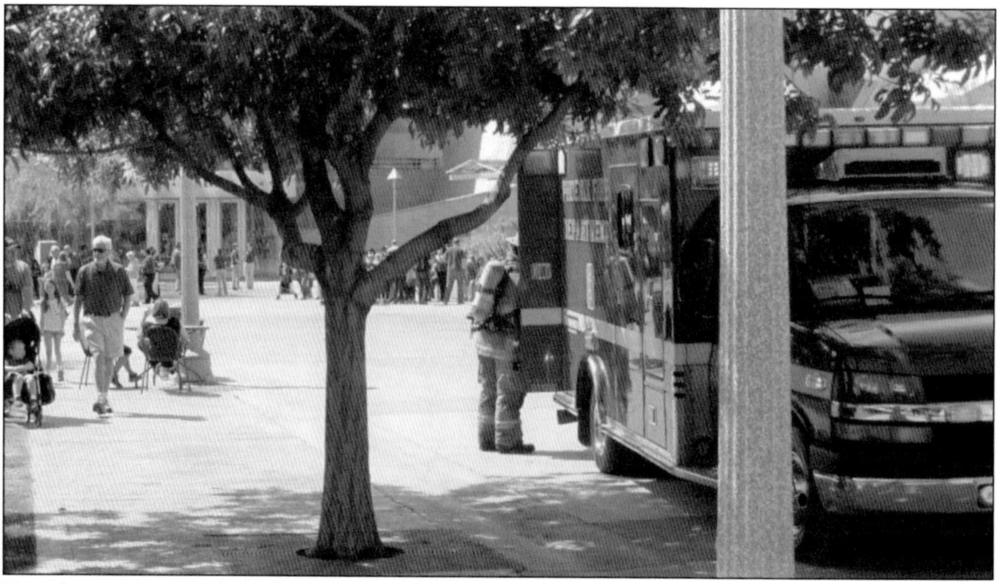

Fire alarms rang out from the Arizona Science Center, located on the south end of Heritage and Science Park. While there appeared to be no real danger, the appearance of fire trucks on the square attracted lots of attention. (Photograph by Marilyn Sklar; RHHSFG.)

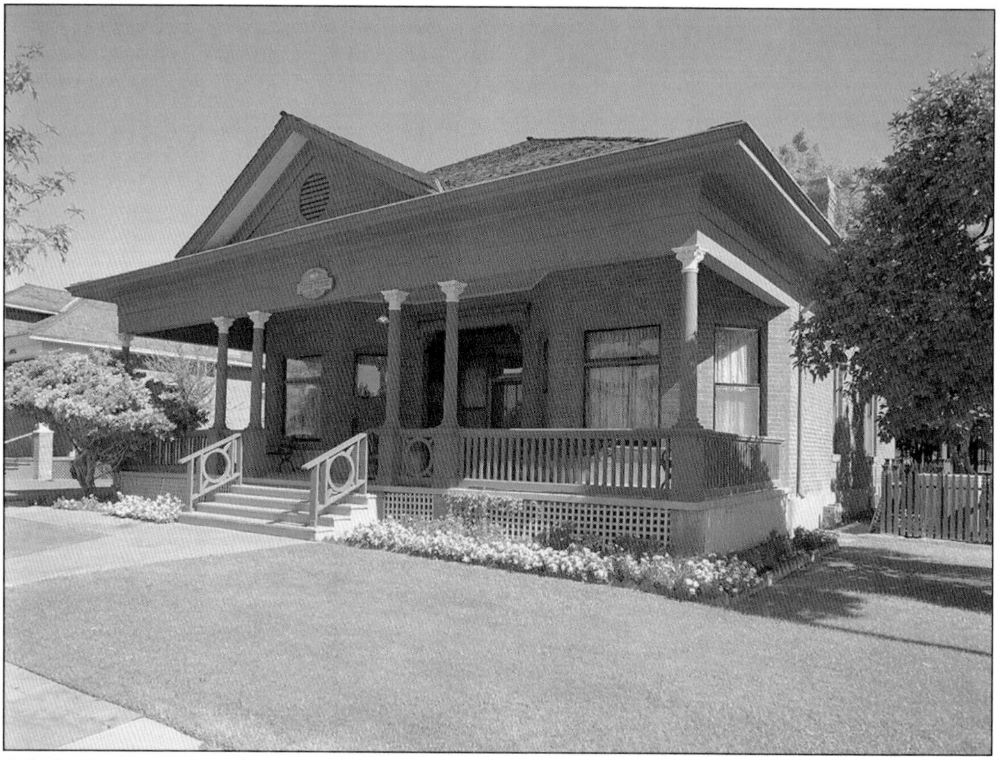

Salt River Project (SRP), a major power and water provider in the Valley, donated $50,000 toward the renovation of the Silva House with the encouragement of Mayor Driggs. In exchange, SRP maintained a history center in the house for nearly 20 years, where visitors could explore items used in early-20th-century homes. (Courtesy of SRP Heritage.)

In the early 1980s, an Oktoberfest celebration was held in the Lath Pavilion and filled the square. Much like such festivals in Germany, the pavilion featured tables where people ate and drank while enjoying the autumn season. The Phoenix Union High School building is visible in the background. (PPD.)

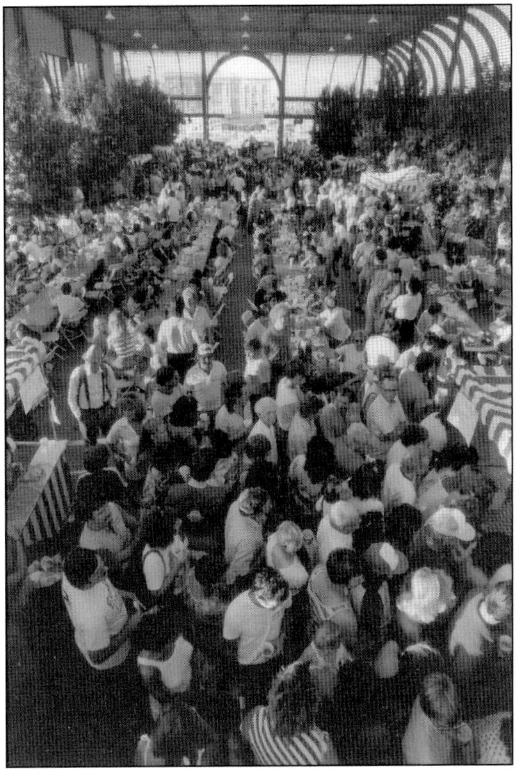

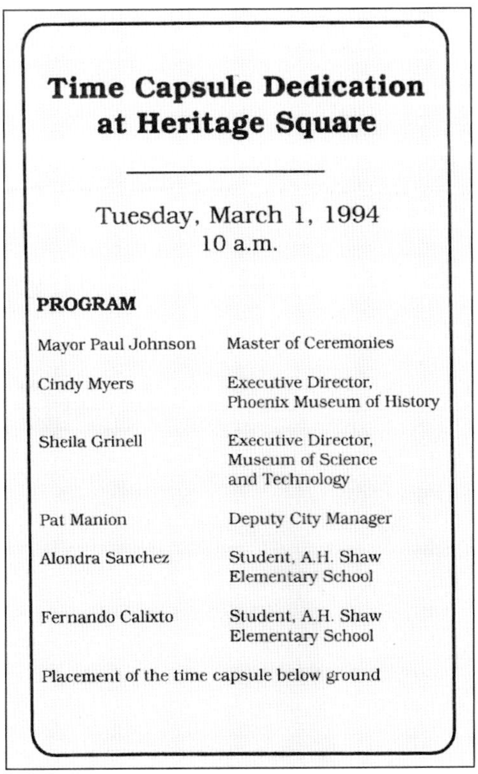

Time Capsule Dedication at Heritage Square

Tuesday, March 1, 1994
10 a.m.

PROGRAM

Mayor Paul Johnson	Master of Ceremonies
Cindy Myers	Executive Director, Phoenix Museum of History
Sheila Grinell	Executive Director, Museum of Science and Technology
Pat Manion	Deputy City Manager
Alondra Sanchez	Student, A.H. Shaw Elementary School
Fernando Calixto	Student, A.H. Shaw Elementary School

Placement of the time capsule below ground

Historic Heritage Square is the site of two time capsules. Students from A.H. Shaw Elementary School, seven blocks east of the square, buried a time capsule in 1994. The students included predictions of what life would be like in 2009, when the time capsule was unearthed. The other capsule will be opened in 2080. (PPD.)

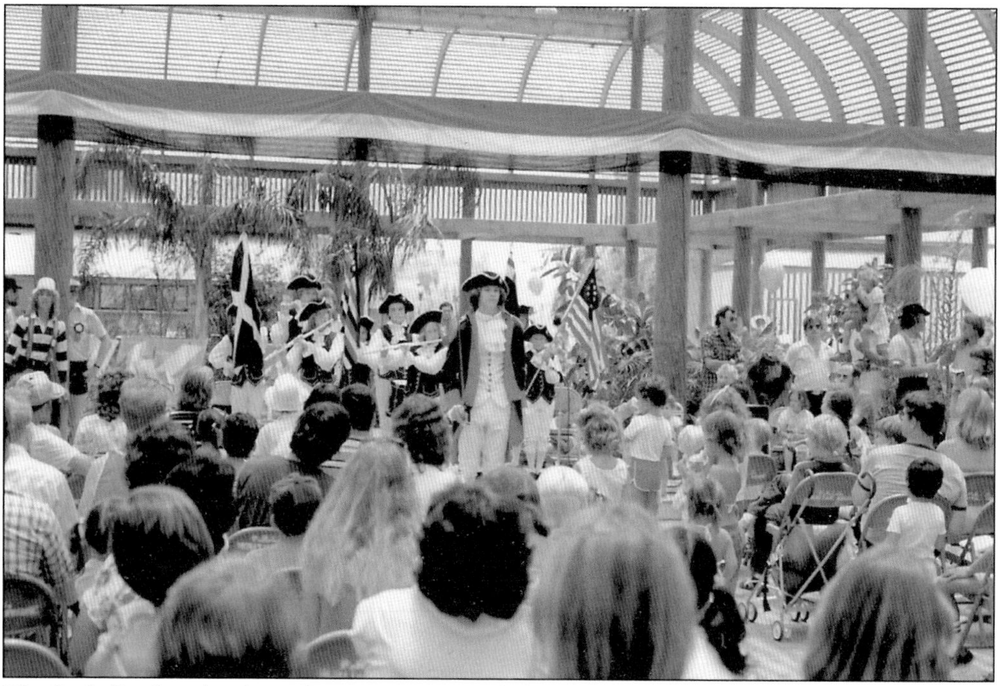

The Lath Pavilion has hosted many events, including this 1983 Fourth of July celebration. No fireworks display took place, due to the proximity of so many buildings. Above, a student group dressed in Revolutionary War uniforms entertains the crowd with some peppy music, including "Yankee Doodle." Below, a local Boy Scout troop raises the flag in the grassy area just south of the Rosson House in a fitting tribute to the holiday. (Both, PPD.)

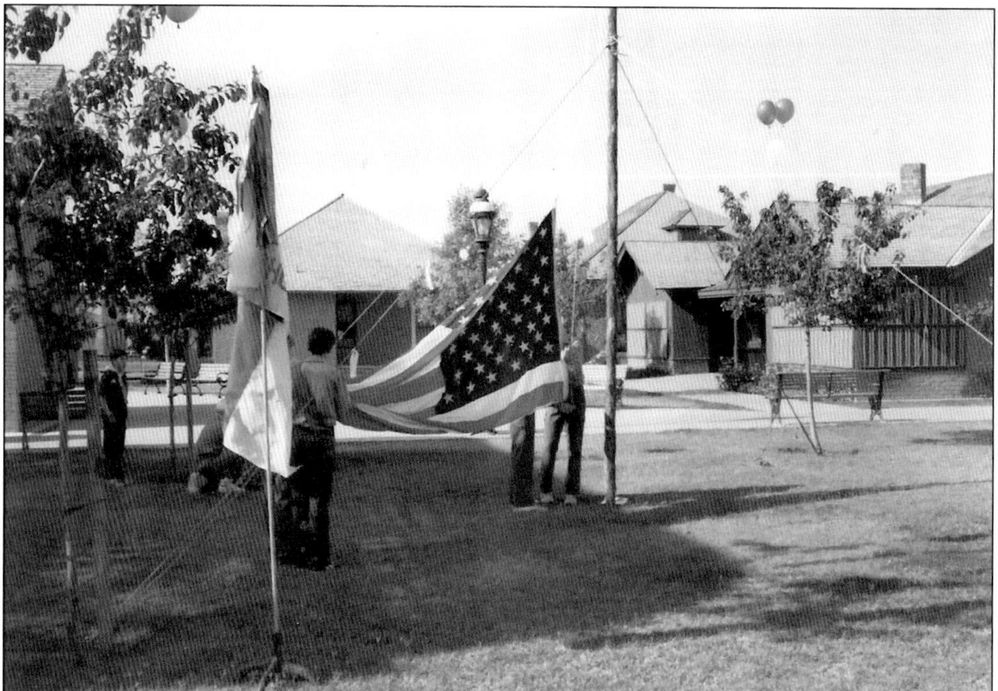

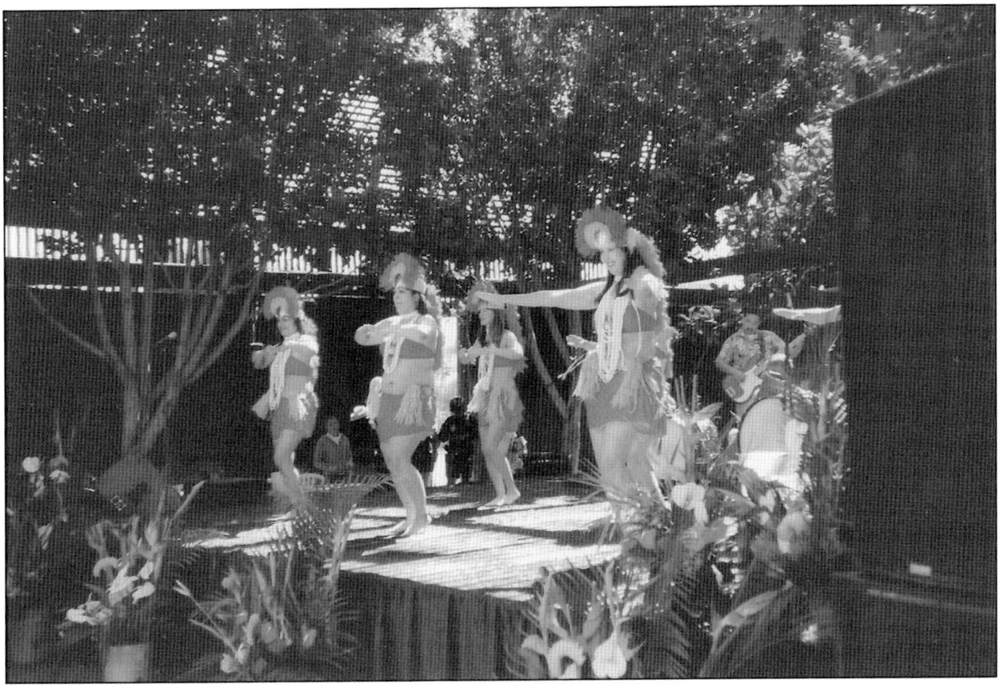

The Aloha Festival is an annual March celebration of Hawaiian and Polynesian culture featuring dance, music, and food. The two-day event was held for a number of years at Historic Heritage Square until its popularity forced its move to a larger venue at Tempe Beach Park. (PPD.)

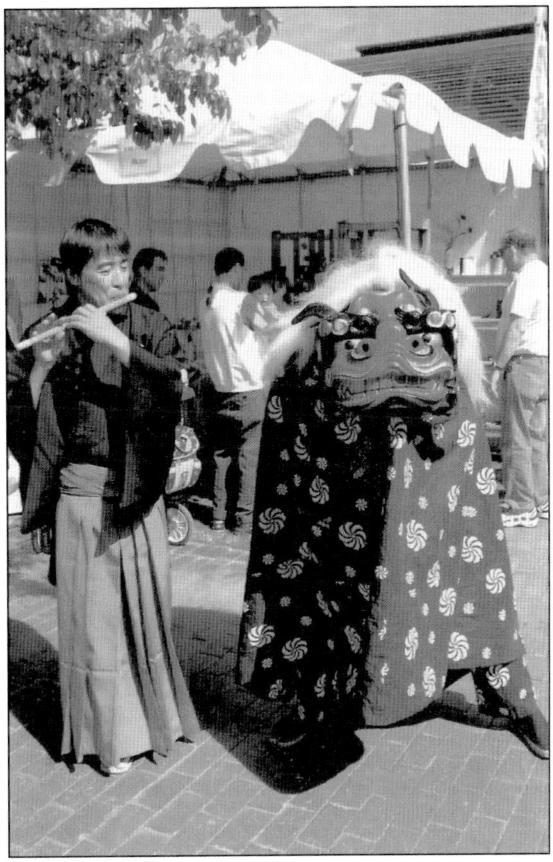

Matsuri is the largest two-day cultural festival now held at Historic Heritage Square. Himeji, Japan, is a Phoenix Sister City, and this festival celebrates that friendship. Japanese costumes, food, entertainment, and crafts fill the square in the last weekend of February. (RHHSFG.)

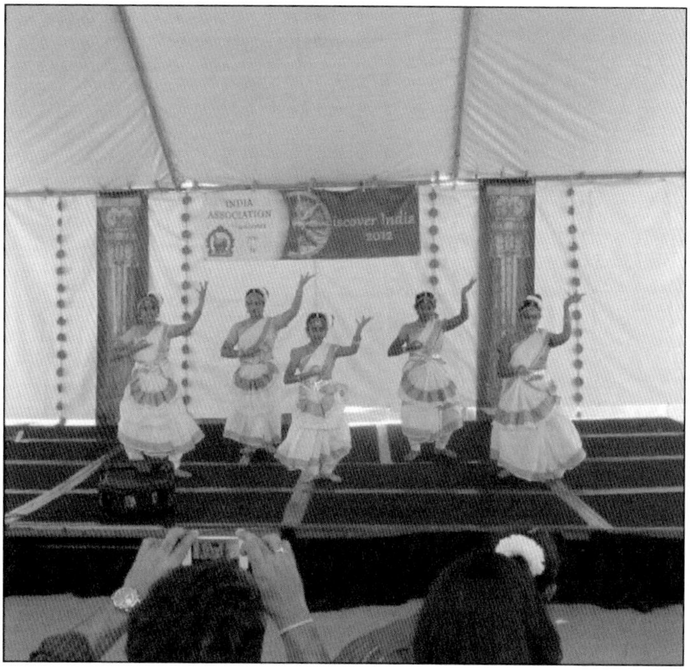

The Discover India Festival, which highlights the rich cultural traditions of India, is another popular festival at Historic Heritage Square. A stage was erected in the Lath Pavilion, where dancers and musicians performed for the 2012 celebration. As with other cultural festivals, it is an excellent opportunity to sample new foods. (Photograph by Marilyn Sklar; RHHSFG.)

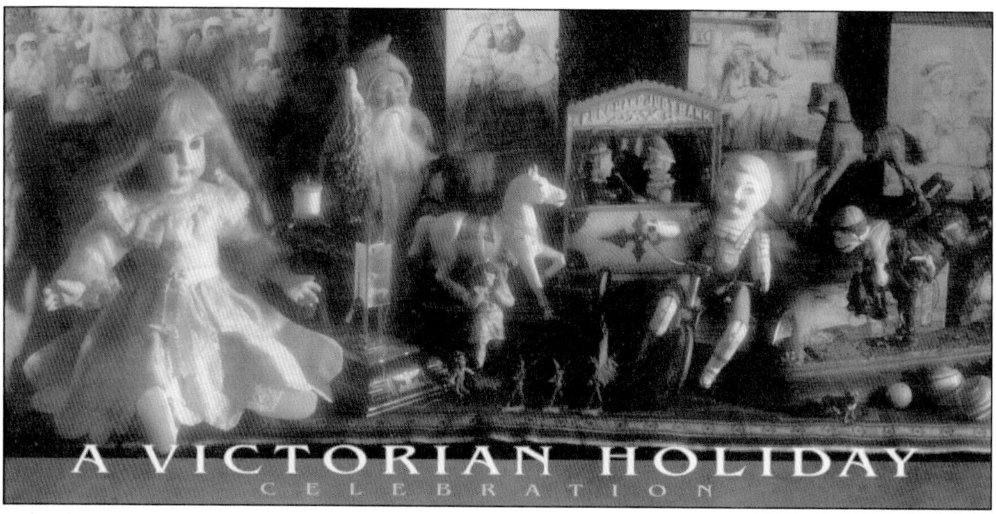

What better theme for a winter celebration in Historic Heritage Square than "A Victorian Holiday"? For many years, this was the park's biggest event. The celebration eventually ended, however, as a result of competition from other holiday activities. The Rosson House Museum, however, still uses decorations that maintain the Victorian atmosphere. (PPD.)

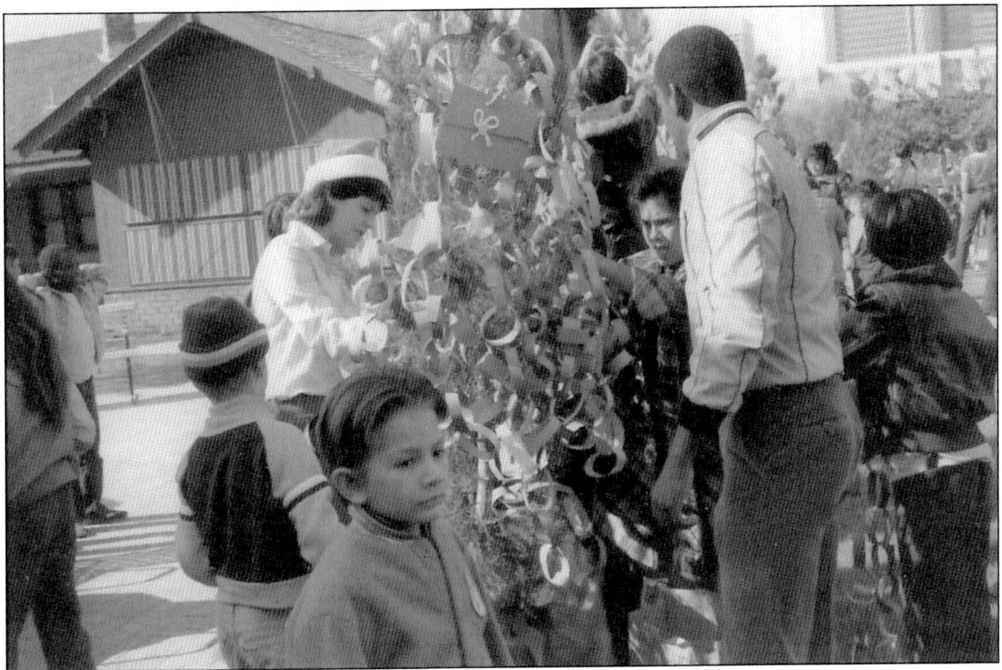

For a number of years, the City of Phoenix decorated the park during the holidays by placing live Christmas trees along the walkways, as seen in this 1983 photograph. The holiday trees were trimmed with decorations created by elementary school children. The students were very imaginative in what they recycled into ornaments. (PPD.)

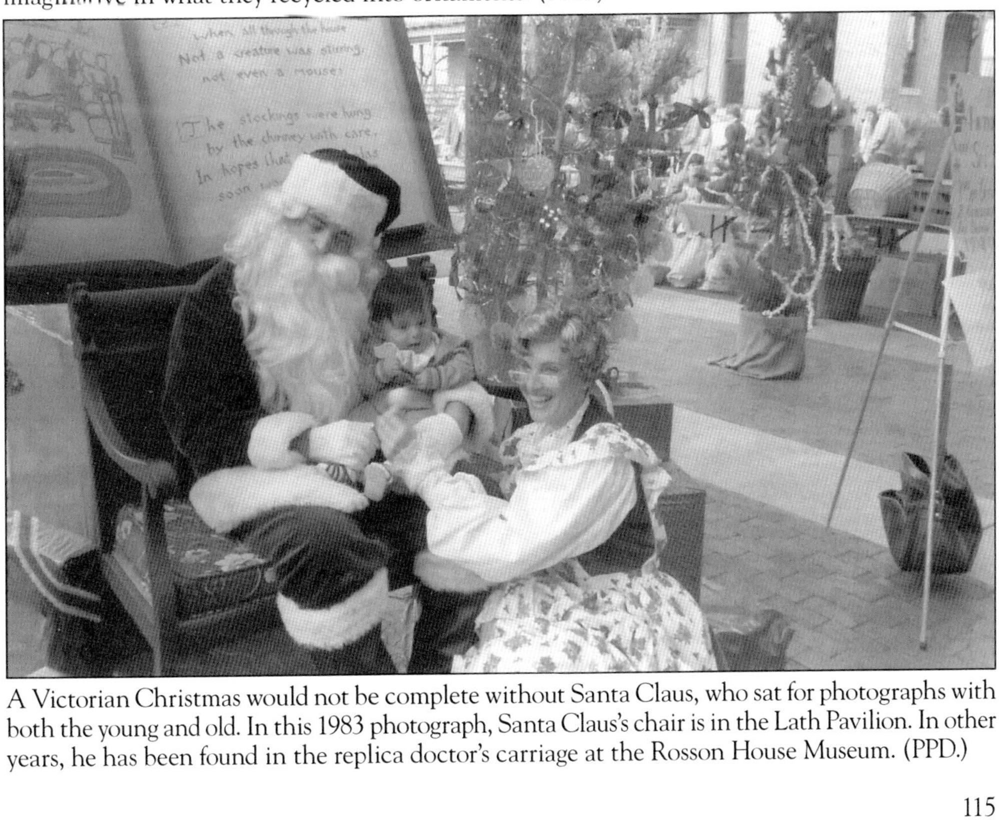

A Victorian Christmas would not be complete without Santa Claus, who sat for photographs with both the young and old. In this 1983 photograph, Santa Claus's chair is in the Lath Pavilion. In other years, he has been found in the replica doctor's carriage at the Rosson House Museum. (PPD.)

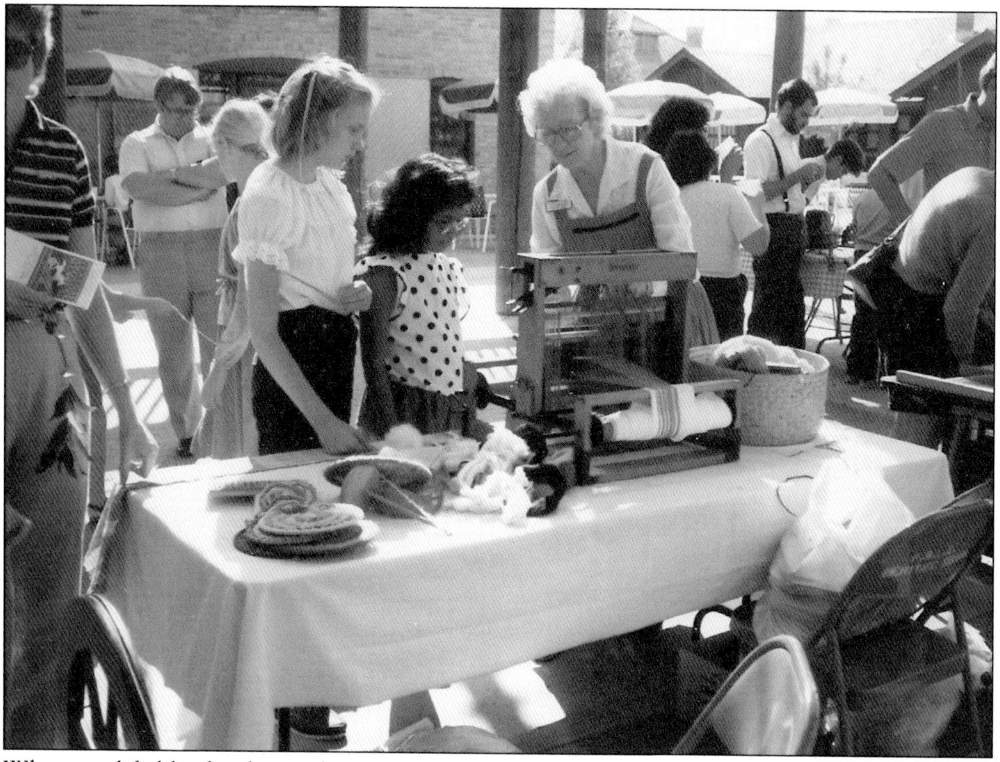

What was life like for those who lived in Phoenix during the Victorian era? Attendees of the Victorian Chores and Games Day witnessed weaving and spinning demonstrations and had the chance to churn butter. Certainly no one could say that life was boring as they tried to play hoops and sticks and other popular games of the era. (PPD.)

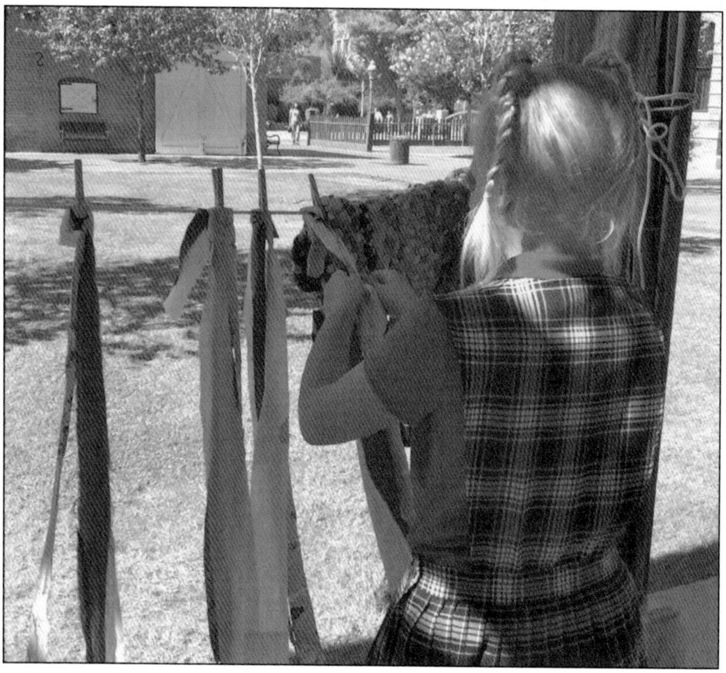

During school field trips to the Rosson House Museum, students partake in rug braiding as they learn about a child's life in 1900. That the young girl photographed has braids is pure coincidence. Surprisingly, the children seem to enjoy the Victorian-era chores. (RHHSFG.)

For the Birds! was a design-oriented competition open to Phoenix area professionals for the creation of a birdhouse. Designers selected a favorite architectural style and then constructed it. Winners received monetary prizes and the birdhouses were auctioned to raise funds for the Rosson House Foundation. Current Rosson House board member Abraham James (on the left, at right) designed the "Birdseye" house seen behind him, and Thomas Niesen constructed it. The birdhouse received an honorable mention for the team in 1993 (below). The previous year, they won third place with their "Dowel House." (Courtesy of Abraham James.)

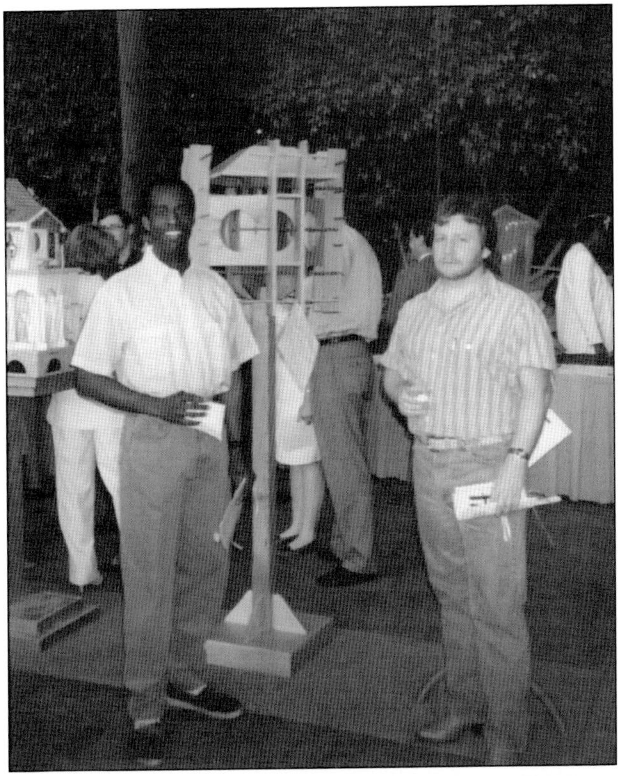

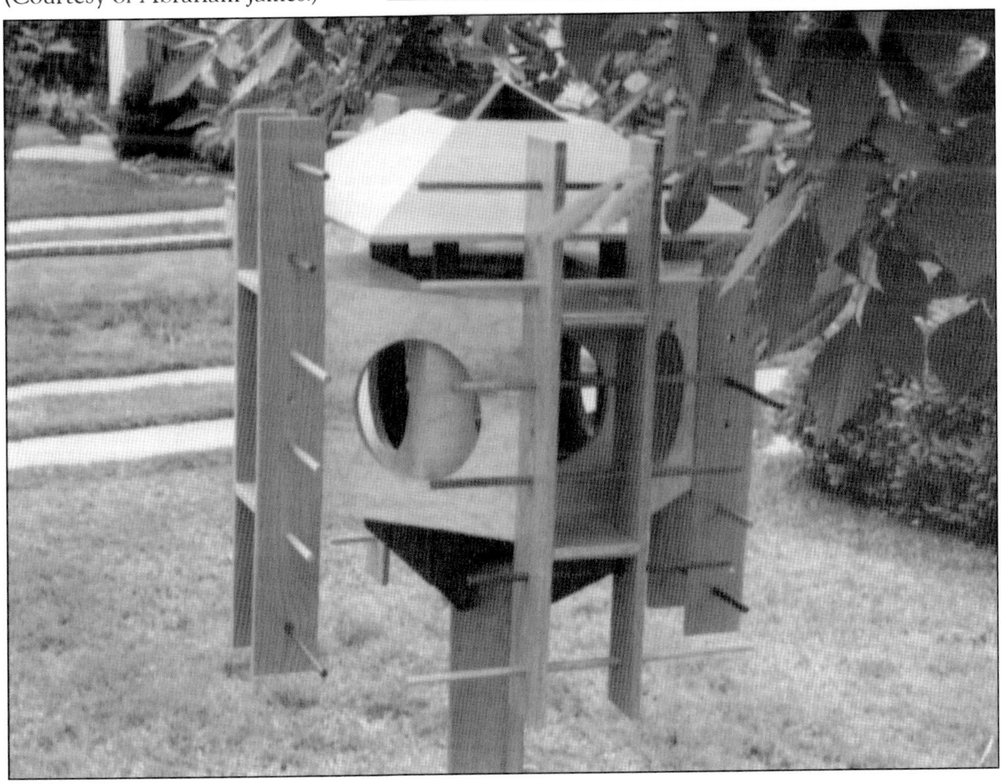

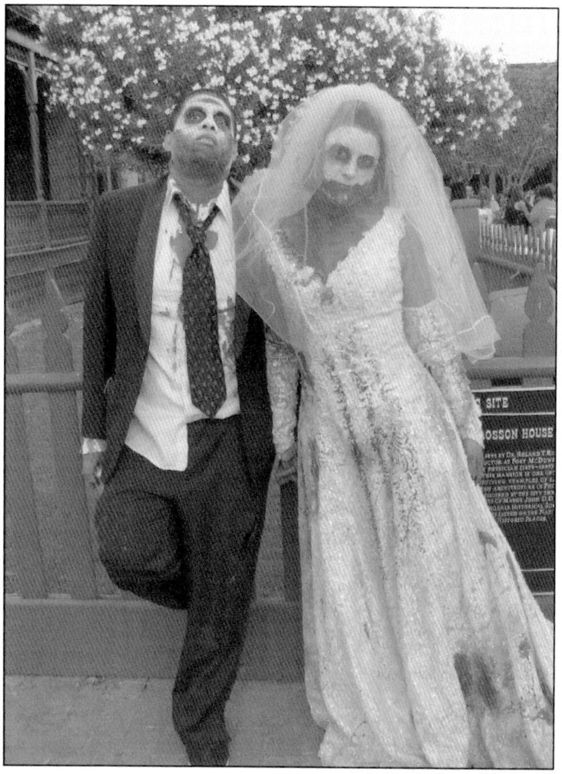

The Zombie Walk has become an annual affair sponsored by the Downtown Phoenix Partnership. The walk begins and ends at Historic Heritage Square. Bridezilla and her mate (left) and three friendlier zombies (below) are just some of the estimated 5,000 gruesome undead that parade through downtown Phoenix one evening in October. (RHHSFG.)

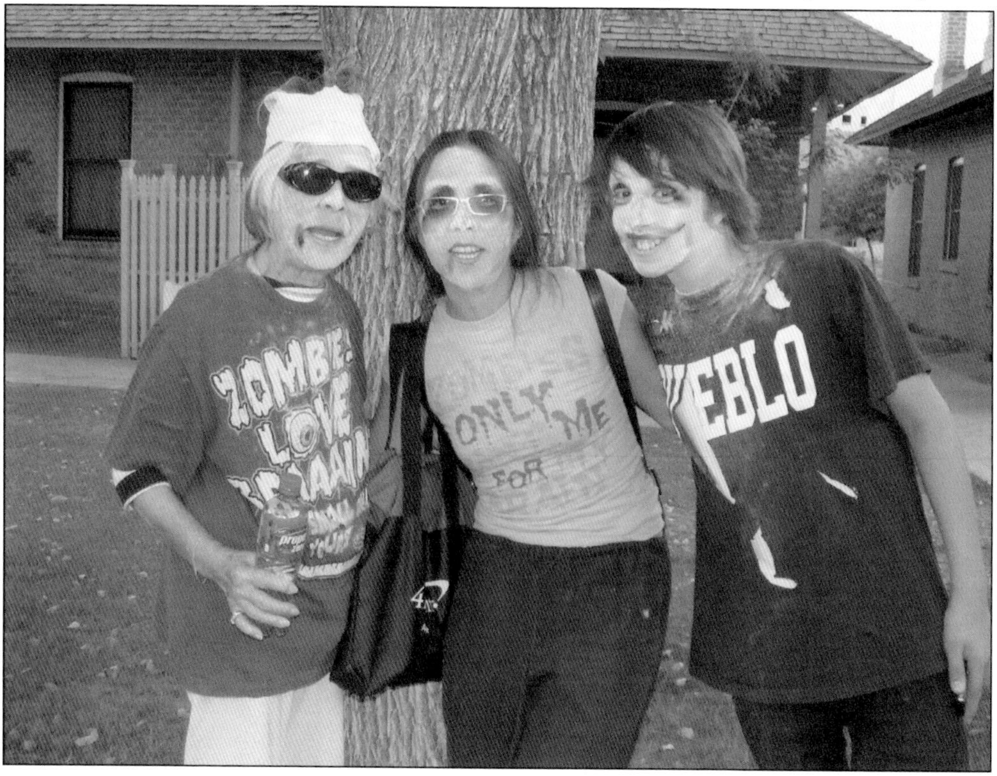

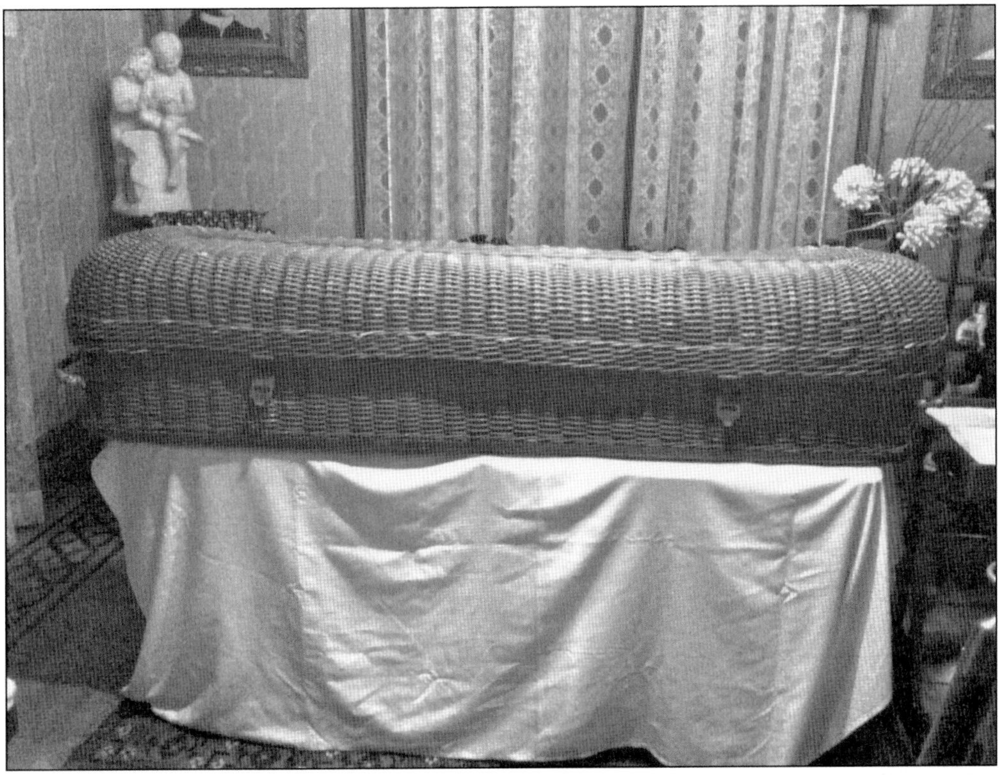

This oblong wicker casket dates from the 1920s, when it was used by the A.L. Moore & Sons Mortuary, a local firm, to transport bodies. Wicker caskets were often used for temporary display of the deceased. The Rosson House Museum displays this one in the parlor during Halloween and the annual Zombie Walk. (RHHSFG.)

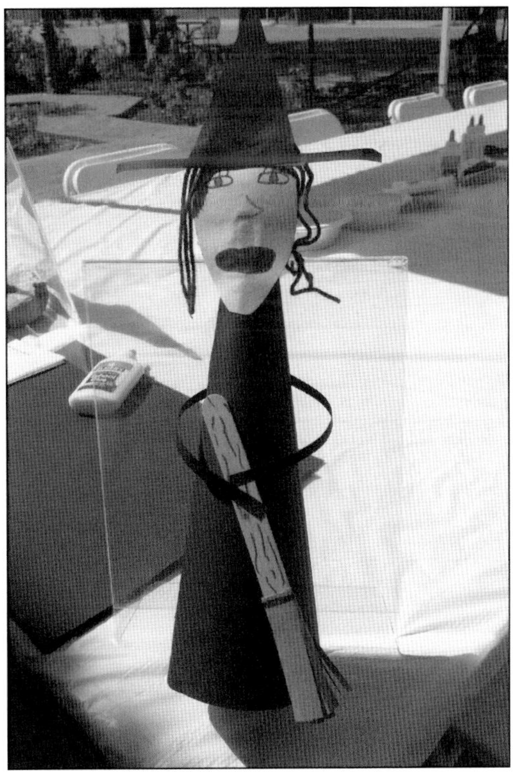

Heritage Saturday at Historic Heritage Square is sponsored by the Rosson House Museum. On the second Saturday of every month, families congregate at the park's white tent, where they can make a Victorian-era craft. This photograph was probably taken in October, as the participants were creating paper witches. (RHHSFG.)

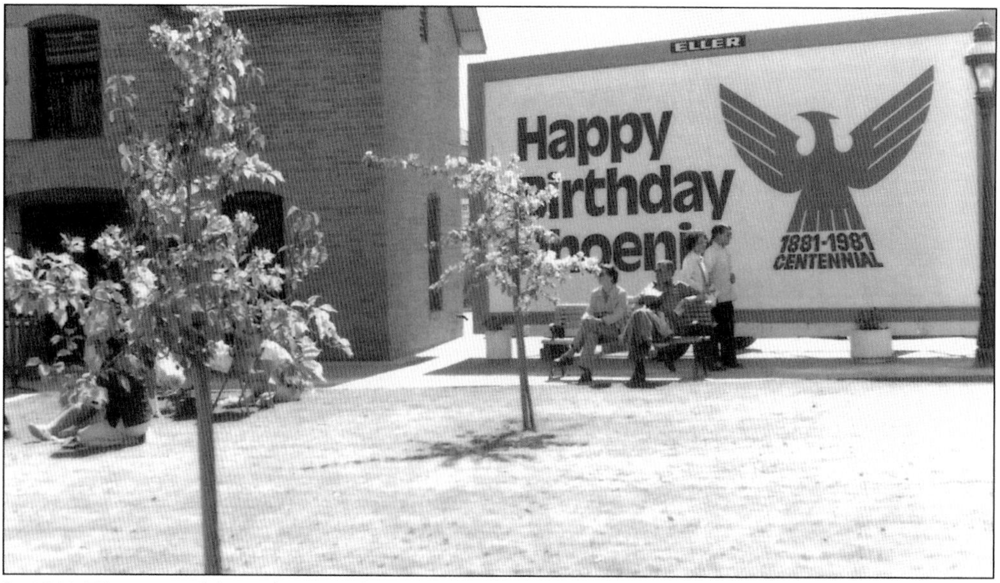

In 1981, Phoenix celebrated its 100th anniversary as an incorporated city, and some festivities were held at Historic Heritage Square. The billboard in the above photograph, sponsored by a local firm, Eller, says it all: "Happy Birthday Phoenix." In a century, the city had grown tremendously, in terms of both population and land area. Dr. Rosson, the first resident of the stately Victorian home on Historic Heritage Square, had been the ninth mayor of Phoenix; his brother-in-law, John Alsap, was the first. Below, JJ Higley Lane and three of her great-grandchildren stand in front of the Rosson House. This was JJ's home for 10 years. The connections to the past are continually being recognized in the square. (Above, PPD; below, courtesy of the Higley family.)

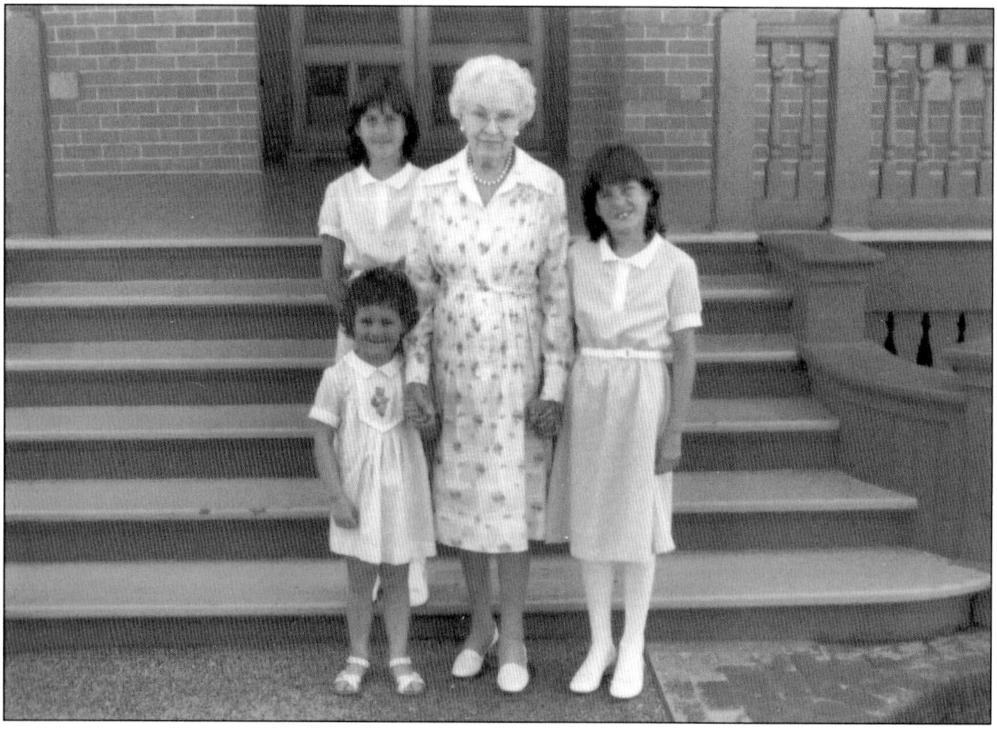

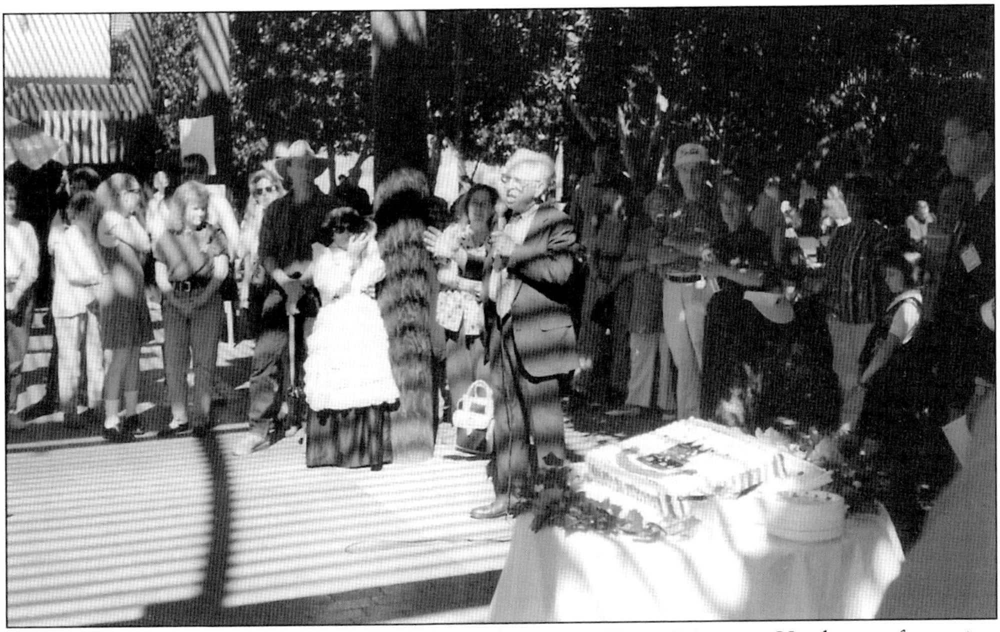

Former mayor John Driggs welcomed visitors to the Rosson House Museum. His dream of restoring the home to its original luster having been achieved, a celebratory cake decorated with an image of the Victorian mansion was warranted. (PPD.)

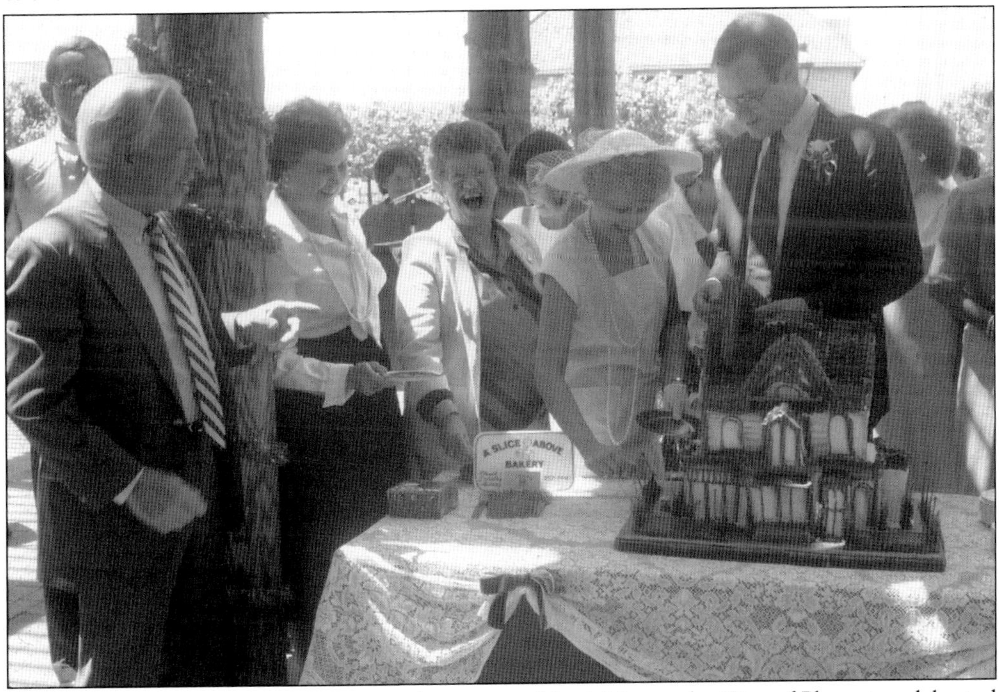

In 1981, Historic Heritage Square was the center of festivities as the City of Phoenix celebrated its centennial and the Rosson House Museum observed its fifth anniversary. For the momentous occasion, a cake was fashioned in the shape of the 1895 house. Among those attending the ceremony were former Phoenix mayor John Driggs (left), guild president Asta Hagadorn cutting the cake, and then-mayor Terry Goddard (right). (PPD.)

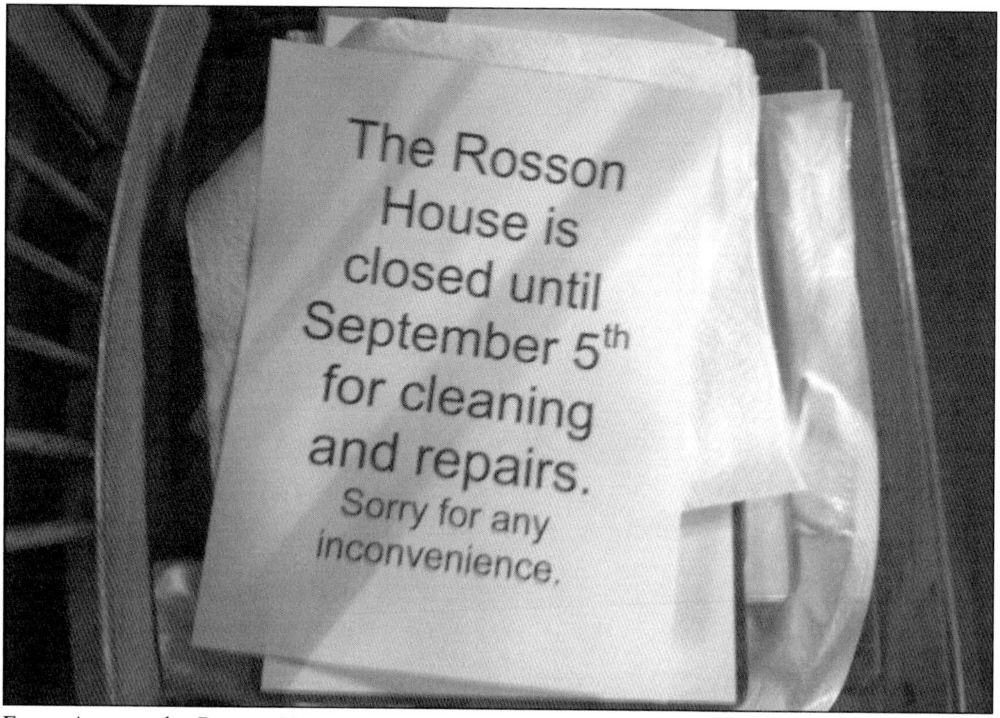

Every August, the Rosson House Museum is closed for two weeks. Volunteers spend that time inventorying, repairing, cleaning, and painting. Volunteers are recruited from the membership and local businesses. The closure is also an opportunity to assess the condition of the artifacts and to display new items. Below, Kim Kasper (left) and Pat Ihsen, both museum volunteers, inspect items in the dining room. (Photographs by Marilyn Sklar; RHHSFG.)

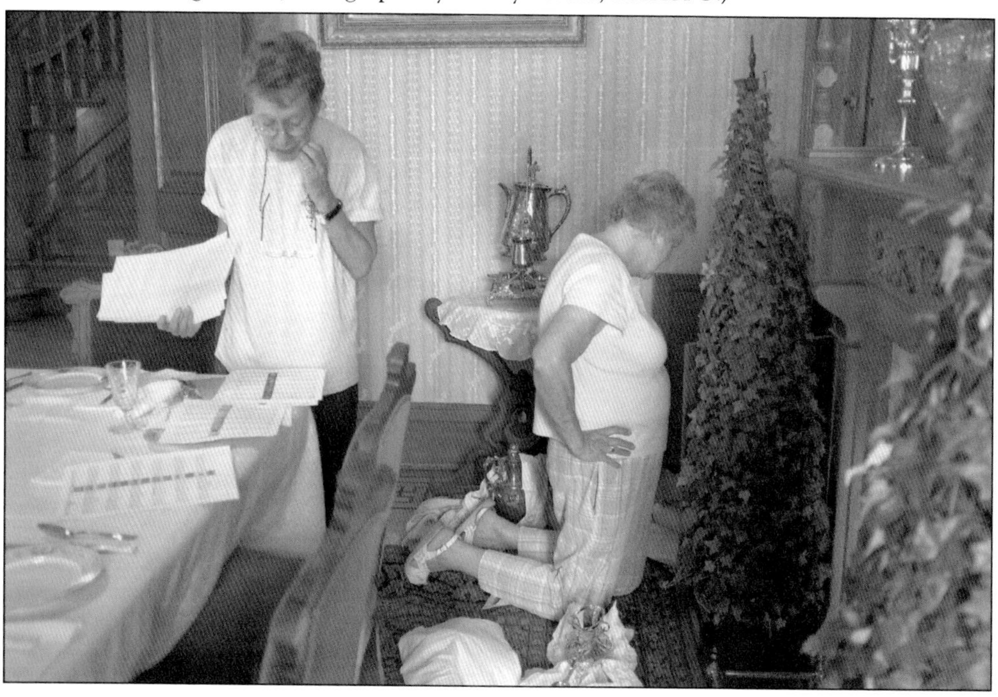

The Rosson House and Historic Heritage Square are often featured in an array of publications. Being the last intact residential block of the original Phoenix townsite, it was only natural for Historic Heritage Square to be part of the city's observation of National Preservation Week (right). The City of Phoenix employee newsletter featured the Rosson House and a vintage bicycle on its cover in February 1983 (below). Today, the foundation prefers to present Historic Heritage Square as a glimpse into the past. (PPD.)

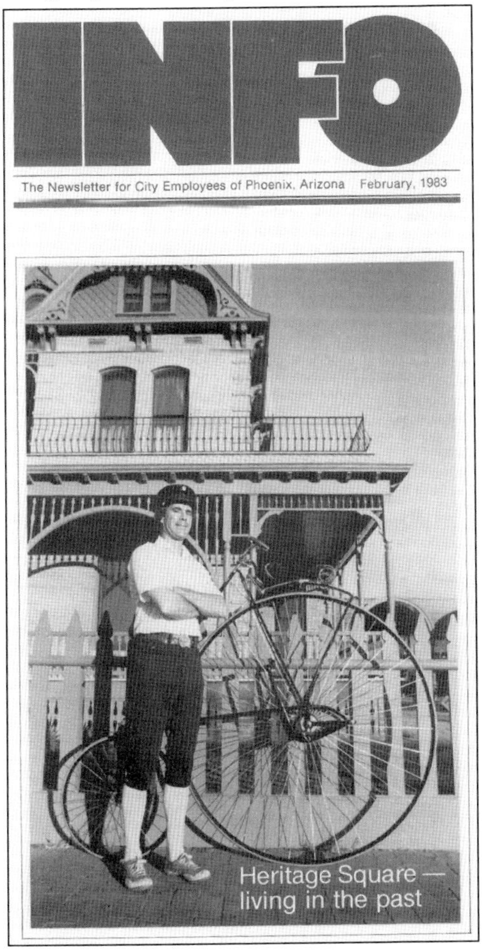

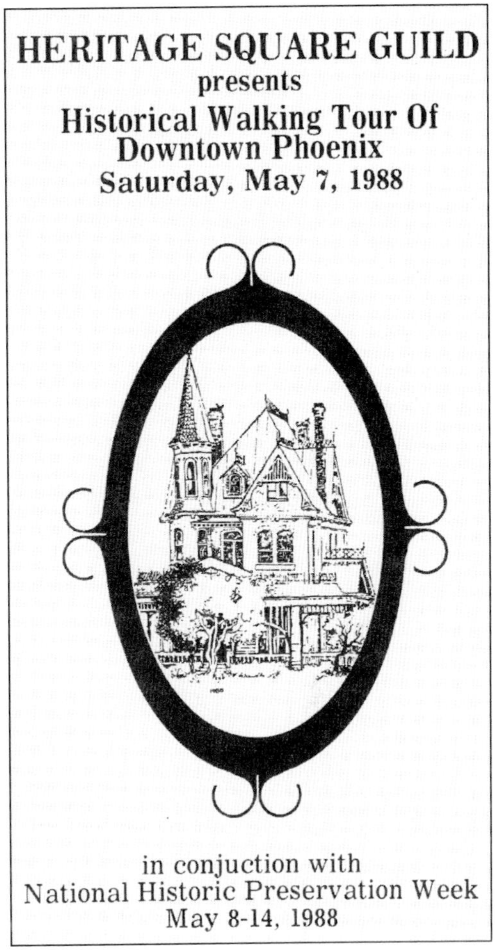

HERITAGE SQUARE GUILD
presents
Historical Walking Tour Of
Downtown Phoenix
Saturday, May 7, 1988

in conjuction with
National Historic Preservation Week
May 8-14, 1988

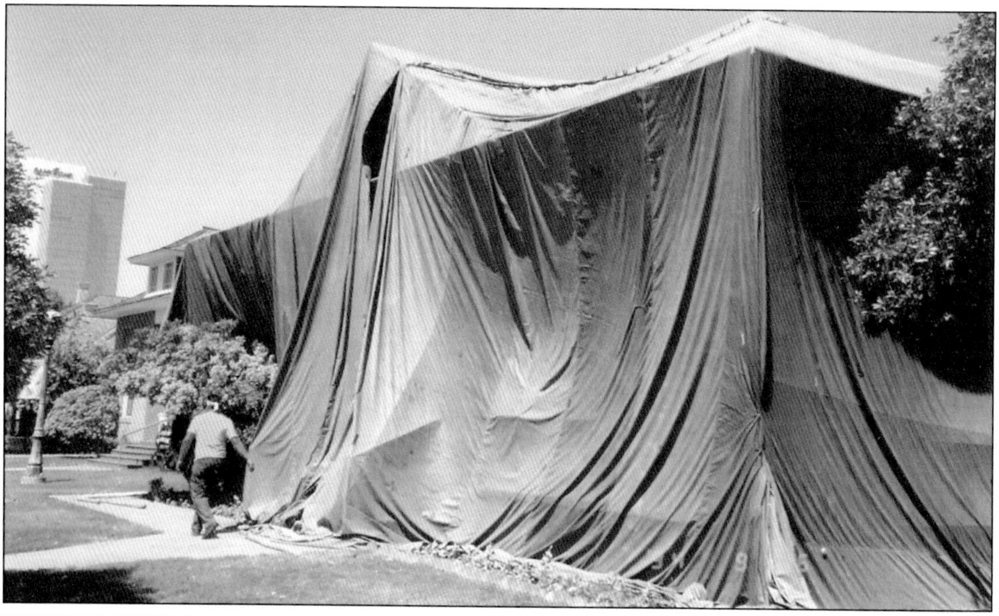

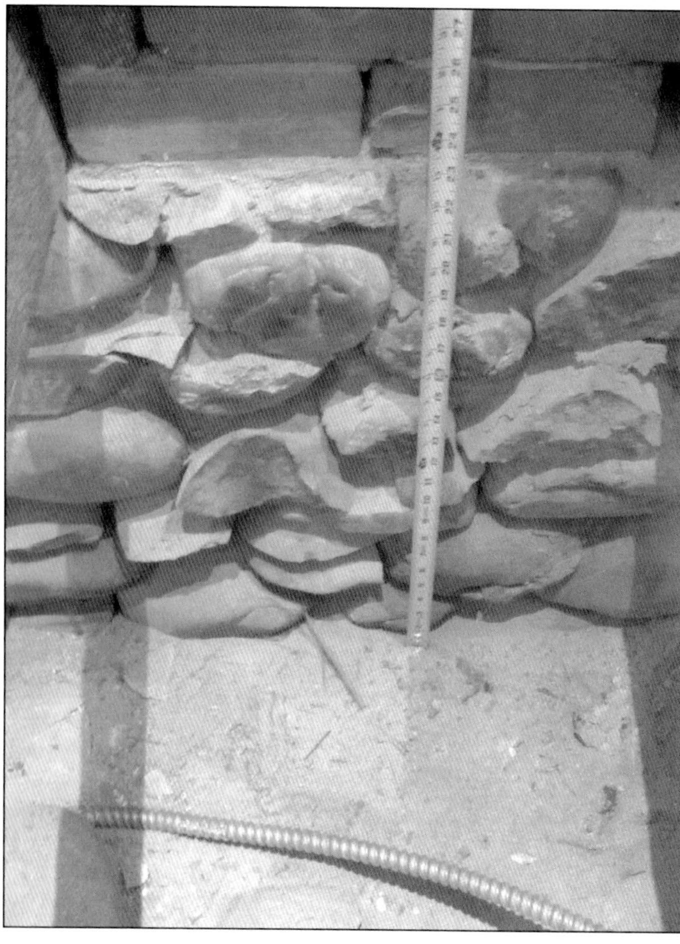

Even brick houses can suffer from termites. The above photograph, taken in 1994, shows the Silva House tented for treatment. Historic houses do require upkeep, especially when their current use as a popular bar and restaurant, like the Rose and Crown Pub, differs from their original residential use. During maintenance to the floor at the Silva House (left), its foundation was discovered to be river cobblestone, although the exterior walls are brick. (Above, RHHSFG; left, photograph by Marilyn Sklar; RHHSFG.)

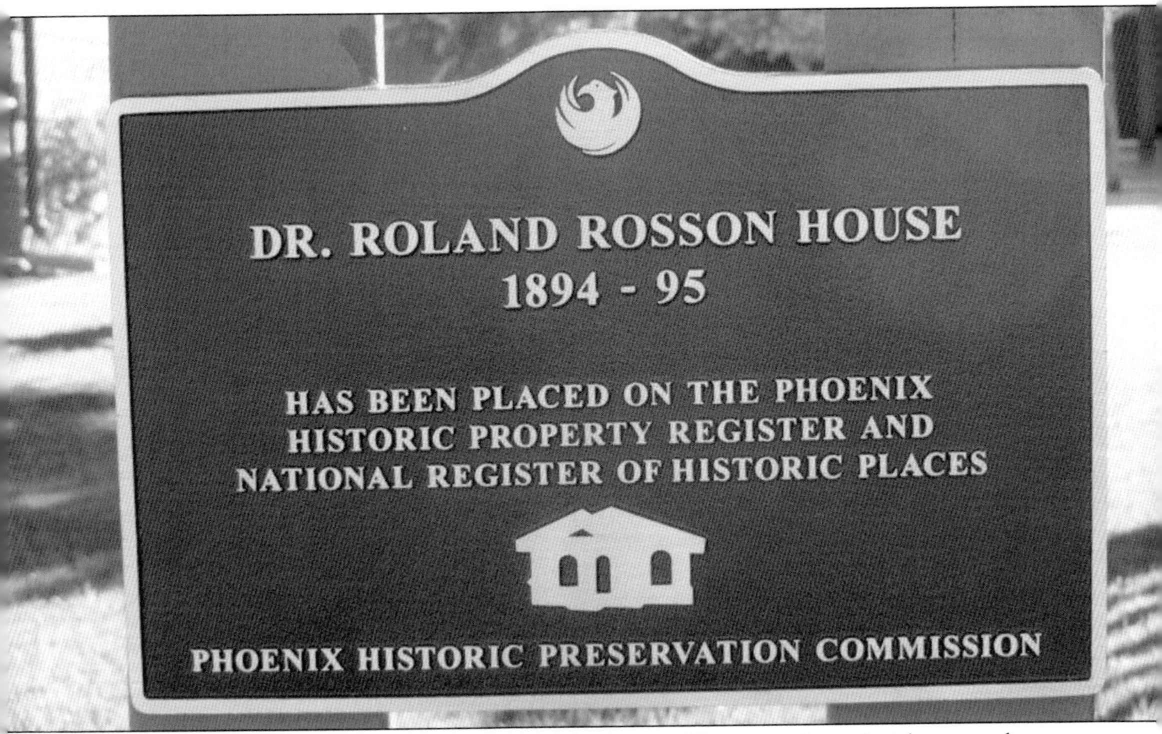

The picket fence that surrounds three sides of the Rosson House is adorned with many plaques commemorating the house. The most recent marker, stating that the Victorian mansion is listed in the National Register of Historic Places, was presented to the Rosson House–Heritage Square Foundation and Guild by the City of Phoenix's Historic Preservation Office in 2012, during Arizona's centennial year. Even before Historic Heritage Square was planned and the Rosson House had been purchased by the city, this magnificent example of Victorian architecture was listed in the national register. Some forwarding-thinking people knew in 1971 that this building must be honored, even with all its alterations. Through the efforts of former mayor Driggs, ultimately, the City of Phoenix recognized its worth, bringing it back to its original state. (RHHSFG)

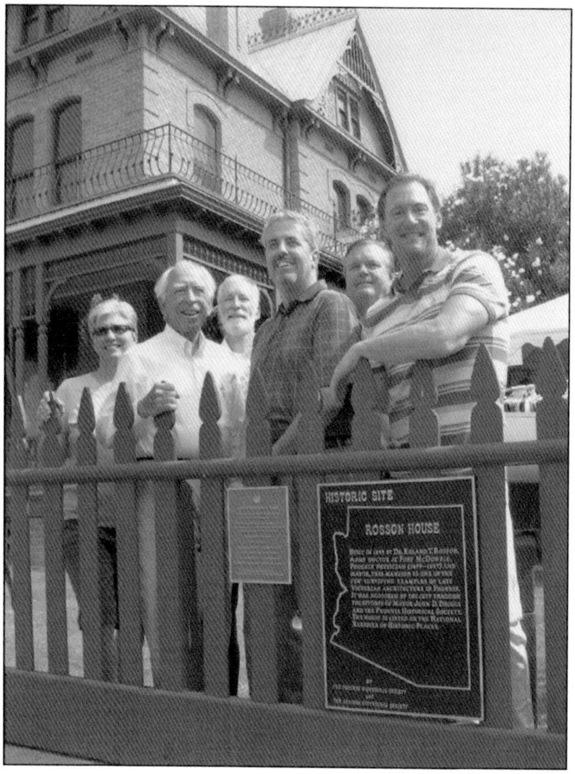

In July 2010, the Phoenix City Council named the Rosson House as its first Protocol House, a special designation allowing city officials to host visiting dignitaries for small meetings or receptions. In attendance at the plaque's unveiling (left) were, from left to right, Karen Williams of the parks department; former mayor John Driggs; Tom Walsh, executive director of the Rosson House; Jim Burke, acting director of the parks department; Don Keuth, CEO of the Phoenix Community Alliance; and District 4 councilman Tom Simplot. The marker (below) is one of many on the Rosson House picket fence. (RHHSFG.)

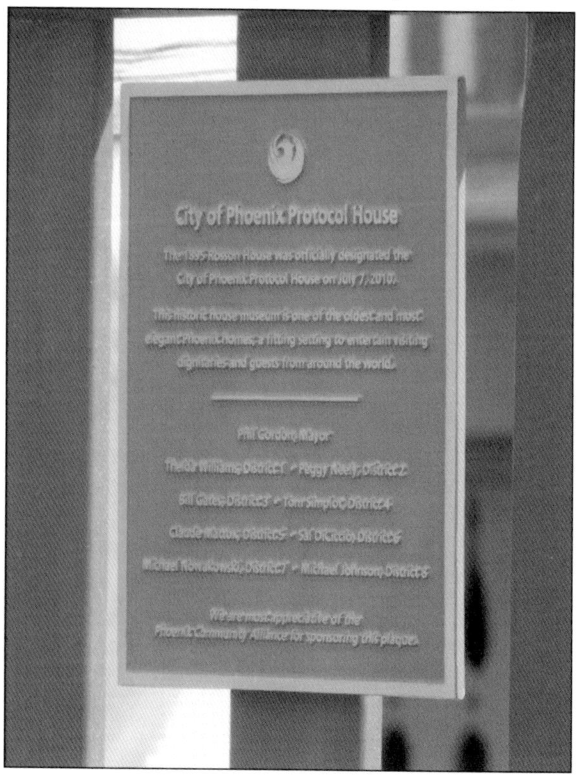

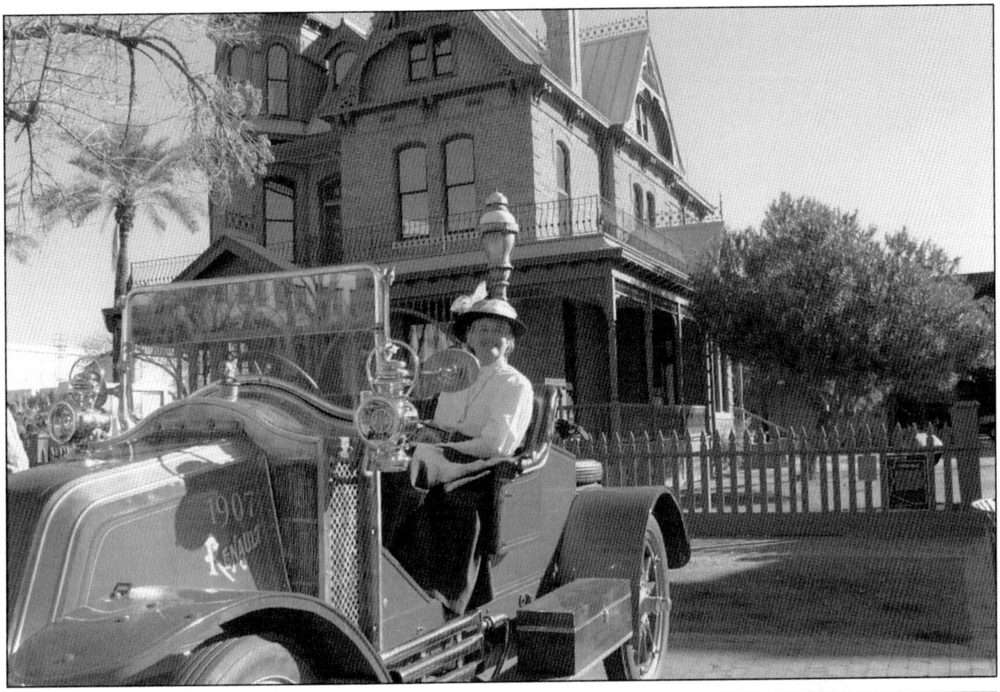

The Step Back in Time Players dress as and impersonate individuals connected with the Rosson House in 1895. Each actor researches the person they are portraying. The actresses portray members of the Lamson Literary Society, a Phoenix charity group whose purpose was to raise funds to create a city library. In the above photograph, Mrs. Jerry Millay (portrayed by Vicki Beaver) sits behind the wheel of a 1907 Renault race car during the Motoring Thru Time car show, which is held on the square each February. At right, Floy Rosson, played by Karina Gordon, sits on the back porch. She urges readers of this book to visit "her" house. (RHHSFG.)

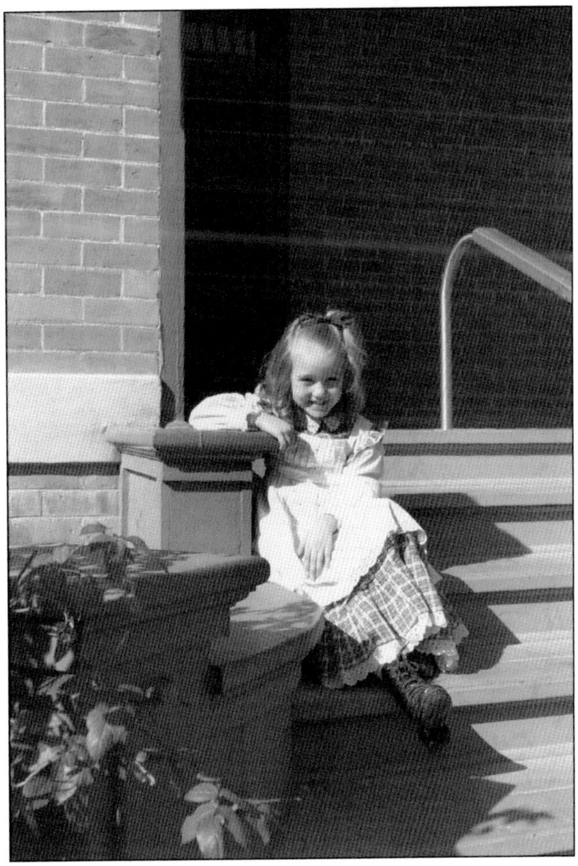